C000134954

STARTUP
GUIDE

#startupeverywhere

STARTUP GUIDE JAPAN

In partnership with
Impact Hub Tokyo, **Monozukuri Ventures**,
Innovation Hub Osaka and **Fukuoka Growth Next**

With thanks to our Community Partners

fgn. FUKUOKA GROWTH NEXT

Proudly supported by

Japan External Trade Organization

Information-technology
Promotion
Agency, Japan

Hankyu

仙台市
SENDAI CITY

CITY OF
KYOTO

OSAKA CITY
大阪市

福岡市
FUKUOKA CITY

manifesto

Startup Guide was founded on the mission to guide, empower and inspire people to start their entrepreneurial journey anywhere. Though helping entrepreneurs start their businesses has been the goal of our guidebooks since our inception in 2014, this is no longer enough. We need to begin evaluating what impact, both negative and positive, a business can and will make.

As a media and publishing company, we have a responsibility to use our role to contribute to the narrative of what good business means today. Therefore, we want to help drive the shift toward sustainable businesses and impact entrepreneurship. Until now, we've talked about technology, funding and growth, but what we haven't talked enough about is how we can solve the world's largest and most important challenges and how to create businesses from that. Thus, we need new businesses to take new measures – to find ways to tap into their power and realize creative entrepreneurial solutions to the problems we're facing now and in the future. In moving over to this vision for our guidebooks, we found it necessary to begin highlighting the ecosystems that advance impact innovation through businesses, working toward a greater good in more ways than one.

We hope that this guidebook will inspire you both as a reader and an entrepreneur to start focusing on how you can personally create a positive impact. Our world depends on it.

Sissel Hansen

Startup Guide

We're thrilled to continue our journey into purposeful entrepreneurship with our next regional impact book, *Startup Guide Japan.*

In Japan, you'll find an incredible mix of traditional culture and design and innovative technology that borders on the futuristic. You'll also find an impressive and still-growing community of startups and organizations tackling local and global challenges, best-in-class research institutions, acceleration and incubation programs with corporate and government backing, and corporates opening up to startup collaboration.

Following in the footsteps of our impact guide in Switzerland, we have chosen to focus on five cities that are generating exciting and purpose-driven companies. In recent years, the startup ecosystems in Fukuoka, Kyoto, Osaka, Sendai and Tokyo have received attention from public and private organizations. Locally and country-wide, entrepreneurs are receiving the support required to inspire the work culture in Japan to grow leaner, more creative and more globally minded.

Covering regional initiatives, startups, programs, coworking spaces, schools, investors, industry leaders and more, this guide helps you take your first steps into Japan's stunning entrepreneurship environment.

We'd like to extend our deepest gratitude to everyone who contributed to this book, with a special thank you to our community partners who helped bring this massive undertaking to life. The book was created during a time when the world was hit by the COVID-19 pandemic, and we were deeply inspired to see our entire team and partners pull together to make sure this book was published just as we envisioned it.

We hope this book will inspire you to make an impact of your own. Happy reading.

Sissel Hansen
Founder and CEO of Startup Guide

how to use the book

What To Expect

This guide features five of Japan's main impact ecosystems, among others. We take a focused, in-depth look at Fukuoka, Kyoto, Osaka, Sendai and Tokyo but also extend to a few smaller cities in the Japanese ecosystem that straddle multiple areas yet are equally as beneficial to the entire region (see chapter **Regional Initiatives**).

Our guides aim to give you a view of the whole region, so we have also included cities not necessarily considered the main Japanese hubs. Some were voted in by the advisory board, and others were selected by our team due to the cities' important contributions to the ecosystem.

This impact guide also features expert interviews, entrepreneur stories and other useful tips and tricks that are the core of the *Startup Guide* series.

Finding Your Way

This book begins with an introduction and a **Regional Initiatives** chapter that gives you an overall view of the area covered and some exciting initiatives happening in Japan. Following this, the next five chapters cover the book's main focus: five of Japan's innovation hubs.

After these city chapters, our **Experts** chapter collects some of the most experienced and knowledgeable experts across the region to share their insights about entrepreneurship in the ecosystem.

The Not So Obvious

→ In this guide, websites do not begin with prefixes, which might not work on some browsers. You may need to add the '**www**' prefix for them to work.

→ The back of this guide includes all the resources you might need, including an address **directory**, contact details, a **glossary** and other self-help points.

→ Japan uses the **Japanese yen (¥)**. The average currency exchange rate over the twelve months before publication (April 2019–April 2020) was **¥1 = USD($) 0.009226**

criteria

Startup Guide's impact books highlight the most innovative startups and entrepreneurs in the region's most socially impactful cities. What we aim to describe in writing about impact are the processes of making changes, both big and small, that help to make the world a better place. Though impact does not exclude negative outcomes that may also occur, this guide aims to highlight the stories of initiatives fueled by businesses with a clear positive vision for impact on both people and the planet.

This regional guidebook has been curated specifically with a focus on impact when it comes to the startups and founders featured. To assess the impact of nominated candidates, Startup Guide uses five dimensions from the Impact Management Project (**impactmanagementproject.com**) tool. These include:

what

the outcomes they contribute to

who

the people who experience the social and environmental outcomes

how much

the scale of the outcome

contribution

the depth that businesses assess their contribution to the depth of an outcome

risk

the probabilities and consequences of risk events if they are realized

Startup Guide also uses its own criteria to select and assess the ecosystem based on startup **purpose**, **vision**, **transparency**, **profits** and **value.** These criteria are rooted in the United Nations' seventeen Sustainable Development Goals (SDGs), which are used as a framework for building businesses. Finally, local city and community partners help to fairly evaluate the selections and later take part in the impact-eligibility process. Startup Guide's main goal for its regional impact books is to highlight local actions for global good, thus providing a perspective for readers and assessing how the ecosystems and entrepreneurs featured have helped provide local value that could be harvested at the global level.

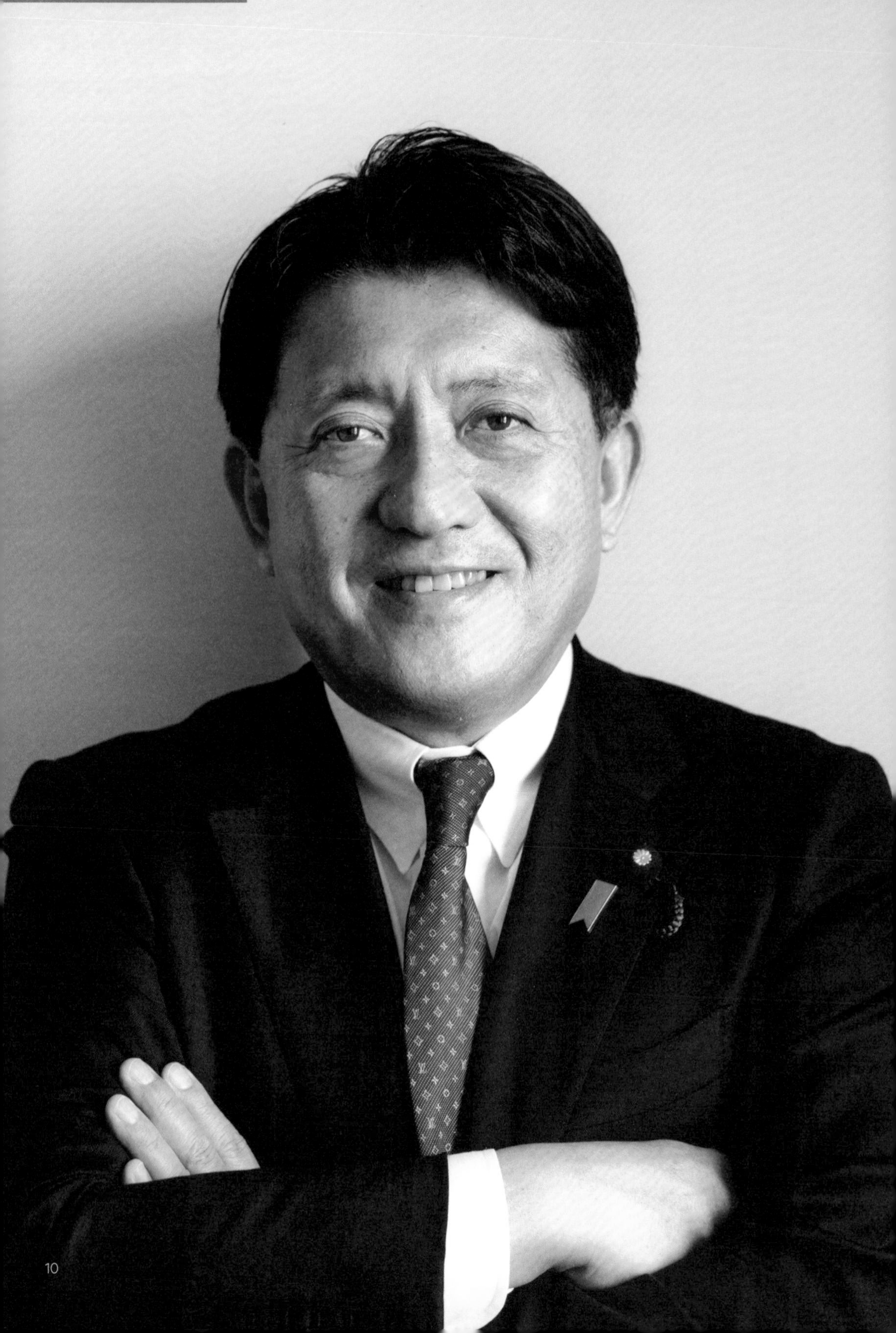

Five Reasons to Connect to Japan

Takuya HIRAI, Former Minister of State

Japan's startup ecosystem is emerging. For Japan, the coming decade will be a historic moment to create a new prosperous society, and startups will be a central player of the challenge. For the following five reasons, we welcome you to start your business in Japan or to collaborate with Japan's startups.

Reason 1: Exciting culture and nice environment

You may know about Manga comics, ninjas and Zen meditation, but upon starting your business here in Japan, you'll be able to experience a deeper understanding of Japanese culture. Japan's cities are safe and clean. Foreign entrepreneurs can easily find convenient workspaces, lively entertainment areas and many comfortable residential areas within the city.

Reason 2: Large sophisticated market

With a GDP of $5 trillion, Japan's market is the third-largest economy in the world. Sophisticated Japanese customers are seeking new solutions to many challenges, such as the social issue of Japan's aging society, environmental sustainability and other issues that can also be found around the world.

Reason 3: Open-innovation movement

Recently, large corporations in Japan have awakened to open innovation. Aiming to connect their business resources to startups for innovation, many corporate acceleration programs and corporate venture capital initiatives have begun. Open innovation has become a major movement among Japan's many industries.

Reason 4: Cutting-edge university R&D

With many Nobel laureates and high-level researchers, Japanese universities are famous for their cutting-edge R&D. By collaborating with startups and engaging in technology transfer, top-ranked universities empower the commercialization of their research.

Reason 5: Government policy programs

The Government has announced a new startup strategy: "Beyond Limits. Unlock Our Potential." This strategy empowers the development of the startup ecosystem with many policy programs being activated, such as gap financing, acceleration programs, public procurement, etc.

Now, the world is confronting the COVID-19 crisis and seeking a better post–COVID-19 society. We are mobilizing our talent and resources to contribute to controlling the epidemic in the world. We would like to support major game changers for the new era. Please collaborate with Japan to make a better world. We hope this guide will encourage you to connect with and join the Japan startup ecosystem.

Takuya HIRAI,
Former Minister of State

contents

Japan Region **16**

Getting Started
in Japan **18**

REGIONAL INITIATIVES **25**

EDGEof **26**

Le Wagon Coding Bootcamp **26**

Open Network Lab **27**

Venture Café **27**

FUKUOKA **29**

Community Letter:
Fukuoka Growth Next **30**

Local Ecosystem **32**

In partnership with
Fukuoka City Government
& Fukuoka Growth Next (FGN):
How the Fukuoka City Government
is Fostering the Next Generation
of Startups **34**

Startups
Doreming **38**

Kids Code Club **40**

Kyulux **42**

On Grit Engineering **44**

Founders
Tom Brooke **46**

Kumiko Sasaki
& Eihiro Saishu **50**

Programs
Co-Necto **54**

Hirameki Sprint **54**

Jump Start Program **55**

Updraft **55**

Spaces
The Company Canal
City Front **56**

Engineer Cafe
- Hacker Space Fukuoka **56**

fabbit Global Gateway
"ACROS Fukuoka" **57**

Fukuoka Growth Next **57**

Schools
Kyushu University Business
School (QBS) **59**

Fukuoka University **59**

Investors
Dogan beta **60**

FGN ABBALab **61**

GxPartners **62**

KYOTO **65**

Community Letter:
Monozukuri Ventures **66**

Local Ecosystem **68**

In partnership with
Kyoto City Office:
How to Make a Strong
Ecosystem Even Stronger **70**

Startups
aceRNA Technologies **74**

Atomis **76**

mui Lab **78**

Space Power Technologies **80**

Stroly **82**

Founders
Isshu Rakusai **84**

Kenshin Fujiwara **88**

Programs
KGAP+ (Keihanna Global
Acceleration Program Plus) **92**

ME310/SUGAR **92**

Phoenixi **93**

Spaces
engawa KYOTO **94**

Impact Hub Kyoto **94**

Kyoto Makers Garage **95**

SPACE KANTE at Co & Co
KYOTO **95**

Schools
Doshisha University **96**

Kyoto Startup Summer
School **97**

Kyoto University Graduate
School of Management **97**

Investors
Kyoto iCAP **98**

Monozukuri Ventures **99**

OSAKA **101**

Community Letter:
Osaka Innovation Hub **102**

Local Ecosystem **104**

In partnership with Osaka City
Government and Osaka Innovation Hub:
Building an Ecosystem through
Government, Academic and
Corporate Collaboration **106**

Startups
Gochiso **110**

Next Innovation **112**

Remohab **114**

Review **116**

Wefabrik Inc. **118**

Founders
Genki Kanaya **120**

Mitsuki Bun **124**

Programs
AIDOR Acceleration **128**

OIH Seed Acceleration
Program **128**

Startupbootcamp
Scale Osaka **129**

RISING! **129**

Spaces
The DECK **130**
Global Venture Habitat
Osaka **131**
GVH#5 **131**

Schools
Kansai University **132**
Kindai University **133**
Osaka City University **133**

Investors
Hack Ventures **134**
HHP Co-creation Fund **135**

SENDAI 137

Local Ecosystem **138**

Startups
Adansons **144**
AI Silk **146**
Brain Innovation **148**
Co-LABO MAKER **150**
IoT.Run **152**

Founders
Kenji Suzuki **154**
Miho Koike **158**

Programs
DA-TE APPs! **162**
Sendai X-Tech Innovation
Project **162**
Tohoku Growth Accelerator **163**
Tohoku Social Innovation
Accelerator **163**

Spaces
cocolin **164**
enspace **164**
INTILAQ Tohoku
Innovation Center **165**
THE6 **165**

Schools
Miyagi Gakuin Women's
University (MGU) **166**
Tohoku Gakuin University **167**
Tohoku University **167**

Investors
Makoto Capital **168**
Tohoku University Venture
Partners **169**

TOKYO 171

Community Letter:
Impact HUB Tokyo **172**

Local Ecosystem **174**

Startups
Crono **180**
Heralbony **182**
Holoeyes **184**
Infostellar **186**
JobRainbow **188**
WOTA **190**

Founders
Emi Takemura, Naofumi Iwai
& Yuji Fujita **192**
Toshiki Abe **196**

Programs
ETIC **200**
FoundX **201**
Team 360 **201**
In partnership with:
J-Startup **202**

Spaces
Anchorstar **204**
Impact HUB Tokyo **205**
Ryozan Park **205**

Schools
Eirene University **206**
Graduate School of Management,
GLOBIS University **207**
i.school **207**

Investors
D4V (Design for Ventures) **208**
DEEPCORE **209**
SEA Fund **210**

EXPERTS 213

In partnership with:
Hirofumi Ukita / Fujitsu
Accelerator **214**
Chikara Takagishi / Hankyu
Hanshin Properties Corp. **218**
Kiyoshi Nakazawa / Japan
External Trade Organization
(JETRO) **222**
Koichi Noguchi / PwC Japan
Group **226**
Hiroyuki Suzuki / Keihanna
Science City **230**

directory **235**

glossary **245**

sources **248**

about the guide **251**

JAPAN REGION

As an island nation, Japan has developed along a unique path. Culturally tight-knit but nonetheless reliant on external trade, the country is increasingly opening up to a new wave of innovation and investment in the twenty-first century. Between 2013 and 2017, investment in the Japanese startup ecosystem increased by more than 150 percent. Foreign investment has surpassed ¥2 trillion for two years in a row. Domestically, the government has launched a number of programs aimed at inspiring young companies to base themselves in cities across Japan, including a startup visa and the creation of National Strategic Special Zones aimed at foreign investment. From the glimmering lights of Tokyo, a pioneer in robotics manufacturing for years, to Fukuoka (the up-and-coming "East Asian Silicon Valley") and a number of other leading startup cities such as Sendai, Osaka and Kyoto, Japan's pivot to a startup economy is real and growing.

For Japan, a 4.0 society is no longer good enough; the country has set its aims even higher, on Society 5.0. As a national initiative to support social impact innovations ranging from smart mobility to AI, the Society 5.0 plan highlights the broader effort to focus on business innovation for good. This vision is not entirely new. Japan has focused on social impact since the 2011 earthquake, tsunami and power plant explosion shocked the country. Social impact interest accelerated after that and now represents about one-quarter of a billion dollars in total. Each city represents a different specialty: Tokyo is alive with startups developing robotics, Fukuoka has an advanced manufacturing sector and has pioneered smart city startups, Sendai has become known as a hub for disaster management startups, and Kyoto and Osaka, both cities with large student populations, are known for biotechnology and life sciences, respectively. Across the country, Society 5.0 is taking form. •

PAGE 29

FUKUOKA

Area: **343 km²**
Metropolitan Pop.: **1,595,365 (2019)**
GDP: **$71 billion USD (2016)**
GDP per capita: **$34,523 (2014)**
Metro Area Unemployment: **2.9% (2019)**
Average Salaries: **¥4,126,332 per year**
Cost of Living: **3% lower than the national average (2017)**
Impact: **Kyushu University in Hakozaki, just 5 km from Fukuoka City, is part of a project to redesign the future of cities to be greener and more efficient.**

✳ The city's population is increasing by 7.1% annually, which is the largest increase among all cities throughout the country.

PAGE 101

OSAKA

Area: **225 km²**
Metropolitan Pop.: **2,690,000 (2018)**
GDP: **$185 billion (2016)**
GDP per capita: **$41,660 (2014)**
Metro Area Unemployment: **4.0% (2016)**
Average Salaries: **¥4,567,968 per year**
Cost of Living: **¥118,583 without rent.**
Impact: **The Osaka Community Foundation, founded in 1991, was Japan's first public philanthropic institution focused on social impact.**

✳ Osaka is home to the world's second largest aquarium, the Osaka Kaiyukan Aquarium.

Check our sources - page 248

PAGE 65

KYOTO

Area: 828 km²
Metropolitan Pop.: 1,475,183
GDP: $95 billion USD
GDP per capita: $37,379 (2014)
Metro Area Unemployment: 3.1% (2016)
Average Salaries: ¥5,507,040 per year
Cost of Living: ¥150,000, including rent
Impact: **Plus Social Investment, founded in Kyoto, received ¥30 million for socially focused investing from the Japan Social Impact Investment Foundation (SIIF).**

✳ In 2007, Kyoto banned billboards and flashing signs on all buildings taller than 31 meters in an effort to reduce urban "clutter."

PAGE 171

TOKYO

Area: 2,187 km²
Metropolitan Pop.: 9,262,046 (2016)
GDP: $1.6 trillion
GDP per capita: $68,776 (2014)
Metro Area Unemployment: 3.2% (2016)
Average Salaries: ¥4,339,116 per year
Cost of Living: ¥119,774 without rent
Impact: **Tokyo hosted the Impact Investment Forum 2019, which brought together entrepreneurs focused on achieving the SDGs.**

✳ Tokyo's metro was built in 1927 and is the busiest in the world, with nearly nine million daily commuters.

PAGE 137

SENDAI

Area: 786 km²
Metropolitan Pop.: 1,090,454 (2020)
GDP: $46 billion dollars (2014)
GDP per capita: $35,675 (2014)
Metro Area Unemployment: 6.9% (2019)
Average Salaries: ¥3,915,235 per year
Cost of Living: ¥52,000–¥62,000 per month
Impact: **After the 2011 earthquake, the UN World Conference on Disaster Risk Reduction was held in Sendai in 2015 and prioritized community involvement in disaster preparedness.**

✳ Sendai is home to a number of government offices, due to its seat as the capital of the Miyagi prefecture.

Impact Initiatives

💡 As part of Japan's Society 5.0 initiative, the country has placed a special focus on smart agriculture (SDG 2), healthcare (SDG 3) and smart city infrastructure (SDG 11).

♥ Biotechnology startups, such as those focusing on regenerative medicine, have received an increasing amount of investment and now number nearly six hundred across Japan.

💧 Despite its small land area, Japanese startups are pioneering so-called digital farming techniques to address coming water shortages around the world.

∞ Japanese cities are known for their advanced mobility infrastructure. The Japanese government's "sandbox" program is aimed at innovating around travel and transportation, among other things.

REGION ESSENTIALS

Getting Started in Japan

GETTING YOUR PAPERWORK RIGHT

To start a business in Japan, you must establish your right to reside in the country and conduct business activities. The first step to getting any visa for Japan is to apply for a Certificate of Eligibility (COE) at your nearest regional immigration authority, a preliminary visa-screening process that ensures you meet the basic requirements. Next you can begin your application for the relevant visa. The process for prospective entrepreneurs from overseas is convoluted, so the best place to start is Japan External Trade Organization (JETRO), who will advise you. Most will apply for a Business Manager Visa; however, this has many requirements that can be difficult to fulfill initially, so the government has created what is unofficially called a "startup visa" and is available in National Strategic Special Zones: Tokyo, Hiroshima and Aichi prefectures, and in the cities of Fukuoka, Sendai, Niigata and Imabari. Depending on the area, this can grant you a six-month or one-year temporary residence permit while you undertake the necessary startup preparations.

The exact documents required vary depending on where you want to establish your business, but expect to submit a detailed business plan. Like anyone heading to Japan on a long-stay visa, you'll

receive a residence card on arrival that you'll later need to take to your local ward office to register your details. If you're also registering family members, you'll need marriage and/or birth certificates translated into Japanese. Once this is done, you'll be mailed a My Number card (with a twelve-digit ID number) that will be used for administrative purposes.

STARTING A COMPANY

Japan, which ranks 29th out of 190 economies on the World Bank's Ease of Doing Business, has made great efforts in recent years to attract overseas companies. Begin your journey by consulting with JETRO, who provide excellent advice in English. You'll need to obtain a Business Manager Visa, which requires you to open an office and either invest at least ¥5 million or employ at least two people. If you're bringing employees from overseas, you must sponsor their visas too. Finding an office space can be expensive and time consuming, but you may be eligible for a temporary free office space provided by JETRO. Also look into local startup-support options in the area where you're launching; for example, Kobe Enterprise Promotion Bureau (**global.kobe-investment.jp/ english**) and the Global Startup Center in Fukuoka (**startup.fukuoka.jp/journal/global-startup-center**). Once you've obtained your visa, you can begin the incorporation process. You'll need to open a corporate bank account, which can be difficult as some Japanese banks are known to be reluctant to deal with customers who do not speak Japanese. JETRO may be able to assist you with introductions and refer you to accountants and specialists in registering for social insurance. All documents must be submitted in Japanese, so you may need to hire a *shihō shoshi* (judicial scrivener) or a *gyōsei shoshi* (administrative scrivener) to handle the process. Venture capital spending by Japanese corporations reached an all-time high in 2018 as they shift towards growth through open innovation, so it's an exciting time to be entering the market.

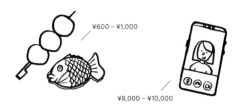

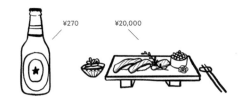

COST OF LIVING

The Economist Intelligence Unit's Worldwide Cost of Living 2020 survey announced a surprise: Osaka rose to joint first place for high cost of living, alongside Hong Kong and Singapore, whereas Tokyo took joint eighth place. However, life in Japan is not as expensive as you might think. In Tokyo, most people expect to spend only about 25 percent of their salary on rent as opposed to over 50 percent in a city like London. The average cost of a studio or one-bedroom-plus-kitchen apartment in central Minato Ward is ¥129,000, compared to just ¥63,900 in Katsushika Ward in the north. Meanwhile, Fukuoka's central Hakata Ward averages only ¥51,500 per month. Eating out at lunchtime is cheap, with set meals for ¥600 to ¥1,000, but fine dining can easily set you back ¥20,000. A 330 mL bottle of beer costs around ¥270 in Tokyo and Osaka. Smartphones are typically sold on two-year contracts with data included and cost between ¥8,000 and ¥10,000 per month. However, mobile virtual network operators are on the rise, offering SIM-only plans for as little as ¥1,400 per month, although you'll need to pay extra for phone calls.

RENTING AN APARTMENT

Finding an apartment as a foreigner in Japan can be a laborious process. Flat sharing is uncommon so there are many small apartments. However, if you prefer to live with others, several share-house companies operate in major cities and offer furnished rooms and a bills-included monthly rate.

The first step in an apartment search is deciding the area in which you wish to live. You can then search online (**suumo.jp** is a popular rentals-search website, but in Japanese only) or visit the real estate agencies in your target areas to compare their listings and fees. Be warned that many landlords are unwilling to rent to foreigners, so you may only be able to view a fraction of available properties. Contracts are normally signed for a two-year period and moving may require more than three months' rent upfront, including a deposit (usually one to two months' rent), the agency fee and *reikin* ("key money"), which is a nonrefundable payment to the landlord. You'll also need a guarantor in Japan willing to cover you should you default on your rent. Several companies provide this service for roughly 50 to 100 percent of one month's rent. Apartments are almost always unfurnished, so be prepared to buy everything, even light bulbs!

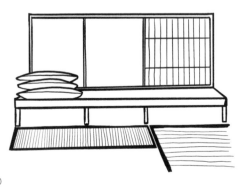

CULTURE AND LANGUAGE

Japanese culture is often portrayed as a unique mystery by both Japanese and foreigners. In reality, it just takes some getting used to, and there's a good reason why many people describe Japan as an easy and pleasant place to live. Perhaps the most pervasive stereotype of Japanese culture is politeness, and it's true that service is generally excellent, demonstrating great attention to detail. You'll quickly notice that interactions are framed by set phrases in certain situations, from simple greetings to sayings like *"otsukaresama desu,"* which can be used between colleagues as a farewell at the end of the working day. This can make communication seem overly formal with a lot left unsaid, but socializing at an *izakaya*, a Japanese-style pub with sharing plates, is a great way to build up rapport. Ordering a beer in Japanese can earn you effusive praise, and locals are usually delighted to hear you making an effort with the language.

Japanese is notoriously difficult: not only are there two alphabets, but learners must contend with around three thousand *kanji* (Chinese characters), each of which have two or more pronunciations. Japanese pronunciation, however, is simple, and so daily conversation skills are relatively easy to acquire. Try flashcard apps to help with kanji memorization and dictionary apps that provide a handwriting function for looking up characters. Google Translate also has a camera function for auto-translation. There are plenty of language schools, or consider taking private lessons – teachers often offer a free trial lesson, so try out a couple before making a decision.

"The burgeoning startup ecosystem has stoked the fire of innovation in Japan."

[Q&A] — **Gen Isayama**
General Partner & CEO, World Innovation Lab (WiL)

[Q] How would you describe the Japanese startup ecosystem in terms of its level of collaboration, cooperation, openness and accessibility to new connections (i.e., the people)?

[A] The burgeoning startup ecosystem has stoked the fire of innovation in Japan, resulting in a six-fold increase in venture investment into Japanese startups in the past six years. Corporations are launching innovation labs and becoming open to partnerships with startups. The government is spearheading multiple programs to nurture entrepreneurship and provide financial support for startups. Pursuing entrepreneurship, which used to be an option only for oddballs given Japan's risk-averse culture, is turning into a legitimate career option for the elites.

[Q] What do you think makes a successful entrepreneur in the Japan ecosystem, and do you feel it's different from other regions in any particular way?

[A] Being resilient, passionate and creative. These are not different from other regions, but if I could name one thing that makes a successful entrepreneur, particularly in Japan, it is civility: courtesy and humility. In Japan's collectivist society, people remember how you act and tend to make business decisions based on your personality and past behaviors more so than in the US. "The nail that sticks out shall be hammered down," is a well-known Japanese saying. A humble nail realizes a better outcome than an arrogant nail. •

MEETING PEOPLE AND NETWORKING

Startup networking spaces and events have proliferated across Japan in the past few years, so it's definitely an exciting time to be an entrepreneur. There are networking nights, seminars and startup events held across the cities on a weekly basis. Coworking spaces are a great way to rapidly embed into a community and get those business ideas bouncing back and forth. Moreover, they are often the venue for events that both support and celebrate creatives and innovators. For example, Hive Jinnan is a coworking space in Shibuya, Tokyo, that regularly holds events from startup-founder talks to art exhibitions. Innovative and entrepreneurial communities are also burgeoning. Kyoto Makers Garage provides tools and a space for anyone to create; government-backed Osaka Innovation Hub hosts Hack Osaka, an annual international conference on innovation; and Ignite Sendai Startups, led by a group of foreign professionals, launched Sendai's first ever startup conference in English in 2019 and is working to grow the Tohoku entrepreneurial community. Fukuoka, the first city to launch the startup visa, styles itself as a "startup city," and government-backed Startup Cafe Fukuoka City provides a coworking space, offers free advice and holds weekly events. In general, Facebook or other social media are the best way to keep track of what's going on, and Meetup is also popular, especially for coding and tech-related events. For startup news in English, follow **thebridge.jp/en**, and for a great podcast, including inspiring interviews with founders, listen to Tim Romero's *Disrupting Japan*. •

REGIONAL
INITIATIVES

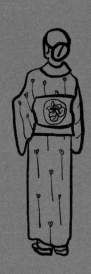

EDGEof

global collaboration platform

EDGEof, one of the most internationally-connected organizations in the Japanese ecosystem, is a collaborative platform for startups, entrepreneurs, researchers, government entities and artists to work together on game-changing projects. On top of match-making between startups and corporates, EDGEof produces innovative projects and helps international startups break into the Japanese market. As a guild of freelance innovators, the organization leverages its community to create teams, provide management support and connect talent to opportunities. Startups that have worked with EDGEof have participated in many unique projects, including helping a car manufacturer reengineer the interior of their cars as "experience platforms," collaborating with a big Japanese real estate company on edutainment content and integrating technologies into shopping malls. EDGEof has no specific entry requirements for collaboration.

SECTOR sector-agnostic
AREAS Japan-wide, international
FACTS EDGEof has supported Japanese market entry of 123 companies from thirteen countries and organized fifty-three official events with government support and seventeen official organizational partnerships in ten countries.
APPLY info@edgeof.co
WEB edgeof.co

Le Wagon Coding Bootcamp

school

"Le Wagon is on a mission to change people's lives by teaching them the skills and entrepreneurial mindset needed to thrive now and in the future," says Le Wagon Japan's course founder Sylvain Pierre. Participants, who are typically looking for a career change or in the midst of launching a company, learn coding fundamentals via a product-oriented, nine-week program. An optional career week can be tagged on to the program. This week is focused on building a resume and an online presence as well as offering technical-interview practice. The course utilizes an open and practical approach, favoring paired programming and asking questions over book theory. Le Wagon boasts a global community of more than 6,500 alumni and a network of over fifty companies that regularly hire its graduates. Its students are international, from forty countries, and with varied backgrounds in everything from marketing to finance, design and tech.

AREA Japan-wide
FACTS Over three years, 200 students have graduated, 3,500 community members joined and 160 events and workshops were organized. Student diversity: forty nationalities, 25 percent women, with the average age of twenty-nine years.
APPLY lewagon.com/tokyo/apply
WEB lewagon.com/tokyo

Open Network Lab

program

Open Network Lab (Onlab) is Japan's longest-running seed accelerator program and one of the most successful. Since 2010, more than 150 participating startups have received investments of up to $100,000. During the intensive three-month program, founders work side-by-side with dedicated mentors from a range of specializations. Follow-on investment is possible through various funds via parent company Digital Garage, and a team of bilingual professionals serves as a conduit to the Japanese market and startup ecosystem. Startups also have access to Digital Garage's formidable global network of startups, venture capitalists and corporations. Free coworking space is available for a year after graduation. Through Onlab's various partnerships, access to more than thirty startup tools and resources are available at discounted prices or for free. Later-stage startups can pursue proofs of concept and joint ventures with Japanese incumbents through industry-specific and regional programs.

AREA Japan-wide
SECTOR sector-agnostic
FACTS More than 150 startups have received investment (of up to $100,000 each), with a 14 percent exit rate.
SELECTED PORTFOLIO SmartHR, Fril (acquired by Rakuten), Fond (first Japanese company to participate in YC), giftee (IPOed in 2019)
APPLY onlab.jp/en

Venture Café

nonprofit innovation support organization

Venture Café Global Institute launched its first Asian branch in Tokyo in 2018 to further its mission of building open, innovative communities around the world. Its signature program in Tokyo and other cities is the Thursday Gathering, which offers networking opportunities, educational sessions and mentoring. These weekly events are open to the public and free to attend. Visitors can pitch their startup ideas, attend information sessions or book a mentoring appointment. "We are here to break barriers and move Japan and the globe towards a common goal. In 2020, we are aiming to become one of the biggest multilingual communities here in Tokyo," says Takuo Urushihara, director of operations. To further this goal and continue encouraging innovation and collaboration, Venture Cafe is expanding to several new cities. The program director Ryusuke Komura "invites and welcomes anyone who wants to connect with the ecosystem here in Japan."

AREA Currently expanding from Tokyo to new locations in Japan.
SECTOR sector-agnostic
FACTS Since launching in March 2018, Venture Cafe has hosted more than one hundred events with approximately twenty thousand visitors from more than one hundred countries.
SELECTED PORTFOLIO Zoi Meet, AC BIODE, D Free, mymizu, YSpace, MESHWell, AXELSPACE, Empath, FiNC Technologies
WEB venturecafetokyo.org/en

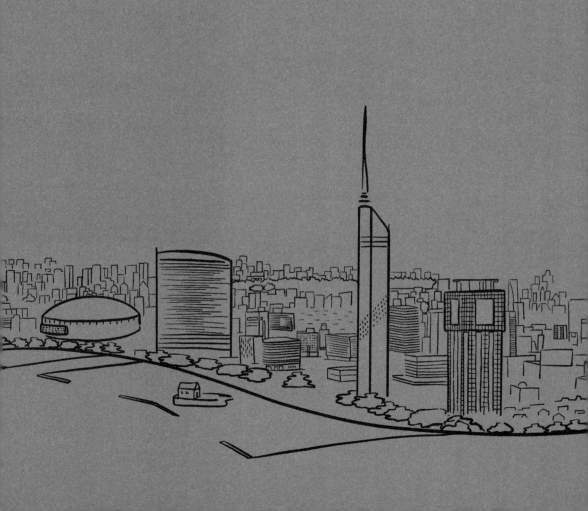

FUKUOKA

Young, multicultural and ambitious, Fukuoka has
already made a name for itself as a startup city,
investing heavily in its startup ecosystem for nearly a
decade. Now, with an increasing number of foreigners
settling here, work spaces opening up to rival larger
cities, and a vibrant cultural life with a number of
international festivals and well-known startup events
that bring attendees from around the world, Fukuoka
is ready to flex its muscles as Japan's startup capital.

Fukuoka Growth Next

Fukuoka Growth Next, the largest startup hub in Japan, was established through a public-private partnership with the goal of fostering innovation and supporting startups for a better future.

Fukuoka City is known as the number one startup city. In Japan, the population is flowing out from rural areas to urban areas, which has become a challenging issue for the entire society of Japan. In such situations, I believe that creating attractive business is an effective solution. The city government and the local private sector have been working together closely to create an environment where new innovative businesses are created, making Fukuoka a unique role model for other cities in Japan.

Our purpose at Fukuoka Growth Next is to create an ecosystem where people who take on risks and challenges are respected. I feel that often local established businesses are not fully aware of startup ecosystems, and this results in hampering their innovation and support for startups. This is a common issue in Japan's local regions. As evangelists, we connect local established businesses and startups to create open innovation in Fukuoka. Our organization and other local experts featured in this book have made every effort to build a unique ecosystem in Fukuoka, and I would like to take this opportunity to express my appreciation to the local experts for making this an amazing place for startups.

One of the hottest topics in the city is "Fukuoka Smart East," a large five-hectare redevelopment project. The city is teaming up with various tech startups to create a smart city. We believe the next five years will be a "spark joy" moment, with the city changing energetically with state-of-the-art innovations.

We believe that strengthening international exchanges will be the key to growth for the startup ecosystem. By participating in *Startup Guide Japan*, we hope that this wonderful local startup community will be introduced to the world and lead to global collaborations.

Yuichiro Uchida,
Chief of Secretariat, Fukuoka Growth Next

Fukuoka
Local Ecosystem

As a port city located in the south of Japan, where the mountains meet the sea, Fukuoka is idyllic – but the city is more than just a nice place to visit. What it lacks in population (it's smaller than Tokyo, Osaka, Yokohama and other cities), it makes up for in innovation. Over the past decade, the city of 1.6 million people has carved its niche in the Japanese startup ecosystem, focusing on creative industries, research and development and smart-city technology, among other things. In fact, Fukuoka has been called "Japan's most innovative city" and even its "next Silicon Valley."

Fukuoka was the first city in Japan to offer a startup visa for foreign entrepreneurs, and it has the fastest-growing, youngest and most multicultural population in all of Japan. It also has the fastest-growing foreign population, a boon for its emergent startup ecosystem. In addition, the city offers various economic support systems such as rent subsidies for startups and is one of the most affordable cities in Japan. Office space here costs less than half of that in Tokyo. Attracted by cheap rents and the generous tax benefits for startup founders, entrepreneurs are flocking to Fukuoka, which already has more than forty international companies established, including Steampunk Digital, a 3D-scanning tech startup, founded by Canadian entrepreneur.

Fukuoka has the third-largest proportion of the number of student population in Japan and third-largest number of international students, with increasing numbers of students eager to start up their own companies. Kyushu University has unique startup club activity, attracting many ambitious students. Over the next five years, the city's startup department wants to develop one hundred new startups from idea to Series-A and build a "Fukuoka-style" startup ecosystem in which unicorn companies are born.

FACTS &
FIGURES

- In 2018, the business entry rate in Fukuoka, which indicates the ratio of new businesses to existing businesses, reached 5.9%, the highest in Japan.

- Between 2005 and 2019, the number of foreigners living in Fukuoka increased by 193%, the highest increase of any major large Japanese city during that time.

- *Monocle* rated Fukuoka the world's seventh most livable city in 2016.

- The labor participation rate of women in Fukuoka City was 53.3% (3.3% higher than the 50% country average).

- Fukuoka City is one of five MICE (Meeting, Incentive, Convention and Exhibition) destinations in Japan. In 2016, 383 international conferences took place in the city, the second-largest number in Japan after Tokyo.

- Through the Fukuoka Smart East project, Fukuoka aims to become the most liveable smart city in the world. The project involves 50 hectares of smart city redevelopment projects with a focus on wellness, mobility and sharing.

NOTABLE
STARTUP
ACTIVITY

- Tenants of Fukuoka Growth Next, a startup hub that serves as a so-called "one stop shop" for entrepreneurs, raised ¥11.6 since the facility opened, which accelerated the startup scene in Fukuoka. Today, more than 165 companies work out of the space.

- LINE Corporation, the creator of the most popular messaging app in Japan, has its offices in Fukuoka. Since being founded in 2013, the company has created more than 700 jobs. In addition, it has a comprehensive cooperation agreement with Fukuoka City and is working on a project that solves the social issues of the city with its own cutting-edge technologies and services and leads to the improvement of civic life.

- Nulab, a local startup developing collaborative apps, has now expanded across the globe with offices in Amsterdam, New York and Singapore. It is a foreigner-friendly company with a multicultural background.

How the Fukuoka City Government is Fostering the Next Generation of Startups

An interview with

Soichiro Takashima / Mayor of Fukuoka City

Entrepreneurs and startups coming to Fukuoka City will be happy to find more than clean air, verdant mountains, proximity to transport hubs, excellent food and a culture brimming with art, technology and relaxation. Fukuoka has a growing startup community, and in recent years the city government has taken great strides in developing this ecosystem into a high-tech hub that adventurous and experimental companies can call home.

"We believe that startups will be essential for the future growth of Fukuoka City," says Soichiro Takashima, Fukuoka City's mayor and a passionate advocate for entrepreneurship and innovation. For Soichiro, supporting startups will create employment opportunities, attract international talent to the region and foster an environment of risk-taking and purpose-driven innovation. "We need to create a society in which people who take risks and take on challenges are respected," says Soichiro.

> *" We need to create a society in which people who take risks and take on challenges are respected "*

Bringing in startups is also essential to the existing corporates and organizations in the area who hope to connect with their local markets and the global ecosystem. "In a society where smartphones and IoT have become so convenient, it is not possible to meet the needs of consumers with traditional services and products," Soichiro says. "In order to provide products and services that consumers want today, it is necessary to create never before seen, state-of-the-art technology and innovative business models, which is the essence of the startup."

This sentiment carries over to the environmental and societal aspects of the city. Creating support options for startups strengthens the city and region quickly for innovators now and for the next generation of entrepreneurs. Soichiro and his office have been working hard to foster an environment where startups are respected and supported.

To kickstart the startup movement and ecosystem, Soichiro and his office designated Fukuoka as "Startup City Fukuoka." At first, established businesses and media outlets doubted the cost-effectiveness and importance of this new startup support movement. "Generally in Japan, since visible results and effects in the short term are required for government administrations, concentrated investment for the future is often criticized," he says.

However, Soichiro and his office forged ahead and received the designation of National Strategic Special Zone for Global Startups and Job Creation from the national government. With this designation, the city government was able to open the Startup Café to familiarize the local communities with startups and to deregulate startup visas enough to welcome more international entrepreneurs to the region.

With the demand for support growing with the ecosystem, the city's next step was to launch the huge startup hub Fukuoka Growth Next (FGN). "At FGN," says Soichiro, "startups, aspiring entrepreneurs and members of the public can exchange ideas, grow businesses and find inspiration to create a better society." As one of the main hubs, FGN is bustling with entrepreneurs from Fukuoka and abroad, as well as investors and established businesses.

In addition to FGN, the city has launched Engineer Cafe in Tenjin, Fukuoka's downtown area, as a meetup locale to attract engineers seeking networking and growth opportunities. Soichiro believes that engineers are not only integral to developing technology but also for creating new, "engineer-driven" business ideas. The growth of both FGN and Engineer Cafe is important for driving the creation of social-impact businesses.

This focus on startups has already made an impact on some of Fukuoka's and Japan's social challenges. In Japan, the birthrate is in decline and the population is aging, so there is a lack of personnel and productivity in the welfare workforce. The number of people responsible for community activities and child monitoring has also decreased. "It is difficult to solve those problems alone," says Soichiro, citing the importance of working with startups.

To tackle some of these challenges, the city government launched "mirai@," a program which accepts tech proposals from startups and tech businesses working in AI and IoT with a focus on solving important social issues. "With this program, demonstration experiments can be conducted throughout the city," says Soichiro, "and if those technologies are recognized as good services, then other municipalities will have an easier time introducing such technology, as it sets a good precedent." This exemplifies Fukuoka's potential as the perfect hub for tech innovators who celebrate risk-taking and purpose.

Moreover, the city is planning a remarkable urban-development project for tech startups all over the world, called "Fukuoka Smart East." This project aims to redevelop fifty hectares (124 acres) of the former site of Kyushu University into a smart city to strengthen the infrastructure for disruptive, purpose-driven innovators and make a leading example of a smart city as a solution for social challenges. "For example, unmanned-operation buses and delivery drones can be solutions for the aging population in Japan," says Soichiro. "However, existing urban infrastructures make it difficult to introduce new technologies in an ideal way. With this redevelopment project, we will make new urban infrastructures that are compatible with such new technologies."

" I feel that the challenge mindset of taking risks and creating new values and businesses, which is the essence of startups, has been steadily fostered in our local startup ecosystem "

All of these initiatives have made the city a close-knit community of startups and the organizations that support them. More and more international entrepreneurs have come to Fukuoka, especially to experiment with new business ideas. "I feel that the challenge mindset of taking risks and creating new values and businesses, which is the essence of startups, has been steadily fostered in our local startup ecosystem," says Soichiro. Fukuoka is set to become an ideal experimental space for startups who want to tackle social innovation challenges..

[ABOUT]

Fukuoka Growth Next (FGN) is a startup hub with coworking and acceleration facilities on-site. Created via a public–private partnership with the mission to foster innovation and support local and international startups, FGN gives startups, entrepreneurs and people in the community the opportunity to exchange ideas, grow businesses and inspire one another to improve the world via innovation. The initiative is strongly supported by the mayor's office, local government entities and local businesses.

[CONTACT]

WEB   city.fukuoka.lg.jp/keizai/r-support/sougyou/index.html

EMAIL   startup.EPB@city.fukuoka.lg.jp

Doreming

ELEVATOR PITCH

" We provide financial services to people
without a bank account via our free,
integrated platform for HR, payroll
and financial services. "

SECTOR fintech

WEB doreming.com/ja

MILESTONES

Holding a UK-Japan fintech event
in London.

Partnering with Seven Bank
and Nihon Unisys.

Partnering with Lien Viet Post Bank
and Eximbank.

Setting up a business alliance
with Tokio Marine & Nichido Fire
Insurance in Japan and Mitsui
Sumitomo Insurance in Vietnam.

The inspiration for Doreming came from Kizuna Japan Co., Ltd.'s expansion into Vietnam. Most staff members didn't have a bank account into which the company could pay their salaries and they relied on services to get the salary in cash and then convert that money to mobile phone apps. Yoshikazu Takasaki, founder of Kizuna Japan, saw an opportunity to develop a better system, so he set up Doreming in 2015. With his team, he developed a way to record the clock-in and clock-off times of staff, allowing companies to manage attendance and calculate payroll while reducing paperwork. Next came the development of salary payments directly to a worker's smartphone account, removing the need to use cash at all. The user could then make payments or send money immediately.

Yoshikazu personally raised ¥84 million to invest in Doreming. With an estimated two billion adults worldwide without access to a bank account, he saw the potential growth of the business and started expansion. Doreming set up a subsidiary in the US, followed by subsidiaries in the UK (in 2016), Singapore and India (in 2017) and Saudi Arabia (in 2018). However, launching Doreming has not been without its challenges. As the business plan is to offer the service for free to users (both employer and employee), it was difficult to generate income, but the company is steadily preparing to generate revenue from companies that receive payments via Doreming or provide loans and insurance to users.

TEAM

With seven offices across the globe, Doreming boasts a diverse team consisting of members of various backgrounds, skills, experiences and perspectives. The staff enjoys a great work–life balance as each member can work when it suits them; they simply ensure they work their required number of hours per month. Each office operates as an independent business, thereby allowing management to cultivate a sense of responsibility for development, sales, distribution and so on. Staff members in each office are free to work in any Doreming office in the world.

Kids Code Club

ELEVATOR PITCH

" We provide a platform that aims to eradicate child poverty and improve educational opportunities through computer science lessons that are both fun and free. Our goal is to create a society where all children are able to pursue their dreams. "

SECTOR education

WEB kidscodeclub.jp

MILESTONES

Founding Kids Code Club in 2016.

Beginning "Computer science in English" courses in collaboration with SIJP in 2018.

Reaching a total of 1,300 participants (including both parents and children) in computer science workshops in 2019.

Beginning to approach investors for fundraising and launching a tech-learning app in 2020.

Maiko Ishikawa knows what it's like to struggle in life. Financial difficulties forced her to drop out of university, and she found employment as a contract worker, but she grew tired of hopping from job to job by the day and began to think about how she could earn a living with just her computer and an internet connection. She hit upon web design and spent the next three years teaching herself, launching her own web design company in 2008. However, after having a child, she began to reflect on her background and how one out of seven children in Japan lives in relative poverty. She decided that teaching programming would give children greater access to future education and prepare them for life in a society where technological skills are becoming increasingly indispensable.

TEAM

According to Maiko Ishikawa, the best thing about the Kids Code Club team is that everyone's sense of values is different. Maiko heads a small team of four that she assembled through her personal and professional networks, both online and offline. Members range in age from their early thirties to fifties, bringing different perspectives. This means they sometimes clash, but it also leads to productive discussions and the development of fresh ideas. Everyone has other jobs in different fields in addition to their work at Kids Code Club, and this is something Maiko actively encourages, as she believes it's natural for adults as much as children to have many creative ideas, so people should follow their interests. With their full-stack engineer working remotely, daily communication is done via Slack with Zoom video conferences when needed, and a face-to-face team meeting once a month. Around thirty mentors in Japan volunteer to lead the online workshops for children.

In 2016, Maiko founded Kids Code Club to provide a platform where children can learn programming at workshops held in Japanese and English. She collaborates with Seattle IT Japanese Professionals (SIJP) to run workshops in which US-based Japanese engineers at large tech companies such as Google or Microsoft give computer science lessons in English to children in Fukuoka and Kumamoto through online seminars. Kids Code Club is also currently developing a free app using blockchain technology through which children can receive "coins" by completing online programming courses, and these coins can then be used to take further courses. As their revenue comes from donations from corporations and private individuals, this system will enable supporters to track how their funding is being used, so they can directly see the positive impact.

Kyulux

" We are commercializing Hyperfluorescence™, a game-changing, organic light-emitting diode (OLED) display technology that enables highly efficient and pure color emission using rare-metal-free organic materials. "

SECTOR **chemical manufacturing**

WEB **kyulux.com**

- Holding the licenses of two basic patents: the TADF parameter patent and the Hyperfluorescence™ patent.

- Achieving the world's longest lifetime (120 hours) for a deep blue OLED.

- Achieving the target lifetime for yellow and red OLED for smartphone and industrial display applications.

- Launching the world's first Hyperfluorescence™ yellow monochrome display.

Kyulux is a fabless-material company commercializing Hyperfluorescence™ and thermally activated delayed fluorescence (TADF) technologies to OLED display panel makers. It has won numerous accolades, including the 2018 CEATEC Grand Prix Award in Device and Technology, the 2019 Innovation Showcase of Japan–US Innovation Award and the 2019 Minister of Economy, Trade and Industry Award for Academic Startups.

Hyperfluorescence™ was invented by Dr. Chihaya Adachi (cofounder of Kyulux) and his research group at Kyushu University in 2013. The work was built on the team's 2012 invention of TADF, a third-generation OLED technology. It had low color purity, so Hyperfluorescence™ solved this problem by offering highly efficient, pure color without the use of iridium. With the goal of commercializing this new material, Chihaya launched Kyulux in 2015 with cofounders Junji Adachi (CEO) and Akira Minakuchi (CFO).

TEAM

Cofounder Dr. Chihaya Adachi is a world-leading researcher of OLED materials, Junji Adachi is an engineer experienced in commercializing cleantech and OLED materials, and Akira Minakuchi is a global venture capitalist with eight years of experience in Silicon Valley. With members drawn from academia, research, business and management, Kyulux's team has diverse experience, skills and ways of thinking. Each team member has a strong track record in technology or business and many are talented in the OLED field. The team is energetic and lively in its work culture, and, with staff working across Japan and the US, it is global in its thinking. Staff members in Fukuoka particularly enjoy the city's rich food culture. Thanks to the city's compact size and wealth of green spaces, most staff live within thirty minutes of the office, so they enjoy a comfortable, pleasant commute.

Though the technology was solid, funding proved a problem. "Even after more than three hundred negotiations with VCs, panel makers and material makers, we could not raise one cent," says Junji. "It was difficult for most VCs to understand the technology and business of advanced materials." Still, Kyulux raised ¥1.5 billion in 2016 and ¥3.5 billion in 2019, including funding from the Japan Science and Technology Agency and Kyushu University. Fukuoka Prefecture and Fukuoka City also lent their support. The local government and Kyushu University provided Kyulux with access to start-of-the-art equipment and cleanroom facilities at its development center for organic photonics and electronics near Kyushu University.

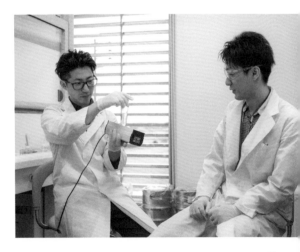

On Grit Engineering

ELEVATOR PITCH

" We use untapped human resources
and technology to ensure the safety
of infrastructure across Japan and
promote a positive work environment
in the engineering industry. "

MILESTONES

Meeting lots of people who
supported business development.

Attracting skilled technicians
to work in the company.

Winning the Yunus & You Social
Business Design Contest 2018.

Becoming certified as having the
seven principles of social business
by Yunus Social Business.

SECTOR civil engineering

WEB on-grit.com

With four years' experience in computer-aided design (CAD), cofounder and CEO Haruna Morikawa created On Grit Engineering with two others in 2018. She was inspired by personal experience: her engineer husband had told her about Japan's shortage of engineers (particularly in depopulated areas), and a friend had told her how difficult it was to find a job as a single mother. She had also learned that the country's aging infrastructure and lack of human resources for surveying was resulting in the closure of some two thousand bridges every year. She decided to address these issues by setting up a company that would hire working mothers and use technologies such as AI and robots to enable them to do CAD. Haruna chose Fukuoka as the company's location due to the city's nurturing environment for new ventures.

TEAM

In the early days of On Grit, Haruna Morikawa found her team members via personal introductions. Most of them had a background in engineering or academia, with expertise in AI or vibration sensors. She recruited a manager from an engineering company, where he had vast experience as a developer. Today, she recruits her staff via advertisements in specialist magazines, but she says that the shortage of human resources continues to be problematic. Most important to her is a person who emanates the company name – grit – who will never give up despite the difficulties he or she faces. Her team is split fifty-fifty in terms of gender and all are Japanese. The team enjoys a relaxed office culture as well as excursions together. The first trip of 2020 was to On Grit's local shrine, where everyone prayed for the success of the company in the year ahead.

On Grit secured an investment of ¥20 million and began creating a database of engineering terms so that CAD could be used by amateurs. It also started offering non-invasive methods of surveying bridges and other concrete infrastructure while developing robots that could assess and fix street lighting. Its image-analysis software uses AI technology that can be rented, so other companies can also employ labor-saving robots. On Grit is one of only four companies in Kyushu to receive support from Japan's Ministry of Economy, Trade and Industry because of its work to maintain local infrastructure and thus help society.

Tom Brooke

CEO
/ Qurate

A digital pioneer from the UK, Tom Brooke's eclectic career has advanced hand-in-hand with the evolution of the internet. Immediately after earning his graphic design degree from Westwood Art College, Tom found himself designing the original Rolls-Royce website, helping to establish the company's initial online presence. After stints of running his own consultancy and traveling the world as a digital nomad, Tom's experiences led him to realize that curation is the key to digital content. In 2014, he founded Fukuoka-based Qurate to transform this vision into a product that helps companies unify their unique content across all digital channels.

ABOUT THE COMPANY

Qurate is an experience platform that allows people to drive their business online through content. The Qurate® Platform enables content creators and managers to unify their brand voice and share content consistently on the websites, apps and social media platforms of their choice.

WEB **qurate.com**

What was your entrepreneurial path?

My first job after graduating was a multimedia designer. It was at that point that I got into the web, systems and content. Before then, I was mostly just creating interactive, artsy type stuff. When I started working, I realized that there was actually quite a lot of depth in digital, and it was all so new.

I worked for Rolls-Royce, built their first website and became head of multimedia because I was literally the only one there who could do that kind of work. It was a very practical job, and I learned a lot in a very short space of time.

Eventually, I left Rolls-Royce and set up my own consultancy in London where I worked as an ideas consultant for brands through various agencies. I was still in my early twenties at this point. I was raking in a lot of money, living with my parents and just commuting to London when I needed to. But I didn't really like this. I knew that there was something more for me in life. I didn't want to simply settle down and become an old guy in the ad industry. So I just left and started traveling around the world.

I got deeply involved in philosophy, meditation and that kind of stuff. I spent a lot of time with myself and had a big think about what I wanted to do. And then, in the middle of these travels, I realized that I could actually still work if I wanted to. I became a first-generation digital nomad. In the end, I settled in Japan, and I quickly discovered Fukuoka.

" The problem with the internet is not about creating content; it's about finding it. "

How did you come up with your business model?

Back in 2005, social media and blogs were just coming about. I believed that the future would be more than a hyperlinked internet. It would be an age of curation. That's where the idea behind Qurate came from.

We are all natural curators. Everything that I'm wearing right now, everything in my pocket, everything in my home, everything in my music library, my film library and on my bookshelf, are all things that I've curated. When people see me, they see the things I've curated – the person I've curated – and digital life is exactly the same as that. We can find anything on the internet. The problem with the internet is not about creating content; it's about finding it. So, how do you do this? That is what I was thinking about for five years. How could I make a natural, inspirational content-discovery platform?

People become inspired by something that is not only about creation but also curation. After realizing this, I started architecting the platform. I was working for agencies, and I realized that all of these agencies have the problems that my technical solution would solve. That's how the business model emerged.

How exactly does your business model work?

There are two main ways that we generate revenue: one way is selling directly to businesses, and the other is selling through agencies. We're selling to the agencies so that they can use our platform with their customers. We work with agencies like Toppan, the largest printing company in the world. They have fifty thousand customers in Japan and ten thousand salespeople. Those salespeople carry our platform with them, and when they sell it, they take a cut and we get a cut. We actually have a fifty-fifty revenue share split with them, so that incentivizes them quite a lot because they can make billions of yen off of our platform. They're striving to become more technical. They're a printing company; they need to get into digital marketing, and we make it easy for them. So we've established a joint venture with them.

That being said, we're also working direct, selling directly to organizations such as Fukuoka City, Kyoto City, Nishi-Nihon City Bank and so on. We're not at the stage where we can efficiently sell to companies like Shiseido or Meiji directly, but agencies such as Toppan and NTT Data can, so we're able to reach medium enterprises directly, and we're able to reach the larger enterprises through our partners.

What challenges did you encounter during the early stages of your startup?

To begin with, our product was a bit too disruptive. Big businesses in particular would rather go with a market leader. No one gets fired for going with IBM, right? It's taken us a few years to scale our product down to the level where it's acceptable and to learn how to actually sell it to companies.

I also struggled with delegating and managing. As I mentioned, at one point I had become a digital nomad. I was essentially a one-man band. I was living on my own, traveling on my own and I could do everything myself. I didn't really depend on other people. I worked with other talented people like writers, animators and illustrators for things that I didn't specialize in, but I didn't have a team of people, and I wasn't a good manager or a delegator. It took me a while to adjust. Now I spend most of my time delegating and managing people. I'm not a doer anymore, and I don't really make anything anymore, which is kind of sad because I like making things. So that was really the hardest bit: making the transition from a creator to a manager.

Conversely, what did you do well?

I didn't struggle with making the company. I also didn't have problems finding people or raising money, to be honest. It wasn't easy but, at the same time, it wasn't hard; whereas management and sales are an entirely different thing.

What mistakes did you make as you grew your business? What do you wish you had done differently?

I would have put a lot more emphasis on sales and marketing early on. When you're working on something that you consider to be your baby, it's never going to be ready, and you just keep working and working on it. You develop a false sense of confidence that you've made something that everyone wants. When it finally reaches the point where you think it's ready to launch, you realize that fundamental thing: you realize that no one is ready for this, that it's going to be a pain to sell, or that what they want is something super simple, which you could actually have made in three or four weeks.

In hindsight, I also needed more experience and a good mentor, but I didn't know that I needed them at the time. I had the vision and the confidence, and we had the skills, but mentorship was the real thing that was missing. Had I known a successful startup founder who could listen to me, understand me, validate my idea and help me bring my product to market earlier, I would be in a completely different place right now.

What advice would you give other people in the early stages of their startup?

Validate. That's it. I don't even need to think about it. Whatever your idea is, you've got someone in mind who you think would use it or benefit from it. Go and talk to as many of them as early on as possible and ask them if they like the idea, but don't leave it at that. Ask them if they'd pay for it. You need overwhelming evidence to support your idea. Don't make it easy by finding people who like to be nice. You have to really drill down and test your hypothesis. Doing that at an early stage will make all the difference. So few people really do that – I certainly didn't.

What do you love about living and working in Fukuoka?

Fukuoka is essentially the same as the rest of Japan. This means that everything is very high quality and you get great service. Additionally, people tend to respect your privacy. What I've found, however, is that Fukuoka is a slightly more concentrated version of that than Tokyo. For example, you get something a little bit better and a little cheaper as well. The quality here is so high that if you come in with a shoddy business plan or your restaurant serves rubbish food, you just won't survive. So, you have to be good at what you do.

We have a word in Japanese, *kodawari*, which means the never-ending perfection of your skill. I love the fact that everyone here – whether they're working in a skateboard shop or ramen shop, whether it's a super cheap place or a super expensive place – is fully into what they're doing. I take inspiration from that. I'm a better version of myself in Fukuoka than I would be in my home country. It brings good qualities out of me. After all of my travels, I found Fukuoka to be the most inspirational place for me to live. It's very easy to live and do good work here. •

What are your top work essentials?
Space. I like having my own space.

At what age did you found your company?
Thirty-four.

What's your most used app?
Slack.

What's the most valuable piece of advice you've been given?
The job is more important than the ideas you have about it.

What do you do every morning (or the night before) to prepare for the day ahead?
Coffee. I can't live without coffee.

What book has most influenced your career?
Start with Why.

What favorite positive habit have you cultivated?
Pausing – a very short meditation between projects.

Kumiko Sasaki
Founder and Chairman

& Eihiro Saishu
President and CEO

/ Groovenauts

Kumiko Sasaki is a lifelong Fukuoka resident and passionate entrepreneur with an extensive background in engineering. Eihiro Saishu was born in Osaka and built a successful IT and entrepreneurial career in Japan and the US. After the two successfully collaborated on a joint project, they decided to found Groovenauts in 2011. Ever since then, these innovative leaders have been working tirelessly to democratize complex technology and break down the technological, geographic and cultural borders that impede the progress of modern businesses.

ABOUT THE COMPANY

Groovenauts provides a cloud-based platform that brings the power of big data, AI and quantum computing to all. With MAGELLAN BLOCKS, Groovenauts democratizes technology with solutions that customers of all skill levels can use. Groovenauts also provides high-tech educational opportunities for children through their after-school childcare service, TECH PARK.

WEB groovenauts.jp

What challenges did you face during the early stages of your startup?

EIHIRO In the beginning, the company focused on cutting-edge technology designed to handle the heavy technological demands of the gaming industry. Our first challenge was learning how to apply that specialized technology to a wider range of businesses. We believed that if we could satisfy the strict needs of the gaming industry, we would be well positioned to serve other industries that required massive amounts of data to be transferred quickly and reliably. We started off catering to experts and professionals, but we quickly realized that if our technology was to be used widely, we needed to reach out to general audiences. Making this transition was the first major problem we had to solve.

What was the greatest mistake that you made during your entrepreneurial journey?

EIHIRO When we started out, our product wasn't fully developed, so we survived by designing custom solutions to serve our clients' needs instead of finalizing our original product. This was a mistake because our attention was divided. We couldn't focus on what we wanted to build.

In a sense, we were offering consulting services instead of an original product or service. Transitioning away from relying entirely on the consulting business

model to being a service provider was also one of our early challenges. We failed to quickly complete the original product that we had envisioned. When we reached the point when we could finally realize our original vision, the transition was difficult and we suffered a deficit. This was a difficult process that took many years to complete.

Can you tell us more about your business model?

EIHIRO We currently have two businesses under our brand. First, we have MAGELLAN BLOCKS, which I oversee. Our other business is TECH PARK, which Kumiko is in charge of.

MAGELLAN BLOCKS is our cloud platform that unlocks the power of machine learning and quantum computers for all. Our technology enables anyone, regardless of their technical background and knowledge, to harness the power of cutting-edge technology such as big data, AI and quantum computers. On the other hand, TECH PARK is a high-tech childcare center where children can enjoy and learn about technology with programs tailored to their individual skills, personalities and needs.

KUMIKO Regarding MAGELLAN BLOCKS, these days creating cutting-edge software requires a lot of skilled engineers. Therefore, there's a high demand for engineers in Japan, and companies are struggling to find exceptional talent. Additionally, even the most talented engineers find it difficult to keep up with how

quickly technology changes and evolves. We created MAGELLAN BLOCKS to solve this problem. In a sense, we are democratizing advanced technology so that any company can thrive, even if there is a shortage of talented engineers.

As for TECH PARK, we wanted to create a trusted place where working parents could leave their children without hesitation or concern. Through this initiative, we hope that children can gain a certain level of awareness regarding technology, IT and AI while also learning the skills they'll need to become the next generation of engineers. I want to share how fun engineering is and build a network around that. I hope they can also use programming, digital art, digital fabrication and more as new tools to express their ideas.

That's the main reason I started TECH PARK. However, I also discovered that there's a need for the public to learn more about AI, and TECH PARK is a great gateway to get more people involved in the field.

EIHIRO One unique aspect of our company is our intense focus on the city of Fukuoka. There's a big cultural difference between Tokyo and Fukuoka. In Tokyo, there's a clear separation between work and personal life. However, in Fukuoka your personal life tends to blend with your professional life, so here a good company is one that lets us consider the needs of our families. We appreciate companies that can sympathize with our personal needs.

Speaking of Fukuoka, what do you like about living and working in this city?

EIHIRO First of all, there's a strong sense of teamwork and trust among employees. Of course, this also exists in Tokyo, but I feel that sense is greater here. We don't just bond as employees but also as human beings. This bond is critical when it comes to innovation and trying new things. It's what keeps us going.

Additionally, the people in Fukuoka are open minded. We welcome people from overseas and Japanese people from all over the country. We believe in diversity – not isolationism.

KUMIKO There are many reasons I could have left Fukuoka, but finding work wasn't one of them. People would often ask me why I didn't work outside of Fukuoka. I was raising children, so I didn't want to leave this supportive community just for a different job. I valued my children above all, and I wanted to raise them in a familiar environment. I can still do the work I love and enjoy a great life here in Fukuoka. A lot of Tokyo-based companies have branch offices here in Fukuoka. These offices don't harbor a culture of innovation and trying new things, so I wanted to challenge those companies to be cutting edge and independent.

EIHIRO People who live and work in Tokyo tend to misunderstand a few things about Fukuoka. There's a disproportionate amount of focus on Tokyo's business scene and an impression that there isn't a significant amount of business and startup activity outside of Japan's capital city. This is a misconception. Just look at some of Japan's largest and most famous companies, such as Toyota, Nissan and Mazda – they don't have Tokyo head offices. Panasonic, based in Osaka, is another great example.

Additionally, Fukuoka's population is about the same size as the population of Estonia, and the population of the Kyushu region matches that of Belgium. In other words, there's the possibility here to generate as much economic activity as an entire country. That's a lot of potential, and that's something that a lot of people living in Tokyo don't realize. You need the experience of living and working here to fully understand that.

" *Establish your vision carefully and work toward it. Society will tell you what your company should be and do. If you realize this and listen to the market, your business can succeed.* "

What advice do you have for aspiring entrepreneurs and those who are in the early stages of running a startup?

EIHIRO Establish your vision carefully, and work toward it. Society will tell you what your company should be and do. If you realize this and listen to the market, your business can succeed. Look for opportunities to address society's needs, and build your business accordingly. Ask yourself what your business can do for society.

KUMIKO I'm a woman, but I don't like being labeled as a "female entrepreneur" or "female trailblazer." Unfortunately, society is primarily perceived from a male perspective. This applies to the startup world as well. There is a lot of bias out there, so I can't simply say "good luck" to women who want to become startup founders. The reality is that you're going to have to work twice as hard as a man would to get your startup off the ground. Even if you do and say the right things, male investors might not take you seriously.

Therefore, I recommend that you surround yourself with experienced women – those who have successfully overcome this challenge and are willing to share their advice with you. This is especially helpful if you have children. Your mentors and network can help you figure out how to balance your work and family life. That's why it's not enough for me to simply say, "Good luck and do your best." •

What are your top work essentials?
EIHIRO Trusted companions.

What's your most-used app?
KUMIKO G Suite.

What do you do every morning (or night before) to prepare for the day ahead?
EIHIRO Think and write down my thoughts on paper.

What favorite positive habit have you cultivated?
KUMIKO Fishing and cooking.

Co-necto

Co-necto is an annual program hosted and sponsored by Toppan Printing, a printing, communications and technology company established in 1900 that connects the innovation of startups to the resources of established businesses. The program is aimed at finding startups that provide new services to Japan (for example, in digital communication, operational efficiency and healthcare services) and at startups that would like to explore the Japanese market. The program's recruitment takes approximately three months and involves both document screening and pitching. Toppan Printing provides the selected startups with resources in the form of financial incentives, client introductions and business collaboration. In 2020, Toppan Printing will invite its client network to join as partners and to work with startups on accelerating commercialization through proof-of-concept trials.

SECTOR B2B services
PREVIOUS PARTICIPANTS yamap, Qurate, VesCir, anect, Payke, thee moment, Hyper Immersion Technology
WHO SHOULD APPLY Foreign startups that want to expand into the Japanese market and that provide new services such as digital transformation, healthcare and business efficiency.
APPLY **toppan-co-necto.com**
WEB **toppan.com/en**

Hirameki Sprint

Hirameki Sprint is an innovation program run by Toyota Motor Kyushu, Inc. aimed at creating a better future for the area of Kyushu. The program's name represents the emergence of ideas and solutions through intense periods of collaboration, such as through the sprints the program facilitates. The program is a three-month intensive, after which selected participants can enter a competition for collaboration and funding from Toyota Kyushu. It accepts applications from not only entrepreneurs and startups but also students, researchers and general office workers. Participants can expect a ¥500,000 subsidy for proof-of-concept production costs, diverse expert mentoring and priority invitations to the competition event. During the program they also have free use of the coworking space, can attend lectures on Toyota Group's principles of manufacturing and have the possibility of expanding their business globally with the Toyota Group.

SECTOR next-generation services for cities
SELECTED PORTFOLIO The program is in its first year and one example collaboration is with Mobby, a company that provides electric kickboards (scooters) for use in Toyota factories in Kyushu.
WHO SHOULD APPLY Ideal participants are those in manufacturing, town-building and Mobility as a Service, but anyone wanting to collaborate for a better future is encouraged to apply.
APPLY **info@garrawayf.com**
WEB **garrawayf.com**

Jump Start Program

The Jump Start program at Fukuoka Growth Next is a one-stop shop that covers all the essential elements of creating a successful startup. The program is aimed at early-stage startups and budding entrepreneurs who need help evolving their business or fine-tuning their business skills. Field experts cover topics ranging from developing a startup mindset to preparing for a pitch, and just about everything in between. The Jump Start Program also seeks to develop local entrepreneur networks and the Fukuoka startup ecosystem. It does this by working with successful local founders, who provide coaching and insights throughout the program. The program also makes participants aware of benefits available from the city government, such as tax reductions for those who register a company. It culminates in a demo day, where participants have the opportunity to pitch to investors.

SECTOR sector-agnostic
SELECTED PORTFOLIO WAAK, Camp Jyoshi, Reright, Toypo
WHO SHOULD APPLY Early-stage startups and budding entrepreneurs who want to learn business essentials.
APPLY Applications open annually, usually in June. See the website for more details.
WEB growth-next.com

Updraft

Updraft is a full-scale acceleration program that provides startup teams with investment, mentors, business collaboration opportunities and educational content covering topics such as marketing and finance. Its mission is to become a world-class acceleration program. Updaft's name represents the strong, upward support it gives. Mentors include venture capitalists, entrepreneurs and specialists from various business fields. At the end of the program, the startup teams participate in demo days in Tokyo and Fukuoka, pitching their ideas to investors. Updraft is mainly focused on tech startups related to AI, augmented reality (AR), virtual reality (VR) and IoT. For example, QUANDO is a successful startup that was able to refine its product and recruit team members during the program, leading to its success launching an original product that uses AR technology for construction sites.

SECTOR tech related to AI, VR and AR
SELECTED PORTFOLIO QUANDO, anect and KINCHAKU
WHO SHOULD APPLY Startups from the pre-seed stage through the seed-funding phase from Japan, South Korea, Hong Kong and Taiwan.
APPLY gx@gxpartners.vc
WEB updraft.asia

The Company Canal City Front

Conveniently located within walking distance from Hakata Station, The Company Canal City Front offers a large coworking space designed to accommodate a wide range of working styles. In addition to wifi, power outlets and flex seating, members have access to a variety of amenities, including lockers, meeting rooms, event space, phone booths, coffee and more. Members can also join The Company's own social media platform, which facilitates connection and collaboration between members across all nine locations (four in Japan and five overseas). For startups and entrepreneurs, The Company offers membership plans that include private office space for up to twenty-five people as well as phone-call and mail-receiving services and other amenities and perks. It also offers a drop-in plan that is paid for by the hour or day.

ADDRESS 1F, 2F Dai-ichi Prince Building, 8-13 Gionmachi, Hakata-ku, Fukuoka 812-0038
OPENING HOURS Mon–Fri: 9 AM–9 PM
USP A spacious coworking space with an international network of locations.
PRICE RANGE Flex desks: from ¥20,300 per month. Private booth/office: from ¥52,000 per month. Drop-in: ¥500 per hour up to three hours or ¥1,500 per day.
WEB thecompany.jp/en

Engineer Cafe – Hacker Space Fukuoka

Engineer Cafe – Hacker Space Fukuoka is a completely free coworking space intended to be used primarily by programmers and engineers. The space is located inside the Fukuoka Akarenga Cultural Center, a historic brick building completed in 1909. Designed by famed architect Tatsuno Kingo, it was named an Important Cultural Property by the Japanese Government in 1969. The main hall features a variety of flex seating and desk space, wifi, power outlets and a library of books. There's also a separate room with six booths designed for deep concentration. On the basement floor is a reservable meeting room as well as a room equipped with a laser cutter for light prototyping. The adjoining cafe stays open until 9 PM serving coffee, snacks and alcoholic beverages.

ADDRESS 1-15-30 Tenjin, Chuo-ku, Fukuoka 810-0001
OPENING HOURS Coworking Space: 9 AM–10 PM. Cafe: 11 AM–9 PM (entire space closed the last Monday of the month or the following day if that Monday is a holiday.
USP A free coworking space for programmers inside a historic architectural treasure.
PRICE RANGE Flex desks: free. Coffee: ¥400 yen. Beer: from ¥600.
WEB engineercafe.jp/en

fabbit Global Gateway "ACROS Fukuoka"

Founded in 2017, fabbit operates several startup spaces throughout Fukuoka and across Japan. In December 2018, it added Global Gateway "ACROS Fukuoka" to its lineup. The coworking space is located inside a unique multipurpose facility that also contains the Fukuoka Symphony Hall and is near government offices necessary for startups' business administration. Global Gateway "ACROS Fukuoka" is focused on international expansion, both for Japanese startups expanding internationally and foreign entrepreneurs looking to enter the Japanese market. All fabbit spaces offer startup support based on four pillars: people, resources, funds and opportunities. In practice, this means providing entrepreneurs with HR services, discounted business services, investments and fundraising support and dedicated events for startups to pitch and connect with other businesses.

ADDRESS ACROS Fukuoka 1F, 1-1-1 Tenjin, Chuo-ku, Fukuoka 810-0001
OPENING HOURS For monthly members: 24/7. For general public reception: Mon–Fri: 9 AM–6 PM.
USP Located in the heart of Fukuoka in a multipurpose facility administered by the government, allowing easy access for collaboration and support.
PRICE RANGE Hot desks: available through a limited-time campaign at ¥1,400 per day or ¥14,000 per month. Private offices: starting at ¥160,000 per month.
WEB fabbit.co.jp/facility/global-gateway-acros-fukuoka

Fukuoka Growth Next

Fukuoka Growth Next is located in an approximately hundred-year-old, renovated elementary school building. The classroom interiors and hallways remain largely untouched, creating a sense of nostalgia. During the day, the on-site coffee shop keeps the resident startups and entrepreneurs caffeinated with local specialty coffees, while in the evening the bar is popular for socializing and networking. There's also a Startup Cafe that offers multilingual consultation services for startups free of charge. The coworking space hosts more than one hundred events on-site each year, with capacity for up to one hundred attendees. Fukuoka Growth Next is located in the heart of Tenjin, with easy access to multiple public transport options and an abundance of dining and drinking establishments nearby.

ADDRESS 2-6-11 Daimyo, Chuo-ku, Fukuoka 810-0041
OPENING HOURS 9 AM–10 PM (Private-office and fixed-desk members have 24/7 access).
USP Fukuoka Growth Next offers a range of workspaces where members can work quietly. It also offers a variety of community spaces that are open to the public.
PRICE RANGE Hot desks: from ¥15,000 per month. Fixed desks: from ¥20,000 per month. Private offices (15–30 m^2): ¥2,600 per month per m^2. Drop-in: ¥500 per hour or ¥1,500 per day.
WEB growth-next.com

Maizuru Park, Fukuoka

Kyushu University Business School (QBS)

Kyushu University is the fourth-oldest university in Japan, but rather than following tradition it aims to become a top global university through innovation and change by setting high standards of research, attracting global talent and developing in tandem with society. For example, the university opened its twelfth undergraduate school based on a model of education new to Japan, and it launched the Robert T. Huang Entrepreneurship Center program (QREC). Undergraduates, graduates and international students can all enroll in entrepreneurship courses offered by QREC, which benefits from having directors who are also professors at the Kyushu University Business School (QBS). Aligning with the entire university, QBS has a strong focus on new business value creation. In collaboration with QREC and the startup ecosystem in Fukuoka, it offers programs for creating science-and-technology-oriented innovation.

LOCATION The main Ito Campus is surrounded by nature in the Motooka area. QBS business-school classes are mainly held in central Fukuoka at the JR Hakata Station.
CLOSE TRANSIT CONNECTIONS Showa Bus service runs between Ito Campus and the nearest train station, Kyūdai-Gakkentoshi Station.
PRICE OF TUITION ¥535,800 per year for both undergraduate and graduate schools.
ENTRY REQUIREMENTS Kyushu University offers three undergraduate degree programs in English and seventy-three international courses at the graduate level. Most QBS classes are taught in Japanese and international students need N1 language certification, but all students must be able to complete two classes taught in English.
WEB kyushu-u.ac.jp/en

Fukuoka University

Fukuoka University is an attractive private university with a large, centralized campus, some of the best research facilities in the country and approximately twenty thousand Japanese and international students. Its mission is to pursue truth and freedom, cultivate creative self-starters and contribute to the development of society. For international students hoping to enroll in undergraduate or postgraduate studies anywhere in Japan, the university's School of Japanese Language and Culture for International Students is a great place to start. This program is intended to equip foreign students with an understanding of the language and culture of Japan and prepare them to enter university. Fukuoka University also offers an extracurricular entrepreneurship course, featuring a range of lectures and events focused on business development. A variety of scholarships, tuition reduction and financial assistance programs are available to help with the financial burden faced by international students.

LOCATION Jonan-ku, Fukuoka
CLOSE TRANSIT CONNECTIONS Fukudai-mae Station
PRICE OF TUITION ¥390,000 to ¥7,600,000 per year
ENTRY REQUIREMENTS Sufficient command of Japanese is required. Applicants must take an admission exam.
WEB fukuoka-u.ac.jp

Dogan beta

Dogan beta's goal is to revitalize the economy on the island of Kyushu by providing managerial resources, finance and advisory services to ambitious entrepreneurs in or connected to the area.

SECTOR all sectors

EMAIL beta@dogan.jp

WEB dogan.vc

Dogan beta Inc. looks for entrepreneurs and startups with a passion for global issues and a willingness to tackle complex or large-scale challenges. Its focus is on geography rather than sector, so startups from all sectors are qualified to apply. Startups can be regional, national or multinational in scope but must be based in or somehow connected to Kyushu. Staff also consider the application according to a number of factors, such as the competency of the management team, the market need for the product or service, the product or service on offer, the competition, the business strategy and the profitability.

Ryohei Hayashi, CEO and partner of Dogan beta, began his career in banking at Sumitomo Bank and then Citibank. As vice president of Dogan, he started work on the venture capital project Dogan beta. Though he didn't have experience in the field, he quickly saw what could be achieved by supporting entrepreneurs in Kyushu. "In 2012, when Dogan beta was created to support a community-based ecosystem, there were few VCs investing in Kyushu," he says. "The potential in Kyushu for investment was overlooked. We believed that the area's climate, culture and open community would create entrepreneurs and that community-based VCs would be able to support the building of the ecosystem." Dogan beta had spotted a gap in the market, and it flourished. When it became independent of Dogan in 2017 and set up as its VC subsidary, Ryohei took on the role of CEO and partner.

For Ryohei, investment is the start of a process of collaboration to grow each business, which often involves developing products and services together rather than simply providing capital. Dogan beta is "part of making things happen" for startups. "We can see the potential before the product or service is completed and share in the process of polishing it together," he says.

FGN ABBALab

FGN ABBALab supports startups in Fukuoka to further the city's goal of establishing itself as an innovation hub. It aims to attract a flow of capital into the city's ecosystem from not only Tokyo but also worldwide.

SECTOR various, including IoT, hardware and ecommerce

WEB fgnabbalab.com

As a company founder himself, Osamu Ogasahara has a good idea of what startups need and an eye for spotting a gap in the market. In 1998, he cofounded Sakura Internet and went to work as a representative for various internet companies. It was through these experiences that he began to develop an interest in IoT and hardware-focused internet. He also saw the need for a greater exchange of creative ideas, and so he established Awabar, a standing wine bar where CEOs of IT companies could socialize. It later became renowned for being frequented by the president of Mercari, Japan's first unicorn. In 2012, he started ABBALab Inc., an investment business specializing in prototyping for IoT startups. He subsequently launched DMM.make Akiba, the largest coworking space for hardware startups. When Sōichirō Takashima, mayor of Fukuoka, approached him to help out with his goal of transforming Fukuoka into an international startup city, Osamu was more than happy to get on board.

FGN ABBALab focuses specifically on businesses that operate in Fukuoka Growth Next (FGN), a coworking space and startup hub designed with the goal of fostering innovation. The fund was established in September 2019 following a major renewal of the FGN space. During this renewal, resident startups were asked about their needs, and these discussions revealed not only a desire for upgraded facilities but also a need for greater access to capital. Osamu and the FGN team managed to convince local banks and large companies to contribute to the fund and also gained the backing of serial entrepreneur Taizo Son. FGN ABBALab's portfolio boasts a range of companies specializing in everything from esports and ecommerce to wearables, AI and even space. It aims to facilitate FGN's goal to support startups and grow Fukuoka into an internationally competitive innovation hub.

GxPartners

GxPartners aims to develop Fukuoka into an international startup ecosystem by supporting domestic and overseas startups and facilitating collaboration with local large corporations.

SECTOR mainly technology (AI, IoT, AR/VR) but also healthcare and agriculture.

EMAIL gx@gxpartners.vc

WEB gxpartners.vc

GxPartners was founded in April 2019, but the team's efforts to support early-stage Fukuoka startups began several years earlier. Back then, Toshihiro Kishihara (now CEO and managing partner at GxPartners) was working with a security company in the underwriting division supporting IPOs. When Fukuoka was designated a National Strategic Zone in 2014, he got together with Takeshi Nakahara and Hiroshi Terai, two finance experts he knew from a discussion group, to consider how they could contribute to growing Fukuoka's startup ecosystem. They decided to set up Startup Go!Go!, establishing a coworking space, acceleration programs and regular pitch contest events. Capitalizing on Fukuoka's excellent location with good access to cities in East Asia, such as Taiwan, Korea and Hong Kong, they began inviting overseas startups to participate in events and to facilitate entry to Fukuoka, including signing a memorandum of understanding (MOU) with the Center of Industry Accelerator and Patent Strategy at National Chiao Tung University Taiwan in June 2018.

However, despite promising growth in Fukuoka's ecosystem, the team saw that early-stage startups still lacked access to capital and that large companies were expressing a desire to invest in startups but lacked the relevant experience.

In April 2019, they established GxPartners and joined forces with another VC firm to launch Kyushu Open Innovation Fund, funded by eleven large local companies, including Fukuoka Bank and Nishitetsu. "Through this, we can solve problems on both sides," says Toshihiro. "A huge focus is on fostering collaboration." Fukuoka, he says, is on the cusp of global recognition, and growth will only accelerate. Its proximity to East Asia provides the opportunity to create a different kind of ecosystem with international impact. Recently, GxPartners has been looking even further afield, having signed an MOU with an accelerator in Finland to smooth market entry.

Atagohama, Fukuoka

KYOTO

Kyoto, the former capital city of Japan, remains
a key node in the Japanese cultural and economic life.
It has the country's largest student population, a
deep focus on research and development, and a long
history of sustainability. One of the world's first major
climate agreements, the Kyoto Protocol, was signed
here. Startups developing prototypes in everything
from creative industries to regenerative medicine
and biotechnology have made Kyoto their home.

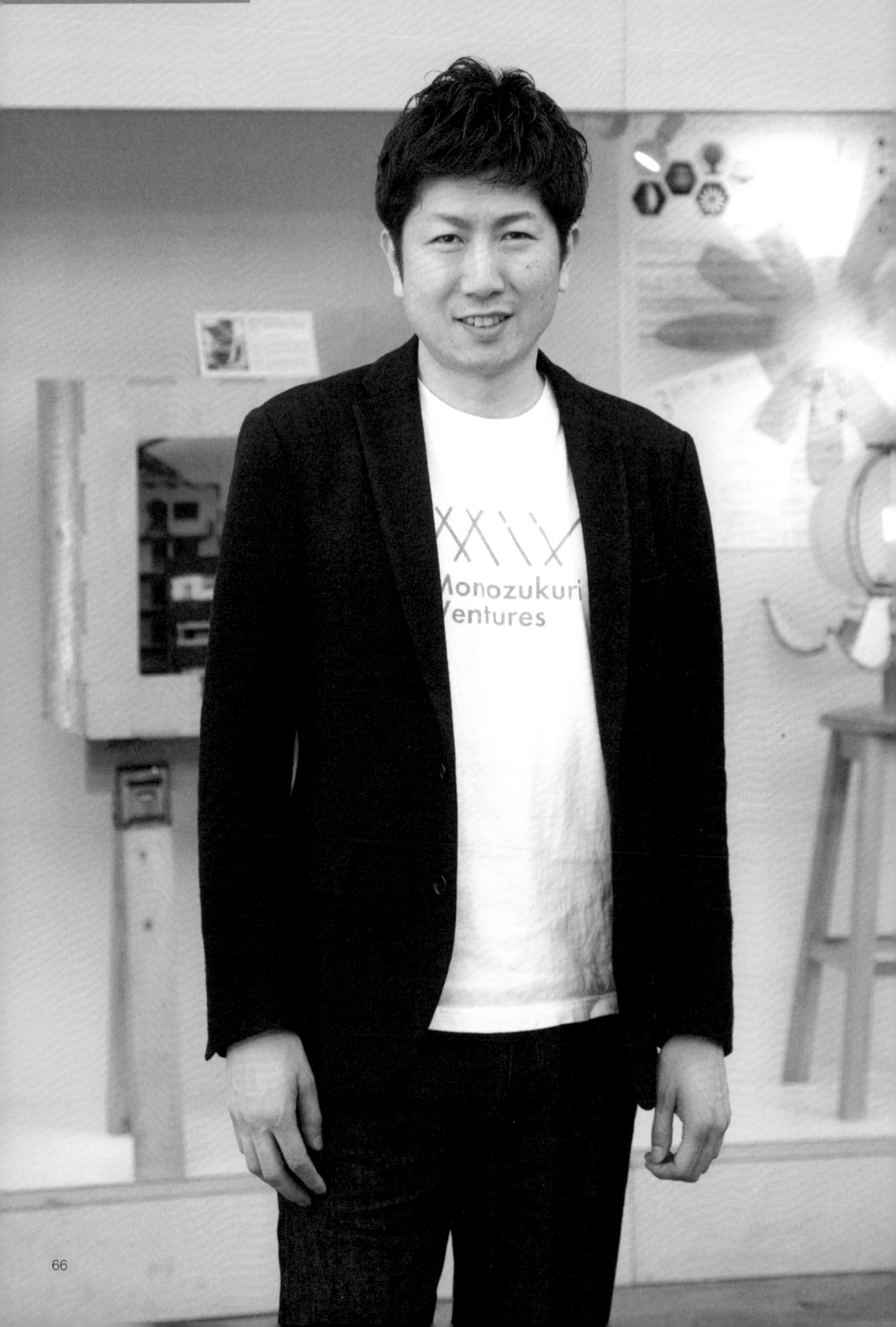
Monozukuri
Ventures

Monozukuri Ventures (MZV)

" We make hardware startups together. It takes more than funding to bridge the gap between idea and product/market fit. MZV partners with startups for the long term and works hand in glove from Kyoto and New York City. "

Kyoto is a well-known area for sightseeing, but few people know that the arts, design, architecture and culture have expanded globally thanks to innovative local entrepreneurs who transformed our lifestyle from ceramics to semiconductors, healthcare products, games and electronic devices. We inherited years of know-how in helping startups to build products at every stage of their business, from prototype to mass production, all highlighting the essence of *monozukuri*: the Japanese art of making things in a creative way.

Our strategic partners include a range of diverse manufacturing experts such as Kyoto Shisaku Net (KSN), a network of prototype professionals that combines its key Japanese best-in-class industrial know-how for hardware product development. Although known as a traditional practice of manufacturing, monozukuri also enables us to create new values by fusing two opposite ideas integrated in harmony, such as old and new, East and West, hardware and software, and historical and modern.

We cohost a series of events with local organizations and international educational institutions at Kyoto Makers Garage, a functional makerspace focused on digital fabrication, in order to foster creativity and critical thinking based on lean startup and agile methodologies. As Kyoto has the largest concentration of students in Japan (10 percent of the population) and over thirty-eight colleges and universities, our space offers free access to local students. In an aging society with so many new needs, we believe younger generations can help us overcome our future challenges, aligning an innovative mindset with traditional and sustainable elements from Kyoto.

Through our current fund, we've been able to invest in startups based in Japan and the US. We invite globally minded startups to visit Kyoto and experience our unique ecosystem as we provide long-term partnerships to startups that aim to build a new future together.

Narimasa Makino,
Monozukuri Ventures
CEO and Cofounder

Kyoto
Local Ecosystem

For many, Kyoto is a place defined by a sense of peace. In fact, the capital city of Japan for more than one thousand years is known for it and was originally called Heian-Kyo, the "capital of stability and peace." Japanese and international tourists alike consider the city a must-visit location for its temples, shrines and gardens. But despite its calm nature, the western Japanese city is also one of the most exciting and fast-moving cities in Japan, especially for startups looking to solve major challenges and innovate across a number of fields and industries.

Part of Kyoto's draw is its world-class educational institutions. One in ten Kyoto residents is a student at one of thirty-eight universities. Kyoto University alone has produced eleven Nobel Prize laureates, in chemistry, physics and medicine. A number of programs for startups have come out of these institutions, such as the Kyoto Startup Summer School, which brings together young entrepreneurs from countries around the world. The Kyoto Research Park and Kyoto Innovation Hub also attract international businesses: combined, they host more than five hundred startups and other companies. Kyoto also has a strong manufacturing sector and is home to Kyocera, Nintendo and Nidec as well as a branch of the Silicon Valley-based accelerator Plug and Play. A hub for academic research and development, life sciences and pharmaceuticals, Kyoto has long been at the cutting edge of sustainability innovation and is where the Kyoto Protocol, a major international treaty aimed at curbing greenhouse gas emissions, was signed.

FACTS & FIGURES

– Compared to Japan's other large cities, Kyoto has the highest proportion of students to population , with nearly 10% of all residents enrolled in colleges, universities.

– In 2020, 28 companies made up the Kyoto Innovation Hub. A number of these are major international companies and startups, including Shimadzu, Nippon Boehringer Ingelheim and AFI.

– Nearly 500 companies work out of the Kyoto Research Park, an office and laboratory space founded in 1989.

– Kyoto University has the largest number of Nobel Prize winners of any Japanese university.

– More than 50 million visitors (domestic and international) come to Kyoto each year, making it a major cultural and travel destination.

– Kyoto was the first Asian country to sign on to the Global Destination Sustainability Index. The city receives 12% of its energy from renewables and 97% of its hotels are "sustainability certified."

– Companies based in Kyoto have more than 1,000 foreign branches in 50 countries worldwide.

– Kyoto's public transportation system, which reaches all areas of the city, is safe, easy to understand and punctual. 97% of the city's hotels are easily accessible by public transportation.

NOTABLE STARTUP ACTIVITY

– One of the most active startups in Kyoto, Atmoph has shipped its "smart windows" (which show beautiful natural scenery to urban residents) to over 30 countries through crowdfunding platforms and is backed by specialized cleantech VCs, such as EEI (Energy & Environment).

– DATAGRID, an AI startup from Kyoto University, has received funding from a VC (Deep30) that specializes in deep-learning startups. Their "whole- body model generation AI" announced in April 2019 has attracted worldwide attention.

– Taliki, a social business incubator, has been involved in more than 100 social activities, contributing to the local ecosystem by investing in startups and supporting the creation of spin-offs.

How to Make a Strong Ecosystem Even Stronger

CITY OF
KYOTO

An interview with

Mr. Daisaku Kadokawa / Mayor of Kyoto City

Over the course of over 1,200 years, Kyoto has evolved creatively into a city of innovation, fusing tradition, culture and technology into a hardworking harmony. At the root of Kyoto is the coexistence of nature and mankind, philosophy and religion. We aim to transcend racial, religious and social barriers and contribute to peace with the people of the world under the highest philosophy based on the Declaration of Kyoto as a City Open to the Free Exchange of World Cultures. Startups and scaleups in Kyoto have much to draw on, from talented graduates hailing from the city's excellent universities to the many tech-based companies willing to share their know-how, as well as the city's rich culture that blends the traditional with the contemporary.

"It is ideal to promote the fusion of science, technology, art and culture in Kyoto, and it is easy to imagine that their fusion will lead to the creation of innovation," says Mr. Kadokawa, the mayor of Kyoto City. "I believe that the sustainable development of industry, economy and society is the direction that Kyoto aims for. In the time of post–COVID-19, Kyoto City Office will continuously contribute to solving all kinds of social issues with the principles of the SDGs, especially those related to resilient cities."

Companies such as Kyocera, Shimadzu, NIDEC, Nintendo, Omron, Horiba and NISSHA all have their roots in Kyoto, and their presence on the global stage links new entrepreneurs to the business world outside the city. Kyocera and Shimadzu have also partnered with the open-innovation platform Plug and Play to bring a chapter to Kyoto, and Kyoto University has established Innovation Hub Kyoto and the VC Kyoto iCAP to help entrepreneurs learn and connect with larger international firms.

For entrepreneurs and interested parties outside the startup ecosystem, popular events in Kyoto include the Healthcare Venture Conference (HVC KYOTO), the Kyoto Smart City Expo, the Monozukuri Hardware Cup, and creative, interactive events such as Design Week Kyoto, BitSummit (game) and the KYOTO STEAM-World Cultural Exchange Festival. Several of these events focus on applying traditional and modern artistic practices to business and innovation.

" *I believe that the sustainable development of industry, economy and society is the direction that Kyoto aims for.* "

Kyoto is also home to highly skilled researchers and cutting-edge technology. It is well known as "a city of universities" where 150,000 students (10 percent of the population) are residents and 10,000 are from abroad. There are around 5,000 entrepreneurs, researchers and business people active at the Kyoto Research Park alone, and the city's well-regarded universities have produced eleven Nobel Prize winners to date. The city and the region frequently rank as a top locale for culture and enterprise.

The Kyoto City Office has implemented a plan to continue building its promising startup ecosystem. Part of this process involves creating an environment that is welcoming to capable talent from all over the world, supportive of their development, and better positioned for locals to launch international businesses. Another side of the process is to create startups that leverage Kyoto's leading position as a manufacturing hub, incorporating the region's expertise on robotics and deep tech, and to build support for expanding these startups into global markets. Mr. Kadokawa, his team and the organizations that collaborate with the local government work together to inspire the ecosystem, promote the idea of globalization and leverage the ecosystem's strengths to bolster industries such as life sciences and manufacturing materials.

To help further unlock the region's potential, the Kyoto Startup Ecosystem Promotion Council was formed at the end of 2019. Its plan involves an impressive number of players, both from within the ecosystem and from other pillars of business and cultural development. The Kyoto Economic Center brings many of the city's economic organizations together into one location, and the Open Innovation Café (also known as KOIN) creates new businesses by encouraging people to collaborate. There is also a lot of focus on the SDGs, particularly the goal of building a sustainable city and society.

For local entrepreneurs who wish to start up, and for businesses coming to scale into the region, Kyoto has several notable accelerators, incubators and investors. These include Plug and Play, the global open-innovation platform that supported over 1,100 businesses in 2018; Phoenixi, a communal residence program near Kyoto University's Yoshida Campus that did its first intake in 2019; and Monozukuri Ventures, a VC that offers hardware startups technical consulting, manufacturing support and prototyping networks for Japanese makers.

University of Kyoto - Yoshida Campus

As Kyoto is a student city, the Kyoto City Office offers many seminars for local and international students on how to start businesses and collaborate with bigger industry players. It has also worked with stakeholders from the Kyoto Prefecture and the Japan External Trade Organization (JETRO) to create the Startup Capital Scheme, enabling entrepreneurs from other countries to open businesses in Kyoto under a special visa program. This initiative includes specialized support for incoming entrepreneurs, such as expert advice on Kyoto's industries and markets, one year of free coworking space and consultations on official business filings. To apply, schedule an initial consultation at JETRO Kyoto at the Kyoto Economic Center.

[ABOUT]

The Kyoto City Office (Industrial Tourism Bureau of the Office) is committed to creating a sustainable community and resilient city from an industrial standpoint. In a rapidly changing environment, the office is taking advantage of Kyoto's strengths, including cultural, regional and industrial/academic cooperation, to provide growth and support options to local entrepreneurs and startups. It aims to enrich the lives of Kyoto's citizens and further strengthen the culture and ecosystem.

[CONTACT]

WEB   city.kyoto.lg.jp

EMAIL   chiikikigyo@city.kyoto.lg.jp

aceRNA Technologies

ELEVATOR PITCH

" We aim to further regenerative medicine and drug discovery through the application of our key technology, RNA Switch Technology, to the development of novel cell-purification methods and the discovery of drug target seeds. "

SECTOR **pharmaceuticals**

WEB **acernatec.com/en**

MILESTONES

Receiving ¥80 million in seed funding from Kyoto iCap in October 2018.

Obtaining licenses for use of intellectual properties related to RNA Switch Technology from Kyoto University.

Closing the Series A round of funding with ¥200 million of investment in 2019.

Developing a screening platform for drug target seeds using RNA Switch Technology.

Teruo Susumu was working as a pharmaceuticals researcher when a former colleague invited him to join a newly established venture capital firm. For more than a decade, he managed the fund. During this time, he began to consider launching his own venture, one that would leverage his pharmaceuticals experience. After the fund's life cycle came to an end, he decided it was time to strike out on his own, and so he approached several venture capital firms to ask whether any startups were looking for a business partner. After reaching out to Kyoto University Innovation Capital (Kyoto iCAP), he got lucky: Kyoto iCAP introduced him to Professor Hirohide Saito, an iPS (induced pluripotent stem cell) researcher who had invented RNA Switch™, a kind of technology that enables the detection of active microRNAs in living cells. This technology can be used in drug discovery for an extremely wide number of illnesses, from cancer and autoimmune diseases to neurological disorders.

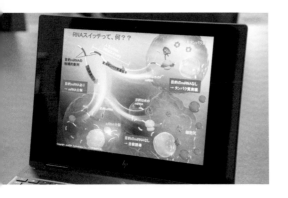

Teruo immediately recognized the potential and, since Hirohide could not manage a company due to his academic position, the two teamed up to launch aceRNA Technologies in April 2018. In October 2018, they secured ¥80 million in seed funding from Kyoto iCAP, allowing them to rent research rooms, equipment and incubation facilities within Kyoto University. The following year, they successfully secured a further ¥200 million in Series A funding. Currently, they are eyeing the US market with the goal of collaborating with large pharmaceutical companies on further research.

TEAM

aceRNA Technologies has a small team of four researchers and two management staff, including Teruo. "We enjoy free discussion," says Teruo on the topic of the weekly team meetings. "Many of us come with different opinions." Being based in Kyoto Innovation Hub at Kyoto University has great creative advantages because although the tenant companies maintain separate offices, the facilities and communal spaces are shared with more than ten different ventures, leading to the exchange of ideas and interesting collaborations. Of course, this also means more opportunities to socialize, and the team joins in the Hub's end-of-year party, barbecues and other events. Members of the aceRNA team also participate in programs and seminars that Kyoto University runs with pharmaceutical companies. These provide a good platform for meeting people in the industry and growing the team's network.

Atomis

ELEVATOR PITCH

" We aim to revolutionize the way
industrial gases are distributed
by using our expertise in chemistry
and materials science to develop
new gas-storage platforms. "

SECTOR chemistry, materials science, big data

WEB atomis.co.jp/en

MILESTONES

Establishing an independent MOF
research and production laboratory
for product development and
large-scale manufacturing.

Developing a new large-scale
manufacturing process for
producing MOFs in bulk.

Completing the first prototype
of CubiTan® in March 2018.

Closing a Series A funding
round in June 2019.

"Metal–organic frameworks" (MOFs) might not be an everyday term but this new class of porous solids that can store and distribute gases is poised to transform several industries ranging from energy to pharmaceuticals. Atomis founder and CTO Masakazu Higuchi was an assistant professor at a lab headed by Professor Susumu Kitagawa, who discovered MOFs. In 2015, he decided to become the first to attempt to commercialize this technology in Asia. He set about convincing his Kyoto University contemporaries Daisuke Asari and Dai Kataoka to leave their jobs in corporate research and bring their business experience to the startup. Won over by the potential of the technology, they came on board as CEO and COO, respectively. They were later joined by Kenji Sumida (executive officer, R&D), who uses his background in MOF chemistry to provide technical expertise.

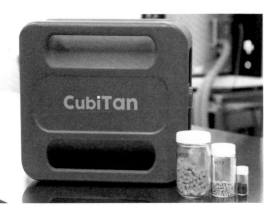

Atomis is currently developing several MOF-based products, including CubiTan®, a compact cube-shaped gas cylinder designed to replace conventional thick-walled high-pressure tanks. It also acts as a smart device that transmits usage and location data, making gas distribution more efficient. Additionally, the company is investigating the potential of MOFs for gas delivery in the human body. As a pioneering business, the company's challenge is to get its products recognized in an industry that has remained unchanged for decades. Its potential has not gone unnoticed; the team closed a Series A round of funding in July 2019, with significant investment from Mitsui Mining and Smelting that also promises research collaboration.

TEAM

The researchers at Atomis come from a wide range of backgrounds, resulting in diverse approaches in the lab that benefit idea generation. That's one of the team's most important strengths, according to Kenji, who says the small size means responsibilities tend to be flexible and everyone ends up getting exposure to different fields. "You really feel like you're contributing to something bigger," he says. "Each of us has a chance to make a unique contribution to something that could be potentially quite big and fundamentally improve the way industries operate." With all members aged forty-four or younger, the atmosphere is quite informal, which makes for more open discussions at internal meetings. This helps to create an environment that fosters creativity and communication, with less of a gap between managers and scientists.

mui Lab

ELEVATOR PITCH

" We're a calm-technology
and design company offering
a better lifestyle-oriented user
experience on connected devices. "

MILESTONES

Completing a management
buyout in April 2019.

Hiring application engineers and
UX designers to speed up product
development.

Moving to work on licensing the
technology to other companies.

Securing $2 million from VCs
in October 2019.

SECTOR smart home, smart city, IoT and UX

WEB mui.jp

mui Lab began as a way of blending technology into people's living environments. Its devices take information from online and connected devices and display it on wood furnishings, allowing users to interact with a natural surface, thereby giving them a better state of mind. Kaz Oki, cofounder and CEO, says the inspiration came from the idea of removing screens from living spaces so that people have a more peaceful and less distracting environment in which to spend time with loved ones. Kyoto has a strong culture of appreciating aesthetics and people's harmony with the environment, seasons and so on, making it a great location for mui Lab. The company is situated on Kyoto's famous Ebisugawa or "furniture street," which Kaz says provides an important community.

TEAM

Everyone in the mui Lab team shares the goal of helping improve people's lifestyles. Thus, they appreciate the importance of community and environment, including at work. When the founders were hiring, they looked for self-motivated individuals who had soft skills and an open mind as well as expertise in engineering or design. The employees are therefore goal-oriented. They enjoy working in Kyoto's famous "furniture street" as it inspires them and gives them ideas about lifestyle goals that can be achieved through furnishings. Most staff members love coffee and also bring treats to the office to enjoy during coffee breaks, when they can have a chat with each other in the office's central kitchen. This practice has resulted in the organic growth of a very social workplace. About 20 percent of the team is female and 80 percent is male. Team members hail from all over the world, and many have worked abroad, adding global mindsets to the workforce.

mui Lab was initially a project at a large corporation then established as a company in 2017. In 2019, five individuals underwent a management buyout from the corporation and are now the second generation of mui Lab. Kaz's background is in global business development, but other cofounders have experience in technology, engineering, design, craftsmanship and materials. Until the management buyout, mui Lab was 100 percent funded by enterprise company NISSHA and, in October 2019, it received $2 million in venture capital. Challenges to date include a lack of resources and difficulty in making the product due to the long time required to develop hardware. In 2019, however, engineers were brought on board to speed up development, and the product launched in 2020.

Space Power Technologies

ELEVATOR PITCH

" We're aiming to start an electrical-
power revolution by using microwave
technology to transfer electricity
wirelessly. Our vision is to realize
ubiquitous power transfer through
the creation of a global network. "

MILESTONES

Founding in May 2019.

Raising ¥230 million from multiple
VCs within the first half year.

Creating WPT prototypes for
logistics and robotics applications.

Developing a wireless charging
mobile battery.

SECTOR factory automation, logistics, IoT

WEB spacepowertech.com

Minoru Furukawa has always been driven to pursue his research interests, even when it wasn't strictly his job. He originally undertook postgraduate studies on "rectennas," rectifying antennas that can convert electromagnetic energy into direct current electricity, which is the fundamental technology for transmitting electricity wirelessly. This led him to join a wireless-transmission company, where he worked as a high-frequency-development engineer. Given the company's relatively small size, he was hoping to have the flexibility to pursue his research interests and participate in academic conferences, but he struggled to find the time alongside his regular responsibilities. Luckily, his boss recognized his passion and granted him permission to use the facilities to continue research into rectennas on weekends.

TEAM

In 2016, Minoru began thinking about taking his ideas further. He teamed up first with Professor Shinohara, an expert in microwave wireless power transmission and solar-power satellites, who leads a laboratory at Kyoto University, and later with Yuji Takeda, who has more than twenty years of experience in the finance industry. In May 2019, he launched Space Power Technologies, and by September he had successfully raised ¥230 million in investment from Kyoto iCAP and other venture capital firms, enabling him to buy simulation software and establish an anechoic chamber for testing microwaves. The company is currently focusing on operationalizing this technology for smaller-scale uses, such as for digital picking systems used to locate items in large warehouses in the logistics industry. Traditionally, such systems relied on sensors powered by batteries. The startup's long-term goal is to provide renewable energy to the globe through solar panel satellites.

Space Power Technologies is the kind of company where creative input is encouraged. Wireless power transmission is in its early stage, and the team has active discussions about the potential uses for this fledgling technology. The six team members – five of whom are in Kyoto and one in Tokyo – all spring from diverse backgrounds with experience in not only microwaves but also robotics, finance, antennas and sensors. This helps to drive their discussions, and they also receive input from outside advisors. The team has close ties with Kyoto University and uses Kyoto University Katsura Venture Plaza as its office. Team lunches are a daily affair. The team kicked off 2020 by offering prayers at Dendengu Shrine in Arashiyama in western Kyoto, which enshrines a deity that represents good fortune for electricity and the electricity industry – rather appropriate in their case.

Stroly

" We're an online platform for maps linked with location information. Anyone can upload and add their own maps or find maps created by others near their current location, all for free. "

SECTOR travel, area management

WEB stroly.com

MILESTONES

Getting noticed by TechCrunch soon after launching the platform.

Securing Japan Travel Bureau, Japan's largest travel company, as a partner for sales.

Being the only Japanese company to pitch at SXSW Pitch 2019.

Attracting 317 submissions from forty-five countries in a map contest, reflecting Stroly's global reach

Stroly Inc. is a spinoff from research institute ATR, where, in 2008, researcher Toru Takahashi created an outdoor guide system based on a paper map of a theme park. He made the map digital to offer a better user experience, and from this the seed for Stroly was sown. Stroly allows users to create and use illustrated, themed digital maps that can track user footfall and turn it into analytical data. In 2016, Toru and Machi Takahashi, then-president of ATR subsidy ATR Creative, bought the patent from ATR and set up Stroly Inc. as cofounders and co-CEOs. There were some initial challenges. "VCs said, 'These are cute maps, but is it a business or hobby?'" says Machi. "It was difficult for them to understand the value of these maps in bringing people to an area." But, with board members secured from meetups and connections, as well as a team skilled in science, the arts and business, Machi and Toru persevered. They met with approximately one hundred investors and in 2017, Stroly Inc. secured $1.4 million, followed by $4 million in 2018.

Stroly uses a subscription business model and boasts customers in travel, real estate, transportation and municipalities that each want to brand their areas or markets through the maps. As travel is a key market for Stroly, Machi says Kyoto is perfect for the company's headquarters. "Kyoto is the old capital of Japan, with a rich history and heavy tourism, so it's a good place to start our map service," she says. "And we have been able to attract engineers and other skilled people who want to work in Kyoto because it is such a beautiful city."

TEAM

At Stroly's offices in Kyoto and Tokyo, about 35 percent of the team is female and most continents are represented. Three of the four board members are female. About half of the team members are from an engineering or technology background while the others have interests in history, culture, art and maps. According to Machi, this diversity and mix allows the staff "to enjoy good interaction and offer a global service." Remote work is supported, with all staff members able to join meetings online if they prefer. Stroly also encourages teamwork and collaboration. Every Friday, staff members in both offices are encouraged to talk to each other informally online during office hours and socialize over food and beer. Every quarter, there is a meeting in Kyoto for all employees to present the work they have carried out in the quarter.

Isshu Rakusai

Founder and CEO
/ Nota

Hailing from Oita Prefecture in southern Japan, Isshu Rakusai discovered his love for programming when he was twelve years old. At the age of eighteen, he coded his first commercial application, and his fate as a tech entrepreneur was sealed. Now, as the founder of Nota, Isshu is on a mission to produce software that eliminates the barriers that separate technology and human creativity.

ABOUT THE COMPANY

Nota is a company that produces software designed to break down the technological barriers that stand between human thought and communication. Nota's software suite includes team collaboration, screenshot sharing and customer support solutions.

WEB notainc.com

How did you become interested in programming?

When I was twelve years old, my father bought a computer, but he couldn't understand how to use it. So I started using my father's computer all the time. I learned programming on my own using books from the library or checking out the programming community on the internet. Back then, the community was small and the amount of books available was limited.

I was motivated to make tools that even beginners could use. So these days, I'm extremely interested in user interfaces that make something easier – something where everyone can make creative content using a computer.

Can you describe your entrepreneurial journey?

My first commercial application was called Kamicopi. *Kami* means "paper" in Japanese, and this was a note-taking application. Microsoft Word was around back then, but you had to save and open files on your desktop or in folders. But my software was kind of like the notebook application you find on Apple Macs these days. There was no manual saving, so when you typed, your work was automatically saved.

Back then, around 1997 or 1998, Windows 95 was so unstable. It often froze, and users were left with just a blue screen. In that case, all the files that they created

> " *We want to help humans become stronger.* "

We had about ten thousand users, but that wasn't enough to run a business.

Survival was very hard, so I did some programming and consulting for other companies. The biggest company I worked for was Dentsu. They needed a lot of designers to make creative products for their customers. That was a good opportunity for me to make money, but it was really hard. It wasn't something I could scale.

Considering your situation, how did you revive the company in Kyoto?

Gyazo, our screenshot-sharing application, started growing rapidly after about three years. We reached three million active users per month. Still, this wasn't making us any money. It cost $3,000 a month just to run the servers. I had to decide between closing the service down or monetizing it, so I decided to try to make money with Gyazo.

were gone. When people used my software, that never happened. This software was a surprise success for me as a young programmer. At that time, I had never worked for a company and I didn't have any advisors or mentors.

Eventually, I joined several startups in Japan, because I was getting interested in entrepreneurship. Then I was able to meet Ken Suzuki, the CEO of SmartNews, who introduced me to Shogo Kawada, one of the cofounders of DeNa, who invested in me and became my mentor. All of this led me to move to Silicon Valley and start a company when I was just twenty-five years old.

Kamicopi was a success in Japan, but I wanted to make products and services that were used globally, not just in the Japanese market. I also wanted to learn marketing and entrepreneurship from Silicon Valley tech companies. This is where I created Notaland.com, which was like a combination of Google Slides and Google Docs, allowing you to share and create anything online, synced automatically in real time.

First, we just added advertisements, and that helped us earn money, little by little. Soon after that, we started offering a premium service, Gyazo Pro. This subscription model provides extra features for users. This simple tool helped us to become a business once again. This allowed me to stop working for Dentsu and start developing our services again. Interestingly, Gyazo also attracted global users. Nearly eighty percent of our users live outside of Japan.

Can you tell me more about your current business model?

We are an SaaS company. Gyazo is a B2C subscription service that helps customers share images. We also have several other products. We're currently focusing on Helpfeel, which is a subscription-based customer-support system for our business customers. It's a tool that helps other people quickly discover knowledge and insights. When it comes to software, most people can't be bothered to deal with manuals and FAQ pages. Our system supports user knowledge discovery by using casual, everyday language.

What were some of the challenges you faced when starting your company and how did you overcome them?

While I was in Silicon Valley, I couldn't attract enough users, and after three years, my company almost went bankrupt. That's why I had to move back to Japan.

As a company, we focus on knowledge. We think of ourselves as a "whole-life knowledge company." This means that we provide the knowledge you need throughout your life. That is our vision.

Our approach to development is also unique. We don't focus on AI, but instead we focus on what we call AH: augmented humans. This is an important approach for whenever we develop something. This is connected to my original story: wanting to help my father use his computer.

With AI, people try to put human brains into computers. They try to simulate human intelligence in computers. But AH goes in the opposite direction. We want to make humans more robotic, in a way – kind of like a cyborg. This is a bit of an exaggeration, though. We want to compensate for human weaknesses by adding algorithms to humans. We want to help humans become stronger.

What was the best decision you made during your entrepreneurial journey?

The best decision I made was not to abandon the company, even when I failed in Silicon Valley. There were many alternative paths available to me at that time. I could have become a freelancer or abandoned entrepreneurship altogether, but I wanted to repay the investors and mentors that supported my company. I just stuck with it and believed in my vision to scale the business.

What mistakes did you make during the startup process?

My biggest mistake has to do with managing human resources. It was very tough to form good relationships with cofounders and initial employees. For example, I didn't respond to personnel issues fast enough, and I don't think I respected them enough.

Now I know how critical it is to maintain great relationships with cofounders and employees. It's important to quickly address any problems that come up. You need to care about multiple things when you start a company. You need to take care of your stockholders and your customers, but it's also important to take care of your team.

What additional advice do you have for aspiring entrepreneurs?

In our company, we have a very important approach that we insist on: we call it "dogfooding." This means that we should create products and services that we also need and want to use. It's really hard, especially for young entrepreneurs, to make something for others. You're not the customer, so you have to do a lot of market research to understand what your

customers need. But if you make something that you need, you become the customer and you can quickly discover your pain points. Then, you can make a product that fits you perfectly. After that, you can grow the market little by little. So, in our company, anyone who creates a service needs to use it themselves. That's dogfooding: if you make food for your dog, you need to be able to eat it too. If you know you're going to have to eat dog food, you're going to get serious and make really good dog food.

Not only does this ensure that you understand your customers well, but it also generates motivation during difficult times. When you know that you're solving your own pain points, you can do what it takes to keep your business alive.

Tell me more about your company culture. What is it like to work for Nota?

As I mentioned before, dogfooding is important to our culture. Also, we work remotely. In fact, we started as a remote company, and that's a big part of our culture. We aren't remote only, though; we do have an office.

Speaking of your office, what do you like about living and working in Kyoto?

This is a city that allows us to focus on software development and uniqueness. There are a lot of universities in this city, and ten percent of the population is made up of students. This is very unique when compared to other cities in Japan. There is also a research culture here.

There are a lot of special, global companies such as Nintendo here. Actually, you can find a lot of unique game companies here in Kyoto. They don't often reveal themselves since they are working on secret projects. A lot of people from all around the world work at these companies, so there's a very diverse development community here. •

What are your top work essentials?
Scrapbox, our knowledge-base software.

At what age did you found your company?
Twenty-five.

What's your most used app?
That would be Scrapbox. I also use Slack.

What's the most valuable piece of advice you've been given?
Find good mentors.

What's your greatest skill?
Discovering something unique and turning it into a business.

What do you do every morning (or night before) to prepare for the day ahead?
Stretching.

What book has most influenced your career?
Recently I've been reading *Thinking, Fast and Slow*.

Kenshin Fujiwara

Founder and CEO
/ HACARUS

Kenshin Fujiwara is the CEO of HACARUS, but the eclectic founder prefers a different title: chief problem fixer. He was born and raised in Shiga Prefecture, but international borders couldn't contain his desire to take on new challenges. He earned his computer science degree in California and then joined Sony as an engineer, developing core features of the PlayStation 2. Kenshin started his first company at the age of twenty-six and has been a serial entrepreneur ever since, with three successful exits to date. He founded HACARUS in 2014 and is currently revolutionizing the use of AI in the medical and manufacturing fields.

ABOUT THE COMPANY

HACARUS Inc., founded in 2014 in Kyoto, is the leading provider of explainable, lightweight AI tools. Its solutions are used in the medical and manufacturing fields to make better, faster and more reliable decisions based on AI-driven insights.

WEB HACARUS.com

How did you become interested in your current industry? What is your origin story?

Encouraged by my wife, I founded HACARUS on the idea of creating ways for people to eat healthier. Originally, the idea took the form of a smart scale that would use small data to generate insights about the nutritional content of what was being placed on it. From that idea (using machine learning to build insights from small data), our unique AI engine grew. Through a series of pivots, all staying true to the original core mission, we have now arrived at applying our technology to the medical and manufacturing fields. What really sets HACARUS apart is our ability to provide lightweight and explainable AI solutions.

What challenges did you face when you were establishing your business? How did you overcome them?

When I set up HACARUS in Kyoto, the startup scene was still in its cradle and didn't have a sophisticated, well-developed ecosystem like you might find in Silicon Valley, Berlin or even Tokyo. That meant that the support these larger regions take for granted wasn't available. In the end, we got through it with dedication, hard work, blood, sweat and tears. I think this experience has made my team more resilient.

" Being a founder is not a job for normal people. You have to be crazy enough to disrupt society. "

at opportunities in North America, Southeast Asia and beyond. HACARUS is built to become a global market leader for explainable AI solutions.

The biggest challenge we face today is customer-expectation management. AI is a field that's very hot at the moment, and more often than not, customers have expectations of systems capable of replacing humans. In reality, it's a tool that helps humans perform better.

What was the biggest mistake you made in your entrepreneurial journey?

My biggest mistake was hiring the wrong people at the wrong time. It wasn't running out of money, because you can always get money from somewhere else. However, bringing the wrong people into the company is something that's very difficult to fix later on.

Honestly speaking, I didn't think that cultural fit mattered much when I started out as an entrepreneur. I understand the importance of company culture now, but when I was running a startup in my twenties, I didn't think of that at all. These days, I always put culture first and treat it as the most important part of the startup. I always choose people who can contribute something to our corporate culture. That's my highest priority at the moment.

Can you tell us about your business model? Is it a challenge to maintain profitability?

We build precision AI tools for use in fields such as manufacturing and medical. We provide solutions both as a service and product offering. We typically sell a consulting package supported by our products and tools.

While most of our traction is still in Japan, we have also expanded into Europe and are actively looking

What was the best business decision you've made so far?

Daring to focus on new markets and opportunities. Our core technology is built using a data modeling technique called sparse modeling. While used extensively in academic research, HACARUS was one of the first companies to apply it to solve business problems. Much larger players have since followed, but we remain at the forefront of its usage.

Similarly, I am now pursuing a new field where I see great potential for our technology: the future intersection between the manufacturing and medical industries, regenerative medicine. I firmly believe that this is the next frontier, and Kyoto is its epicenter. I am now focused on bringing HACARUS into this exciting new movement.

What professional advice would you give early-stage founders?

Be crazy. You have to be crazy enough to make new things. I think all successful startup and big corporate CEOs alike are crazy to some extent – and they have to be. The career path of a founder is a tough one. Many people have an infatuation with being an entrepreneur, not understanding what it takes or that not everyone can be one. It's not a typical job, and it's a lot harder than one would expect. Being a founder is not a job for normal people. You have to be crazy enough to disrupt society.

What personal work habits have you developed over time?

I'm a lot funnier now. I'm trying to be a funny guy, and I think I'm doing all right. I say this because I really wasn't funny at all before. When I was working on startups in my twenties and thirties, I was a CTO. I was a tech guy and not very fun. I changed my personality a lot to become funnier and more charismatic in some way. That's my number-one accomplishment over the past twenty years.

Why did you establish your company in Kyoto? What do you enjoy about living and working here?

People are more creative in Kyoto. Perhaps this is tied to the city's long history (formerly, it was the capital of Japan for more than a millennium) or to its large student population (ten percent, the largest in Japan). In Kyoto, people approach problems in unique ways.

There are more sights to be seen in Kyoto and its surroundings than there are days in a lifetime. This is a hugely humbling fact. Recognizing that we are standing on the shoulders of giants and that we have a tremendously rich heritage available allows us to contemplate how best to contribute and add on to this rich history. With HACARUS, I want to show that Kyoto

has the ability to reinvent itself in a digital age and remain a master of expert craft.

Steeped in tradition, culture and the idea of perpetual improvement, I wanted to create a new business that takes the best from these traditional approaches all the while building a team with a global perspective. Today, we have employees from all over the world. I firmly believe that for Japan to be a global player, a global workforce is necessary.

What is your company culture like? What is it like to work at HACARUS?

When I started HACARUS, I wanted to create a company that not only does right by its customers and partners but also treats its employees well. Having worked in both startups and large companies, I've learned a thing or two about how to create an inclusive environment where employees feel motivated and appreciated.

We have a code of conduct consisting of three main points. First, it's up to you to make your job exciting or boring. Second, don't be domestic; be global. Finally, don't follow the mainstream; be unique.

With the first point, I aim to communicate that it is your responsibility to enjoy your job. This means

having the freedom to be independent in work performance, in decision making around what you want to do to make the company grow, in personal development, and in having opinions that are heard. This also means that you are accountable for the tasks you decide to pursue.

The second point is all about being a global company. Expanding abroad means the company grows and strays away from a traditional corporate culture. This also means hiring members from all over the world and having a global team. We have international talent on the team and a development center in the Philippines.

With the final point, I want to inspire my team to be creative and to attack issues in a new way, creating real innovation. Cultivating a strong company culture is key to building a successful team.

I like to think that we've created a strong team dynamic here at HACARUS. While highly unorthodox for a tech startup, we begin each morning with a companywide gymnastics exercise: yoga-like stretching.

This regime is actually quite common in Japanese firms performing physical labor, such as construction or heavy manufacturing, but we've made it our own by alternating the cheerful instructions to the native tongue of our various employees each day. It's great to start the day with smiles all around, and it allows us to break down the walls that tend to separate specific departments.

How do you envision the future of your company? What concerns or challenges lie ahead?

Looking ahead, I'd like to build a stable company that can stand the test of time. My intent is to provide a space where my employees can grow and gain new skills and where our partners continue to seek out our services for support. The great challenge today and going forward is scaling: hiring, training and building the team to meet growing demand is no easy feat. I hope that spreading the word about HACARUS and our culture will continue to help us attract talent. •

What are your top work essentials?
My laptop and my wife's healthy bento (Japanese boxed lunch).

What's your most used app?
The Microsoft Office suite – still the fundamental key to productivity.

What's the most valuable piece of advice you've been given?
Focus! (from former CEO and visionary of Nintendo, Satoru Iwata.)

What's your greatest skill?
Spotting icebergs. Small surface issues that hide larger problems below.

What do you do every morning (or night before) to prepare for the day ahead?
Look at my son's face: my source of motivation.

What book has most influenced your career?
Iwata San.

What favorite positive habit have you cultivated?
Walking my dog, which is great for staying healthy and appreciating Kyoto.

KGAP+ (Keihanna Global Acceleration Program Plus)

The Keihanna Global Acceleration Program Plus (KGAP+) is a global acceleration program for startups based in Kyoto. KGAP+ is organized by the Advanced Telecommunications Research Institute International (ATR), which aims to promote pioneering and original research in the fields of information and communication. In order to stimulate diversity, the program supports approximately twenty startups a year from Japan and abroad. The program has been running since 2019 and has selected startups from demo days for business expansion in Barcelona and New York. It is interested in startups that have a product or service, or at least a prototype, that enables a proof of concept or pilot test. KGAP+ builds the value of global startups through interaction with local industrial partners and investors.

SECTOR sector-agnostic
SELECTED PORTFOLIO Includes companies in industries such as mobility as a service (MaaS), healthcare, AI, robotics, foodtech, emotion analysis, building management, braintech and digital health.
WHO SHOULD APPLY Startups in any sector, of any size, that are already incorporated.
APPLY bdo-staff@atr.jp
WEB keihanna-rc.jp/en/business/business-support/#kgap

SECTOR academic program with industry partnership (sector-agnostic)
SELECTED PORTFOLIO Yanmar, BMW, Renault, All Nippon Airways, Poggipolini, Rovio
WHO SHOULD APPLY Typically design, engineering and business students at the master's level.
APPLY Check for program announcements every summer at the Kyoto Institute of Technology campus and on the KYOTO Design Lab website. For companies interested in sponsoring projects, contact sushi@kit.ac.jp.
WEB me310kyoto.org

ME310/SUGAR

THe ME310/SUGAR Kyoto program takes students all the way from idea to proof of concept in nine intensive months. The program operates out of the Kyoto Institute of Technology as part of the greater ME310 and SUGAR network. Students from two universities develop innovative products or services utilizing design-thinking methodologies to deliver a detailed concept. Many of the end results have been patented, further developed by the sponsoring company, and have entered the market.

Having a culture of collaboration and community is fundamental to the program. "Our mission is to educate and train the great innovators of tomorrow," says Sushi Suzuki, program lead and founder. "Many of our alumni have gone on to start companies as well as develop amazing products in existing companies."

Phoenixi

Phoenixi is a startup program focused on connecting and developing the creativity of individuals, organizations and society, and on promoting the kind of entrepreneurship that is as concerned with impact as it is with profits. Most of Phoenixi's fellows are intrapreneurs from sponsor organizations, and the program provides them a place and an opportunity to tackle the issues they want to focus on with innovative solutions.

The program lasts one year, and the first four months are the incubation period. Participants live together in Kyoto in the toberu incubator, developing their ideas and going through pitching and mentor sessions in a stimulating environment. For the remaining six months, they are given assistance as needed. The first program cohort began in June 2019.

SECTOR sector-agnostic within the UN SDGs.
SELECTED PORTFOLIO Companies include LAIKA, Fitness Pass, True Juice, MamaOrgana
WHO SHOULD APPLY Entrepreneurs or intrapreneurs who have solutions to social issues using their own ideas or their company technology.
USP The name "Phoenixi" has the dual meaning of the phoenix regenerating and the "i" signifying three different ideas: innovation, incubation and an island where participants are free to create.
WEB phoenixi.co.jp

Kamo River, Kyoto

engawa KYOTO

engawa KYOTO, a coworking space created by advertising giant Dentsu, opened in 2019 in the center of Kyoto's business district. The space, designed by a residential architect, provides a comforting, living-room–like atmosphere with plants, sofas and warm wood accents. It prides itself on its exceptional level of cleanliness, a policy founded on the idea that a clean space is a productive space. The driving concept at the core of engawa KYOTO is the desire to facilitate collaboration and exchange between entrepreneurs, startups and major corporations. Members of the coworking space are also offered entrepreneurship programs divided into three stages: innovation, acceleration and scaling.

ADDRESS 647 Nijohanjikicho, Shimogyo-ku, Kyoto 600-8412
OPENING HOURS Access hours vary by membership level.
USP A space centered around connection between startups and corporations.
PRICE RANGE One-day pass: ¥3,000. Membership: ¥30,000 per month. Meeting room: ¥3,000 per hour. Kitchen: ¥4,000 per hour. Locker: ¥4,000 per month. Private office: contact for pricing.
WEB engawakyoto.com

Impact Hub Kyoto

Impact Hub Kyoto is a branch within Impact Hub's global network of more than one hundred spaces. The organization aims to drive change in the world (guided by the UN's SDGs) through providing access to space, community events and startup support. Impact Hub Kyoto is located inside a culturally significant building built in 1921 and designed by the famous architect Roku Iwamoto. Originally, the building served as one of Nippon Telegraph and Telephone Corporation's exchanges, and today it still plays an important role in connecting people through its entrepreneurial community outreach. Membership is offered at various levels of thirty, fifty or one hundred hours of access per month, and there is also an unlimited plan and a private-office plan.

ADDRESS 97 Kainokamicho, Kamigyo-ku, Kyoto 602-8061
OPENING HOURS 10 AM–8 PM
USP A coworking space that fosters an entrepreneurial community in Kyoto.
PRICE RANGE Prices range from HUB30 (30 hours per week access) at ¥3,000 per month to HUB Unlimited (unlimited access) at ¥25,000 per month. Private offices with unlimited access are also available.
WEB kyoto.impacthub.net/en

Kyoto Makers Garage

Kyoto Makers Garage, or KMG as it is commonly known, is a makerspace marked by its independent spirit and DIY culture. Rapid-prototyping tools, such as 3D printers, CNC machines, a laser cutter and more, are available to the public. Tools can be reserved hourly after completing one of the hands-on training courses. Monthly membership plans are available for frequent users at ¥10,000 but are not required for training or tool usage. Ongoing events and workshops include KMG's 3D Printing Meetup, IoT and hardware programming workshops, and themed hackathons. KMG is a service of Monozukuri Ventures, a Kyoto-based VC firm that backs and supports both domestic and international hardware startups. The makerspace is also supported by Kyoto City and local business partners.

ADDRESS 73-1 Sujakuhozocho, Shimogyo-ku, Kyoto 600-8846
OPENING HOURS Sat–Wed: 10 AM–7 PM
USP A well-equipped makerspace where all are welcome.
PRICE RANGE Training course: ¥3,000–¥5,000. Tool usage: ¥500–¥1,000 per hour (free for students). Membership: ¥10,000 per month.
WEB kyotomakersgarage.com/en

SPACE KANTE at Co & Co KYOTO

Located in the heart of Kyoto's business district, SPACE KANTE at Co & Co KYOTO is a coworking space with a refined style. The lounge area features a variety of flex seating options, a bookstore, a cafe/bar with a proper espresso machine and a space for events. Meeting rooms, call booths and quiet study booths can be reserved for an added fee. Monthly membership starts at ¥8,880 per month, and daily guest passes are available for ¥2,000. In addition to coworking, the space doubles as a language school, offering lessons in English, Japanese and other Asian languages. Aside from Kyoto, the coworking space has locations in Hokkaido and Singapore, with a new location coming soon to Tokyo.

ADDRESS Kyoto Fukutoku Bldg 2F, 670, Tearaimizucho, Nakagyo-Ku, Kyoto 604-8152
OPENING HOURS Mon–Fri: 10 AM–10 PM; Sat and Sun: 10 AM–7 PM.
USP A coworking space, cafe, bookstore and language school all under one roof.
PRICE RANGE Basic plan: ¥8,880 per month; registration fee: ¥20,000; management fee: ¥500 per month; private booth: ¥500 per day; locker: ¥1,500 per month; one-day visitor pass: ¥2,000.
WEB space-kante.com/en/kyoto

Doshisha University

Doshisha University was founded in 1875 on the principles of liberalism, internationalism and ethics, values that continue to help guide the institution through twenty-first century changes. The school is located next to the Kyoto Imperial Palace in an area "where the traditional and modern coexist," says Philip Sugai, professor of marketing with the Graduate School of Business. Appreciation for this contrast is a particular theme of Doshisha's Global MBA Program, which is focused on sustainability, culture and creativity, and business in Asia while also encouraging deep respect for Kyoto's history. Students in the program have the chance to work with newly established startups as well as with local, traditional companies who have been in business for generations. They are encouraged to learn about Kyoto's traditional culture as well as its startup innovators. Doshisha University also supports student and faculty entrepreneurs through its incubator, D-Egg.

LOCATION Next to Kyoto Imperial Palace and centrally located in the thriving business and startup district.

CLOSE TRANSIT CONNECTIONS Imadegawa subway station, Demachiyanagi train station.

PRICE OF TUITION From ¥1,078,000 for a four-year undergraduate program to ¥1,631,000 for a two-year graduate business program (tuition-reduction scholarships are available for international students).

ENTRY REQUIREMENTS International students should have English proficiency and the equivalent of a high school diploma. For the graduate business school, students should also have a bachelor's degree and a GMAT/GRE score or more than three years of relevant work experience.

WEB doshisha.ac.jp/en

gmba.doshisha.ac.jp/en/index.html

Kyoto Startup Summer School

While most academic startup programs focus on launching a company, Kyoto Startup Summer School takes a content-oriented approach. The program covers a wide variety of entrepreneurial topics in just two weeks. Successful entrepreneurs, investors and academics from around the world run workshops and give lectures on topics like lean startup principles, fundraising strategies and product management. "I wanted to create a program that would introduce participants to all sorts of different topics before they go forth and create a startup," says founder Sushi Suzuki. "You could say our mission is to get aspiring entrepreneurs onto a better starting line." The curriculum is exclusively in English and the school attracts a diverse and international student body, with more than 250 people from forty-five countries having been involved since its inception in 2016. Given the intensive nature of the summer school, there is a focus on creating a social and fun environment, with morning yoga sessions and meetups with local entrepreneurs and communities.

LOCATION North of the city center in Matsugasaki, Kyoto City
CLOSE TRANSIT CONNECTIONS Matsugasaki subway station (Katsuma line)
PRICE OF TUITION ¥70,000–¥150,000
WHO SHOULD APPLY Current students, recent graduates, entrepreneurs preparing to start a company and those working for new startups.
WEB **kyotostartupschool.org**

Kyoto University Graduate School of Management

Following Kyoto University's tradition of academic and entrepreneurial excellence, the Graduate School of Management (GSM) educates global-minded business leaders to tackle important challenges and contributes to great management research in Japan and abroad. Founded in 2006, GSM offers several two-year full-time programs taught in English and more in Japanese, two international double degree programs with Cornell University and National Taiwan University and a PhD in Management Science. GSM supports powerful new approaches to business with its offerings in Global Social Entrepreneurship. As a graduate school with an international mindset, GSM works with research and business partners from all over the world. The university offers a number of extracurricular opportunities. For instance, it supports the live-in innovation program Phoenixi, which helps students to develop groundbreaking ideas. GSM graduates have created the Kyoto University International Entrepreneurs Club, which hosts hackathons, speaking events and more.

LOCATION Yoshida Campus in Sakyō-ku, Kyoto
CLOSE TRANSIT CONNECTIONS Hyakumanben stop (bus line), Demachiyanagi stop (Keihan and Eizan rail lines)
PRICE OF TUITION ¥535,800
ENTRY REQUIREMENTS Ambition to improve business and society, a passion for problem-solving, an interest in research and a high level in mathematics. GMAT is required for certain programs.
WEB **gsm.kyoto-u.ac.jp/en**

Kyoto iCAP

Kyoto University is one of the highest-ranked universities in Japan with an especially strong record in sciences. Kyoto iCAP aims to realize the business potential of this research through investing in university startups.

SECTOR natural sciences, life sciences, engineering

EMAIL info@kyoto-unicap.co.jp

WEB kyoto-unicap.co.jp/en

In early 2014, a legal change took effect in Japan that allowed national universities to provide venture capital and hold stock in private companies. Several university investment companies were born, with Kyoto iCAP among them. "Kyoto University has eleven Nobel Prize winners in natural sciences, out of twenty-eight Nobel Prize laureates nationwide," says Ryosuke Gonotsubo, investment manager at Kyoto iCAP. "We see huge potential in Kyoto's scientific research." Ryosuke is the only member of the fund that doesn't come from a scientific background, but, with several years of business development experience, he brings essential commercial experience to the team and the ability to offer hands-on support to startups. "We begin by talking to the professors," he says. "If the science is good and the business plan is interesting, we'll enter further discussions."

The team maintains strict requirements for proof of concept, asking for strong datasets that clearly demonstrate the science before they make any investment decision. Yet, as with all scientific research, they recognize that these kinds of startups take time to commercialize from the initial launch to exit through IPO. As a result, the fund has a long maturity of fifteen years compared to a more common eight to ten years, reflecting an emerging class of investors worldwide who provide "patient capital." Between 2016 and 2018, more than sixty university startups incorporated in Kyoto, and around half of them were born out of Kyoto iCAP funding. The city has yet to catch up with Tokyo, but recent years have seen a shift in people's perceptions of entrepreneurship. Ryosuke says there has been promising growth and "some really talented people are choosing to join startup companies." Kyoto iCAP aims to help grow this ecosystem and transform Kyoto into an innovation hub with a particular strength in life sciences.

Monozukuri Ventures

Monozukuri Ventures' mission is to help entrepreneurs bring hardware products to market by providing investment, mentorship, prototyping and manufacturing expertise. The name Monozukuri (meaning the art of making things in a creative way) represents how its funds work and what it invests in.

SECTOR hardware startups in fast-growing industries; e.g., AI, clean energy, wearables, spacetech, healthcare, IoT, robotics, smart homes, well-being and industrial IoT

EMAIL contact@monozukuri.vc

WEB monozukuri.vc

Monozukuri Ventures is an international investment funder with offices in Kyoto, where it began as Makers Boot Camp, an acceleration program for startups with physical prototypes, and New York City. Monozukuri Ventures invests in companies with a product at early-development stages, as long as the entrepreneurs are curious, talented and looking for a physical solution to improve the world. Narimasa Makino, CEO and founder, discovered his passion for startups that aim to make a positive impact while completing his MBA at Kobe University. "I realized that startups could create faster innovative solutions to help tackle many of the world's problems," he says. After graduating, he worked in other venture capital firms, learning about private equity, incubation and common problems startups face when launching a business. He founded what is now Monozukuri Ventures because he saw a need for founders with physical products to have access to both funds and mentoring in manufacturing and product development.

One example of a startup Makino has mentored is SmartShopping, Inc., whose founders had no previous experience with hardware. They developed Smart Mat, a weight scale that automates stock management and ordering. Monozukuri Ventures helped the SmartShopping team create a prototype for mass manufacturing and, after building both B2B and B2C services, they are aiming to develop the product to help the elderly with shopping, a growing need in many countries. Making the connections needed to help SmartShopping's founders is why Narimasa loves this industry. "I can't count how many people in the startup ecosystem have been open and kind, providing honest and helpful feedback when founders need it most." In the near future, Monozukuri Ventures wants to extend its portfolio into advanced manufacturing in order to create a platform where any startup can launch a hardware business and create a product, regardless of its own limited resources.

OSAKA

The port city of Osaka, a historical center for trade and commerce, is increasingly opening itself up to new markets and developing a flexible startup ecosystem to rival that of Tokyo. With an emphasis on spurring on SMEs that prioritize craftsmanship and quality production, and with its longstanding and deep connections to major international technology companies, Osaka has found its niche in central Japan and the global economy.

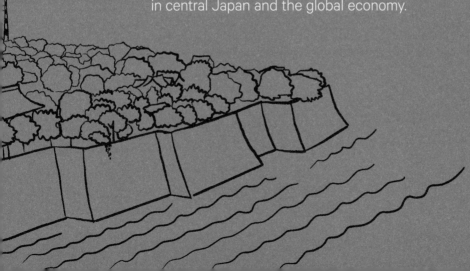

Osaka Innovation Hub

Osaka Innovation Hub connects startups, universities, corporations and investors, stimulating new innovation. We are committed to forming steadfast collaborations with international partners to further enrich the innovation ecosystem in Osaka.

Being part of Osaka's startup ecosystem puts you in a position to connect with major international global players in the tech and electronics industry. The environment is conducive to reasonable startup costs and operating overhead, keeping down fixed costs such as rent, land prices and labor costs, all of which help young companies get on their feet more quickly and spend their precious funds on developing their business.

Osaka is rated as one of the most desirable cities in which to live due to its reasonable cost of living, wonderful healthcare, abundant green spaces, and its "open arms" approach to those coming from overseas. The advantages of operating your business out of Osaka are varied, but first and foremost is Osaka's central location in Japan. Its extensive transportation network offers convenient access by land, sea or air and connects you to Japan's major metropolises as well as to cities throughout Asia and the rest of the world.

The Kansai region's triad of Osaka City, Kobe and Kyoto make this area a golden trio of commerce, culture and business. The cities share easy access to each other through a highly efficient and convenient transportation system. Osaka City is the hub, with Kobe and Kyoto being vital and aspirational branches connected to Osaka's tremendous transportation and manufacturing resources. Osaka's world-famous Kansai Airport is open twenty-four hours a day with an average of 1,260 flights per week to eighty-four cities around the world.

In addition, the Osaka-Kansai World Expo in 2025 (headlined with the theme "Designing Future Society for Our Lives") is already attracting leading technology companies and designers from around the world.

From right to left in the photo:

Nae Nakamura,
Executive Director

Megumi Ishitobi,
Director of Global Network

Osaka
Local Ecosystem

Osaka, the "nation's kitchen," originally got its nickname for being the main port for rice imports from China and other Asian countries. Today, the city of just over 2.5 million people trades more than just food staples. Osaka manufactures a number of high-tech goods, pharmaceutical products and electronics, all with a focus on craftsmanship that's uniquely Japanese. The city has more than 200,000 small businesses, an advanced commuter train system that connects to other cities in the Kansai region (such as Kyoto and Kobe), and a bustling international airport. The region produces about 70 percent of Japan's lithium-ion batteries and is Japan's largest exporter of pharmaceutical products.

Osaka is second only to Tokyo in startup creation. Part of its recipe for success comes from its highly advanced educational system. A number of other top-tier universities and research institutions are based here, including Osaka University, the National Cerebral and Cardiovascular Center, and the National Institute of Biomedical Innovation, Health and Nutrition. Innovation has long been baked into Osaka's DNA, with a range of innovative products coming out of the city, such as the first-ever camera phone and Nissin Foods' instant ramen noodles. Increasingly, life sciences are an important part of Osaka's ecosystem, with a government-formed "life-sciences" cluster and some of Japan's leading pharmaceutical companies based in the city. Osaka, as the host of the 2025 World Expo and a number of startup competitions like Hack Osaka and the Osaka Global Innovation Forum, is making its mark in Japan and around the world.

FACTS & FIGURES

– Osaka, along with Kobe and Kyoto, is part of the Kansai region, which has a population of about 25 million people and a GDP roughly equivalent to that of the Netherlands.

– Startups taking part in the Osaka Innovation Hub's seed accelerator program raised more than $40 million in three and a half years.

– In 2025, Osaka will host the World Expo, whose primary goal is to support the SDGs and the Japanese government's Society 5.0 initiative aimed at using technology to achieve social good.

– The number of international flights out of the Kansai International Airport nearly doubled between 2008 and 2018, to just under 150,000.

– There were roughly 1,000 early-stage startups in Osaka, about 200 fewer than Japan's top startup city, Tokyo.

– Each year the Osaka Innovation Hub hosts more than 250 events for its 1,130 members.

– The *Economist*'s 2019 Global Liveability Index ranked Osaka the fourth-most-liveable city in the world, after Vienna, Melbourne and Sydney.

– Osaka has a dozen "innovation bases," coworking spaces where founders can interact with like-minded entrepreneurs. These include Garage Minato (for precision engineering), Robo & Peace (for robotics) and L-nest Innovation HUB (for bringing together academic research and technology).

NOTABLE STARTUP ACTIVITY

– A number of healthcare startups have come out of Osaka, including At, which developed the world's first-ever capillary-condition analysis system that doesn't need blood testing; Next Innovation, a telemedicine platform; and Triple W, a device that notifies people who have incontinence about when to use the bathroom.

– Cookbiz, a job-search platform for the restaurant industry founded in 2007, has revenues of nearly $20 million per year and grew by about 67 % in 2018.

– Akippa, a crowd-sourced platform for car parking, has gained more than one million users over five years and hopes to create the world's biggest mobility platform by 2030.

Building an Ecosystem through Government, Academic and Corporate Collaboration

OSAKA CITY
大阪市

An interview with

Masaaki Yoshikawa / Founder and CEO of Human Hub Japan Corp.
Chikara Takagishi / Senior General Manager of Urban Management
Division of Hankyu Hanshin Properties Corp.

Osaka has entrepreneurship baked into its DNA. The city is Japan's oldest international port, and ever since the first diplomatic delegation was dispatched to China 1,400 years ago, it has evolved as a commerce hub. The Osaka prefecture has a high level of technological know-how, and its manufacturing capability and economy both operate on impressive scales. Its universities produce abundant talent in many fields, and the cost of living is relatively low given the high quality of life. Another notable advantage for entrepreneurs is its accessibility to Kyoto and Kobe. The three prefectures form the collective urban area called Kansai, which makes knowledge and tech transfer, and collaboration with stakeholders, seamless.

The residents of Osaka are known to be open-minded, generous and welcoming to new cultures, but as the startup ecosystem is still growing, entrepreneurs coming from abroad may still find it challenging to navigate this fast-evolving community. To address this and to bolster the ecosystem, the Osaka City government created the Osaka Innovation Hub (OIH) in 2013 as a gateway to the area's swiftly growing startup and tech community.

Two important players in this initiative are Masaaki Yoshikawa (founder and CEO of Human Hub Japan Corp. and former director-general for Innovation of the city government's Economic Strategy Bureau) and Chikara Takagishi (senior general manager of the Urban Management Division at Hankyu Hanshin Properties Corp.). Both leaders take inspiration from Silicon Valley in growing the Osaka community and have launched initiatives under the OIH umbrella, including the Rainmaking Startupbootcamp, the coworking space GVH#5 and Hankyu Hanshin Properties Corp.' corporate VC.

OIH, along with a number of other organizations in the city, supports the "The Declaration of Startup Friendly Kansai," meaning it is committed to opening the door for startups and willing to provide them with advice and consultation on matters such as business-

building, developing networks, technical support and management of funds. It is creating communities within the Osaka and the Kansai regions for startups to network and grow. Seeking to leverage Osaka's philosophy of open innovation, many companies are actively investing in startups, and there is also a movement to bring in more international startups and acceleration and incubation programs.

According to Masaaki, who believes that entrepreneurs should be moving toward purpose-driven innovation, the OIH initiative stems from an earlier movement, Hack Osaka, which he created to forge connections between entrepreneurs and companies in the city to optimize and maximize available talents and resources toward societal benefit. Hack Osaka is now a well-known conference for entrepreneurs and startups.

Left to right in the photo:
Chikara Takagishi and Masaaki Yoshikawa

> *" Startups are one means of innovation. Every actor, such as major corporations and universities too, should contribute to the creation of innovation. "*

For Masaaki and Chikara, breaking down silos has been vital in leading the ecosystem to create and invest in innovation that tackles social issues. "In order to adapt to rapid changes, we should become more flexible and work together to perform more purpose-driven initiatives," says Masaaki. "Startups are one means of innovation. Every actor, such as major corporations and universities too, should contribute to the creation of innovation."

One of the major initiatives run by the city government and other organizations is the Grand Front Osaka project, centered around the Umekita area, located in the northern part of the central business district. Entrepreneurs are encouraged to seek support and become active members of Knowledge Capital, the creative hub associated with the initiative. In 2024, the Umekita Area Second Zone Development Project, another large-scale initiative, will launch to promote open innovation in the city, especially innovation that aligns with its "Fusion of Greenery and Innovation" focus. The project will prompt the creation of more hubs for innovators similar to Knowledge Capital.

There's also the Kansai Bridge Forum, which helps connect startups and senior executives of corporates. The initiative, which was created to give startups more social credit with established organizations and to mentor CEOs on startups, has led to the Kansai Association of Corporate Executives' "The Declaration of Startup Friendly Kansai," which continues to foster communication that in turn strengthens the ecosystem.

Students and researchers hoping to commercialize the technologies they've developed in one of the region's advanced institutions should connect with OIH, as the organization offers events and resources designed to bolster student and university-led entrepreneurs. Osaka has a strong manufacturing history, so OIH and other initiatives are focusing on boosting the growth of deep-tech startups (especially those spinning off from universities) and helping them enter a more global market. As part of its Overseas Workshop Tour program, OIH also takes groups of young Japan-based entrepreneurs on tours of innovation ecosystems abroad.

Overall, the city government supports both Japanese startups that wish to expand abroad and startups from around the world that want to operate in and invest in Osaka and the Japanese market in general. Startups created in Osaka should approach OIH, as the organization wants to showcase the city and prefecture's talent and technology to the global market. Collaboration with OIH means continuing and building upon Osaka's already strong history of entrepreneurship for a changing future. Osaka is also uniquely welcoming to foreign innovation and investment, and international entrepreneurs who want to make use of these resources can apply for the startup visa offered by the Japanese government.

[ABOUT]

Backed by the Osaka City government, **Osaka Innovation Hub** (OIH) is a broad-reaching startup community for the city and prefecture. The community is situated in the heart of Osaka, Japan's second-largest metropolitan region boasting a long history of entrepreneurship. As of 2019, the community and network consists of over 330 businesses and 800 entrepreneurial individuals. OIH hosts over 250 events per year, including many pitch events, in order to provide local and international entrepreneurs with resources, information and networking opportunities.

[CONTACT]

WEB   innovation-osaka.jp

CONTACT   Innovation-osaka.jp/inquiry

TWITTER   @OIH_Osaka

FACEBOOK   OsakaInnovationHub

Gochiso

ELEVATOR PITCH

" We help companies contribute towards
the Sustainable Development Goals
(SDGs) through better utilization of
their corporate dining expenses and by
converting restaurant marketing costs
into social and environmental value. "

SECTOR social enterprise, IT

WEB gochiso.jp

MILESTONES

Achieving a sales volume
of ¥1 million while bootstrapping
in summer 2016.

Raising our first fund of ¥15.5 million
in November 2016.

Releasing our web application
for connecting nonprofits and
restaurants in November 2017.

Receiving a further ¥22 million
in funding in December 2018.

Many people want to make a difference but don't know how, says Gochiso cofounder Philip Nguyen, whose desire to have a positive impact on society has influenced much of his life. While pursuing a master's and PhD in radiation safety at Kyoto University as the country was recovering from the 2011 earthquake, tsunami and resultant radiation leakage, he undertook an internship at the IAEA. Seeing how a large organization operated drove him towards smaller organizations like startups and nonprofits, as he felt they could move faster towards having a direct positive impact. While trying to launch an education nonprofit, he noticed two key issues: Japan has a low level of charitable donations compared to the US, and young people especially want to make a difference but are the least able to contribute financially. He thought about how to address both issues and hit upon an activity that everyone does occasionally: eating out.

Gochiso began as a platform that allowed people to donate to nonprofits of their choice at no extra cost, simply by dining at certain restaurants. This enabled restaurants to better utilize their marketing expenses to fill more seats while allowing socially conscious diners to enjoy a meal knowing that 10–20 percent of their bill would be put to good use. After encountering difficulties in scaling the number of restaurants to match the many use cases of their diners, Gochiso refocused its growth strategy on corporate dining, helping companies put their business dining expenses toward sustainable SDGs.

TEAM

The Gochiso team is passionate about creating a better society through social business. The team members are from very different backgrounds, bringing diverse perspectives to the table and making Gochiso a dynamic environment. The company's work style is very flexible, with members able to choose to work from the coworking-space office, from home or wherever is most efficient. Team meetings are held by voice call or video conference at the beginning of each week. Gochiso often has team dinners at one of their partner restaurants, and occasionally team members also do volunteer work together. Gochiso owes a lot to local startup and networking events, where Philip met his cofounder Kina Jackson.
The team has adopted a local tradition of celebrating the Toka Ebisu Festival every year on January 10, when they go to the Ebisu Shrine to receive a lucky bamboo branch for business prosperity.

Next Innovation

ELEVATOR PITCH

" We operate an online platform called Smaluna, which provides telemedicine services, including consultation and prescriptions, to women in Japan. We are the major supplier of medicines to medical institutions listed on Smaluna. "

SECTOR **pharma, telemedicine**

WEB **nextinnovation-inc.co.jp**

MILESTONES

Creating a reliable team.

Pivoting from services for men to services for women.

Scaling up to exceed thirty staff members while maintaining the same company culture.

Receiving media attention for our company.

With a degree in pharmacy and more than fifteen years' experience in the field, Kenichi Ishii founded Next Innovation with business partner Koichi Watanabe in 2016. His goal was to maximize on the softening of the law regarding online medical treatment by offering telemedicine to people of working age in Japan. "We dreamed of bridging doctors and people, particularly those with busy lifestyles who don't know how or where to seek medical treatment," says Kenichi, CEO. The pair set up Smaluna, an online platform where patients can connect with doctors and receive consultations as well as prescriptions. Revenue comes from supplying medicines to the medical institutions listed.

TEAM

Next Innovation received ¥75 million in seed funding in 2017 but struggled financially in 2018. As a temporary solution, the founders sought financial support on a non-equity basis from their contacts, before securing ¥100 million in pre–Series A funding in late 2018. Another challenge was pivoting their customer base from men (for treatment of conditions like hair thinning) to women (for oral contraceptives and so on). "We didn't understand women's needs or how to market them, so we carried out surveys," says Kenichi. Osaka's two-hundred-year reputation as Japan's city of medicine has long made the city a hub for pharma companies, which has facilitated collaboration. Having fewer startups in Osaka has also made it easier to attract attention. Kenichi often uses Osaka Innovation Hub and believes the 2025 World Expo in Osaka will draw more healthcare providers to the city, thereby helping the startup grow even more.

People in the Next Innovation team have largely worked with each other before, resulting in a close-knit team with deep understanding of each other. Most team members were recruited from the founders' professional or personal contacts based on their known skills. The team loves innovation and learning from mistakes. Ideas are welcomed and the founders don't say *no* unless they foresee a problem. Attitude and effort are valued more than experience due to the pioneering field of the startup. Two thirds of the forty-five-person team is female. Most team members are from Osaka, with some from elsewhere in Japan. Employees from Tokyo with experience in IPOs were recruited in 2019. Though employees mainly work remotely, they come into the office to spend time socially. Children are welcome at the office, and employees are members of corporate clubs, taking part in activities such as road biking and diving.

Remohab

ELEVATOR PITCH

" Heart disease is the second-most-
common cause of death in Japan.
To tackle this, we provide a remote
system that allows cardiac rehabilitation
at home efficiently. Our innovative
approach can lead to decreases
in heart failure, rehospitalization
or cardiovascular death. "

SECTOR **healthcare, IT**

WEB **remohab.com**

MILESTONES

Being awarded a national grant from
the Ministry of Internal Affairs and
Communications in August 2017 that
allowed us to run a feasibility study
to get a proof of concept.

Successfully completing our first
round of fundraising in July 2018.

Being awarded a national grant for
medical research and development in
July 2019 that allowed us to conduct
our first clinical trials – the first ever
for telemedicine in Japan.

Completing our second round
of fundraising in December 2019,
enabling us to further refine
our product and begin business
development.

Osaka University graduate and cardiologist Tatsunori Taniguchi had never considered joining a startup let alone founding one. Yet in November 2015, he found himself among some of the first participants of the Japan Biodesign Program. This was a spinoff of the Stanford Biodesign Program, renowned for spawning many successful US startups for medical-device development. Through the program, Tatsunori undertook ten months of training with other entrepreneurial medics with the aim of bridging the gap between ideas on how to provide better services for patients and the harsh reality of turning these into viable businesses.

By the end, Tatsunori was solidifying the idea for what was to become Remohab, which he founded in 2017. The company is developing a system to allow cardiac rehabilitation treatment at home, relieving patients of the burden of commuting back and forth to the hospital. Through a medical app, an IoT-equipped exercise bike and an electrocardiogram, healthcare providers can monitor and supervise patients remotely. After six months of funding the venture himself, Tatsunori was awarded a national grant that supports IoT ventures, allowing him to conduct a feasibility study. He subsequently brought on board serial entrepreneur and engineer Yoichi Nakayama as CTO, and the two combined their respective backgrounds in medicine and business to lead the company through a successful second round of fundraising in December 2019. The company is running further clinical trials to gain medical accreditation, with a goal to launch the service in 2022 or 2023.

TEAM

Launching Remohab by himself, founder Tatsunori initially enlisted the support of high school friends to help him get the business off the ground. Another friend introduced Yoichi, an engineer with the valuable experience of taking a startup through an M&A exit. Today, the Osaka-based team is fourteen members strong, with roughly half from a medical background and all joining through personal introductions. The team works well together as its structure is very flat, making communication transparent and allowing issues to be easily addressed. Their individual backgrounds are all highly suited to the roles they fill. Tatsunori, with his cardiologist background, oversees the clinical trials and can communicate well with doctors, whereas other members bring key skills in project management. Due to its growing business, Remohab is considering expanding its team by establishing a Tokyo office within a couple of years.

Review

ELEVATOR PITCH

" We are developers of the business map service Macci, which provides up-to-date information that is not available through web searches. This gives our clients access to key real-time, offline data for everything from monthly parking spaces to disaster prevention. "

SECTOR data, IT

WEB macci.biz

MILESTONES

Receiving mentoring through the Kansai Acceleration Program and launching our app, Macci, in 2016.

Reaching three hundred data gatherers out on the street primarily through word-of-mouth referrals in 2017.

Participating in the Infinity Ventures Summit in 2018, enabling us to gain many investors and customers.

Hiring six new members and rolling out a major update of Macci during 2019–2020.

Shigeo Fujimoto was running his own recruitment firm when he was tasked by a client with collecting a very specific dataset on people in Osaka – data that was not available via Google Search or Street View, and which could only be obtained by sending people out into the city. The project was a success, with Shigeo and his team collecting twenty times more data than what was available online. Yet manpower was needed to undertake this kind of research. Shigeo knew from his background in recruitment that there were many people looking for jobs with flexible working hours. He put two and two together: on-ground researchers would take photos and log information about the city in an app (called Macci), thus building an offline database for clients, whether they be a real estate agency monitoring construction progress, a marketing firm looking to target specific groups or experts investigating crime or disaster prevention. Meanwhile, researchers are free to choose their own hours. For example, parents can work while their children are at school, and seniors can earn while out shopping or even going for a run.

TEAM

Review is a vision-led team with all thirteen members coming through referrals from early business contacts and supporters. Everyone is passionate about the goal of making people's lives more convenient through big data while creating freer and more flexible employment. The result is a diverse group aged from twenty-four to fifty years old, with backgrounds ranging from engineering to PR and marketing. One member was even originally collecting data on the street for the app, but was such a strong researcher and so interested in the business, he became a full-time employee. A small team means that if someone has a problem, those with available hands pitch in. While there are crunch times to meet deadlines, the emphasis is on freedom, and the system developers all work remotely. They hold online team meetings every week and head out for team dinners on a regular basis.

"We didn't have any success stories to follow, and we wondered how come this doesn't already exist," says Shigeo, reflecting on doubts in the early days. Yet the idea received positive media coverage, and the team won the Infinity Venture Summit pitch competition, which led to interest from investors. Currently, their service covers Tokyo's twenty-three wards and Osaka, and they are hoping to expand across Japan and Asia.

Wefabrik Inc.

ELEVATOR PITCH

" We circulate and provide
fashion-industry products to creators
and buyers who can use them as
a resource, thereby reducing waste
and fostering sustainability. "

MILESTONES

Creating the philosophy of the
company with input from all staff
members.

Designing a scheme to increase
sales using data analysis.

Securing funding of $2 million.

Launching a logistics system.

SECTOR **apparel**

WEB **wefabrik.jp**

Tsuyoshi Fukuya worked in the apparel business and at a fiber trading company and was astounded by the fashion industry's mass production and wastefulness. "When I looked into the problem, I discovered that more than twenty billion items of clothing are discarded worldwide every year," he says. Inspired to change the industry, he set up Wefabrik in 2015 with funding of $200,000 from two VCs. Tsuyoshi chose Osaka as the headquarters of the business because it is not only his hometown but also has a large number of manufacturing companies.

TEAM

It has not been smooth sailing for the Wefabrik team. Initially, most of the staff was recruited via referral and employment agencies, but the team didn't gel and almost fell apart during the company's pivot. Tsuyoshi attributed this to a lack of support for each other and set about trying to establish it. He held business camps where all staff members would discuss and set the company's philosophy, vision and mission. Today, all team members and business partners receive a business card featuring that information, so they understand what the company is doing and where it is going. A core requirement of all staff members is to bring creativity to their positions and be driven to help pioneer change in the fashion industry. To be successful, people also need to be team-driven and keen to support their colleagues. Three times a year, the staff participates in business camps to discuss issues at Wefabrik.

Wefabrik purchased fabric, yarn and other materials to upcycle into clothing and lifestyle products. However, the brand didn't take off and Tsuyoshi realized that one upcycling brand couldn't have a sufficient impact on the industry's wastefulness. In 2017, the company pivoted by halting the brand and launching Smasell, an online platform that brings companies holding unnecessary inventory together with buyers in need of stock. Registrations currently total one thousand companies and five thousand buyers. The companies are mostly apparel, fashion and trading companies, while the buyer side is predominately Japan-based consumers who sell at flea markets or via online apps. In 2019, Wefabrik launched a logistics system to analyze purchasing behavior on each item, allowing suppliers to use Smasell for consignment sales. It also secured $2 million in funding from VCs and logistics companies, bringing the total funding received to $3.6 million.

Genki Kanaya

Founder and CEO
/ akippa

A consummate salesman who never hesitates to challenge convention and speak his mind, Genki Kanaya was destined to become a startup founder. After launching his career in sales at one of Japan's largest telecommunications companies, he soon realized the importance of having a purpose in life: creating real solutions to real problems. This inspired Genki to found akippa in 2009. He quickly leveraged his sales experience to bootstrap the funds needed to validate his business idea and fully incorporate in 2011. Now he's determined to transform Japan's premier parking-space-sharing app into the world's number one software company.

ABOUT THE COMPANY

akippa, an IT company, provides a mobility platform that connects owners of vacant parking spaces with drivers seeking places to park. Through its namesake app, users can reliably discover convenient parking at over 33,000 locations nationwide.

WEB akippa.co.jp

Can you describe your business model?

It's actually pretty simple. People who own parking spaces can register with us via our website for free. Drivers who use our app can book a place to park in advance, well before they reach their destination. This eliminates the frustration of driving a long way to a popular destination only to find that there's nowhere to park. We have a fifty-fifty revenue split with parking space owners. For example, if a user pays ¥1,000 to rent a space, ¥500 will go to us and ¥500 will go to the owner.

Why did you start this particular business?

When we originally worked in sales, our lives were all about numbers, meeting arbitrary sales targets. Because of this, we were always dealing with complaints. This made me question my career and the purpose of my work. I felt that I needed a mission and a vision in life. During this time, I experienced a blackout in my home. This incident reminded me of the necessity of electricity in our lives, so I started to wonder about what other things in life are indispensable.

This led me to think about services that solve actual problems, and I started brainstorming. I got together with all of my employees and, by the end of our brainstorming session, we had a list of over two hundred societal problems that needed to be

" Persistence is the most important characteristic that successful founders have. "

What was the best decision that you made during the startup process?

My business idea centered on an app, but when I started out, I had no knowledge or experience in this field, so I hired experts who knew much more about technology and the internet than I did. Doing that made the company stronger. Many founders want to be the best in their company; however, that means that their company's capability can never exceed their own. So in order to continually expand and push our company forward, I try to hire people who know a lot and who can contribute their expertise to the company. We currently have eighty employees, and I'd rank myself somewhere around thirtieth when it comes to technical expertise.

What is it like to work at akippa? What is the company culture like?

Of course, we value skills, but the mindset of our employees is equally important. Even if we interview a highly skilled candidate, we won't hire them unless they have the mindset to match. This mindset – you could even call it our core value – is hospitality. By this, we mean the ability to recognize a problem and quickly take action to solve it, helping those around us.

solved. One of these ideas stood out to me: taking a long journey to a particular location, only to arrive and discover that the parking lot is full. I figured this problem could be solved with a mobile phone application. Instead of dealing with parking machines on-site, I believed that people should be able to reserve parking in advance via an app.

What difficulties did you face during the early stages of your business?

Funding was definitely my greatest challenge. We only had ¥50,000 to start with – basically nothing. There were at least ten times when we had less than ¥10,000 in the bank, and we needed to pay the salaries of twenty people. But the bank did not lend me any money. Thankfully, after our business started growing, we received ¥3.5 billion in seed funding from companies such as Toyota, Japan Railways Group and Japan Post Holdings.

How did you pay your employees during those difficult times?

I had to borrow money from my personal network, including from friends, family and extended family. Sometimes, I would cold-call people, explain what I was doing and ask for their support.

What professional advice do you have for aspiring entrepreneurs or early-stage founders?

As important as education, skills and experience can be, I believe that persistence is the most important characteristic that successful founders have. As long as a founder maintains that mentality and keeps pushing the company forward, the business will survive. So, my advice is to do everything you can to keep going. Push your abilities to the limits.

Also, many companies only pay attention to their current situation, maintaining the status quo, but it's important to set a goal for the future, calculate backward and figure out what it will take to achieve that goal. For example, six years ago, I couldn't imagine our current situation: owning an app with over 1.7 million users. We didn't have any engineers on our team back then. However, because we had a goal to be the world's best, this kept us on track to achieve our current success.

What does the future look like for akippa? What do you hope to achieve and what challenges lie ahead?

We aim to be the number one company in the world by 2040. We want to surpass Google. In the meantime, we're increasing our parking-lot-space inventory. As the world shifts toward electronic and autonomous cars, we need to increase the amount of places where these vehicles can be charged. We expect autonomous driving will depend on the sharing economy, so we'll need to build an infrastructure of hubs to be ready for that. In order to build these hubs in an optimal way, we're currently collecting data on how people move to and from our parking lots.

Does this mean that your business model will evolve beyond software and include the construction of physical infrastructure?

Indeed, our product is just an app right now, but we're planning to build the necessary infrastructure by collaborating with other companies. Then we can use our app to connect users to these physical locations.

What does it mean to be the number one company in the world? What metrics will you use to measure this accomplishment?

Our guiding principle is to become a company that solves the world's problems in the future. This is why we say that we want to become the best in the world. However, since that's difficult to measure, we also want to increase our profit and market capitalization. I should say that this objective primarily serves as our internal motivation – a benchmark, if you will.

What work habits have you developed over time?

Basically, we separate management from execution. We leave business operations to others and focus our attention on management. The advantage of doing this is that it separates the corporate side of the business from core operations, which helps us to clarify our corporate mission, vision and business strategy. We can then consider further diversification and portfolio restructuring. If going public were our goal, then we'd only need to execute; however, our goal is to be the best in the world. I also believe that corporate governance will help us achieve healthy and sustainable growth.

Most business strategies are new to me, so I learn the basics first and then make my own. I find that mentors often lead to obstructive thinking. I believe that it's important to start with diffuse thinking and then narrow my ideas down or change my ideas while consulting with experts. Of course, part of this process requires me to have great confidence in my intuition. I should also note that I address any remaining gaps in my knowledge by reading books.

What are the benefits of starting a business in Osaka?

First of all, land, rent and labor costs are more affordable than what you'll find in Tokyo. Additionally, the food here is excellent. Our office is located in Nanba, which is easy to access from Kansai International Airport, just thirty minutes door-to-door.

Osaka also offers advantages when it comes to recruitment. In Tokyo, the market for highly skilled employees is very competitive. We're actively reaching out to people who grew up in Osaka and moved to Tokyo for employment. We're inviting them back to Osaka and offering them the chance to return to their hometown and do great work. This approach enables us to attract talent from famous companies such as Google and Rakuten. If they work for us, they can work in the communities where their parents live. They can raise their children while staying close to their own parents, all while enjoying a rewarding career. Generations of families can stay together, and that makes working with us attractive.

What local activities, restaurants and attractions do you recommend for business and leisure?

I enjoy reading books at a local Starbucks that is combined with a bookstore. I also enjoy watching live performances of the idol group Momoiro Clover Z, who are famous for collaborating with Kiss. •

What are your top work essentials?
My iPhone. I do most of my work on my iPhone.

At what age did you found your company?
Twenty-four.

What's your most used app?
Uber Eats.

What's the most valuable piece of advice you've been given?
I haven't received much advice. I learn from books.

What's your greatest skill?
Sales.

What do you do every morning (or night before) to prepare for the day ahead?
I think about how I can impact others.

What book has most influenced your career?
The Social Network.
It's a movie, not a book, though.

Mitsuki Bun

Founder and CEO
/ Beautiful Smile

Mitsuki Bun is tackling one of Japan's greatest social problems: food waste. She is a native of the tranquil city of Nara, earned an economics degree from the prestigious Doshisha University in Kyoto and eventually moved to Osaka to work and raise her family. Her desire to work hard while maintaining a flexible schedule for her family catapulted her into the startup world. As the founder and CEO of Beautiful Smile, Mitsuki tirelessly dedicates her energy and effort to promoting ethical consumption through her Loss Zero brand, creating value for food producers, local restaurants and end consumers.

ABOUT THE COMPANY

Beautiful Smile is a company that reduces food waste while creating value for consumers, local businesses and corporate partners. Through the Loss Zero program, Beautiful Smile is able to buy and sell food that would normally be discarded.

WEB beautifulsmile.co.jp

What was your entrepreneurial path?

I'm a serial entrepreneur. After having children, I wanted to return to the workforce. However, in Japanese society, it can be difficult for mothers to find good work. So, in 2001, I came up with the idea of starting a company. That way, no one could fire me. I started working for myself, but I didn't know anything about business at all. I didn't know about the internet or ecommerce, but I was able to start an online shop at home. Although it was difficult, this is how I realized just how much of a good fit running a business was for me. It was so challenging and interesting. I worked hard, learned a lot and gained so much experience. Overall, my business went well.

My first venture specialized in hair accessories. After we sold a lot, I started collecting used accessories via the internet as a corporate social-responsibility project in Japan. We donated and occasionally resold them in developing countries such as Laos and Cambodia. Our success in this venture allowed us to create scholarships and youth vocational programs.

Reusing waste has so much value, and I realized that I could do important and positive things for society with the internet. I decided to focus on one of Japan's major social problems: food waste. That's how the Loss Zero brand came to be.

" Be willing to listen to the market and change your business model quickly in response. "

Originally, these producers didn't want to reveal their brand on the products they sold to us. These days, the situation is different. We live in a society of SDGs – Sustainable Development Goals. Big brands want to be associated with this, so they proudly display their names on the products that we sell. It's a win-win. Consumers can contribute to Japanese society by buying and eating food that would have otherwise gone to waste. And, by selling excess food to Beautiful Smile via the Loss Zero program, food producers can also contribute to Japanese society.

What was the best business decision you've made so far?

My best decision was to do business to solve social issues. I was forty-eight years old when I started Loss Zero, and I was slightly more conservative than when I started my first business. However, I made a decision to take on a new challenge. Thanks to that, I am growing more. Solving social issues is very rewarding.

What advice do you have for early-stage entrepreneurs?

Just act. Acting quickly is so important. Be willing to listen to the market and change your business model quickly in response. Some businesses never change their business model, and that can cause problems. Always think about consumer satisfaction and how you can monetize your business model.

What challenges did you face while starting up and how did you overcome them?

It's so important to solve social problems, but doing so is difficult to monetize. This was my struggle. Fortunately, through my first company and the amazing business relationships I'd been building for over eighteen years, I had numerous acquaintances – including entrepreneurs, social entrepreneurs, administrative personnel and company executives – that I could rely on. People in my network gave me a lot of advice. Also, after some time, I had a lot of business experience and knowledge. All of this helped me solve the business problems that came up. My business environment gradually improved, and I could continue to run Beautiful Smile.

How does your business model work?

I started this business to reduce food waste and connect food producers to consumers – ethical consumption. To explain this more concretely, we buy surplus food, imperfect food and food about to expire at a low price and then sell it directly to customers. We serve both individual consumers and companies. Some customers make individual purchases and some join our subscription service.

We reach consumers in two main ways: through our Loss Zero online store and via restaurants and cafes through Loss Zero–themed events here in the Kansai area. We collaborate with a lot of food producers to make this happen.

What was the biggest mistake you made while running your business? How did you recover from it?

When I was running my first company, I didn't respond to complaints quickly enough. These complaints gradually escalated and festered online, due to my failure to respond to what were initially minor customer complaints. Eventually, some of these complaints became slander, and this made me so depressed that I couldn't even leave home. Thanks to the encouragement of family and friends, I overcame this situation little by little. Since then, I've been working so hard to run my company in a sincere way. It was a very painful experience, but now I think it made me stronger.

Why did you start your business in Osaka?

I built my business here in Osaka while raising two children. My parents-in-law, who live near my house, have always been supportive of me and my husband, and they helped with housework and childcare. I don't think I could work without their support.

I sometimes think about living in Tokyo, because it's filled with information and energetic people. People in local cities, such as Osaka, tend to be slightly more conservative than people in Tokyo. So, in a way, I feel like I have a responsibility to encourage people here. That being said, there is also plenty of opportunity in Osaka. Additionally, there aren't so many women who are entrepreneurs here in Osaka, so I'd like to encourage them as well.

What do you like about living and working in Osaka?

The people here are very kind and have a sense of pride in the Kansai region. We have our own unique style of humor. Also, our food is very delicious. So I always enjoy working and laughing in Osaka. The city gives me so much energy.

From a business perspective, I've developed so many helpful connections since I started the hair-accessory business back in 2001. Osaka's a big city, but it's not as big as Tokyo, so it's easy to meet people and discover new things. The city is a great size for doing business. Also, it's easy to access other Asian countries from Osaka, so the city feels very international.

What local activities, restaurants and attractions do you recommend for business and leisure?

Osaka is one of Japan's manufacturing centers, and there are many companies with excellent industrial technology. If you are looking for a place that can support your business, Osaka may be a candidate.

Also the World Exposition will be held in Osaka in 2025. This event aims to make a significant contribution to achieving the Sustainable Development Goals through the use of technology. At the World Exposition, you'll be able to experience what life will be like in the near future.

Can you describe your company culture? What is it like to work for Beautiful Smile?

These days, a lot of people in Japan are interested in Sustainable Development Goals, especially issues regarding food waste and conserving our environment. That's why we are often interviewed about Loss Zero activities. When our vision was introduced on television or in business magazines, it was easy to attract and hire young, talented university students and people who were willing to quit their jobs at other companies to come and join us.

What personal work habits have you developed over time?

I have two meals a day, so I work without a lunch break. Working in this way allows me to go home early. Of course, business lunch meetings and training time are exceptions to this practice.

When I exercise, I go to the gym, which is a five-minute walk from my company. I can save time and get back to work quickly. This also makes me feel refreshed and helps me work more efficiently.

Lastly, I avoid working at night. Instead, I value having conversations with my family, taking a relaxing bath and going to bed early.

What does the future look like for you? What concerns or challenges lie ahead?

We plan to recruit more staff who sympathize with the vision of Loss Zero: people who are passionate about working with us to solve the problem of food waste. Additionally, we want to propose a new way of food consumption to Japanese society and create a new movement in the market.

This ties directly into our biggest concern. Here in Japan, the majority of the population is still unfamiliar with the issues surrounding food waste, so we want to create a public consciousness about food while simultaneously expanding our business. I believe that this process of generating our awareness and achieving greater business success will be a long-term challenge.

Our main goal is to create a new market in Japan. We are actively developing innovative strategies to achieve this. The continued success of Loss Zero will require working with corporate partners and more media exposure. •

What are your top work essentials?
Energy.

At what age did you found your company?
I started my first company when I was thirty-one. Loss Zero at forty-eight.

What's your most used app?
Google Maps. I get lost every day.

What's the most valuable piece of advice you've been given?
Get a lot of sleep.

What's your greatest skill?
Encouraging people. I strive to be a role model for women.

What book has most influenced your career?
The Seven Habits of Highly Effective People.

AIDOR Acceleration

AIDOR Acceleration is a business-creation program tailored to IoT, robotics and hardware-technology-related startups. During the program's four-month duration, participating entrepreneurs receive support in the form of business-plan mentoring, technical workshops and lectures, networking opportunities and discounts on 3D printing and other rapid-prototyping tool usage. Participants are also given access to commercial spaces and sports facilities where they can test products and concepts with real customers. The program is targeted at pre-seed-stage startups, individuals and students. Expats living in Japan are encouraged to apply, though at least a basic level of Japanese language ability is encouraged. The program costs ¥50,000 for individuals, ¥25,000 for students or ¥25,000 per person when entering as a team. The program's portfolio includes Toraru, makers of GENCHI, a real-time virtual travel service designed for disabled and elderly people who are physically unable to travel.

SECTOR IoT, hardware, robotics
SELECTED PORTFOLIO Toraru, GENCHI
WHO SHOULD APPLY Entrepreneurs with a hardware-technology-related business idea.
APPLY
sansokan.jp/enquete/?H_ENQ_NO=23608
WEB teqs.jp/acceleration

OIH Seed Acceleration Program

The OIH Seed Acceleration Program (OSAP) has been running for four years and holds two programs per year aimed at stimulating the startup ecosystem in Osaka City and the Kansai region. The program is geared toward startups in the position to scale up through venture capital investment or collaboration with larger established companies, and both of these opportunities are offered during the program. Participating startups can also learn about topics such as public relations, finance and marketing, to name a few, and they are invited to participate in the annual alumni event. "OSAP startups have successfully fundraised about eight billion yen and made about sixty business collaborations with large companies," says Yoshiyuki Kuwada, program manager. "Since many startup-acceleration programs have started in Kansai these days, I think OSAP is a pioneer and activated the startup ecosystem in Osaka."

SECTOR sector-agnostic
SELECTED PORTFOLIO Baseconnect, Compass, ACALL, Heart Organization, WEFABRIK, Inc.
WHO SHOULD APPLY Seed-stage startups established within the previous five years or who have released a new service in that time, with yearly sales under ¥50 million.
APPLY innovation-osaka.jp/inquiry
WEB innovation-osaka.jp/acceleration

RISING!

EO Osaka (a Japanese chapter of the Entrepreneurs Organization) founded RISING! in 2019 to help establish a venture ecosystem in the Kansai region to rival Tokyo. Leveraging a network of global entrepreneurs in fifty-three countries, RISING! incorporates EO content developed by some of the world's leading psychologists and management consultants. It is implemented through public–private collaboration, and many founders of listed companies in Osaka are mentors in the program. RISING! seeks startups that are or will be based in Osaka Prefecture with a turnover of least ¥100 million, and a strong motivation for growth is paramount for a successful application. Participants benefit from the extensive network of companies within the Entrepreneurs Organization, while RISING! has a local network of support organizations including financial institutions and venture capital firms.

SECTOR public–private partnership project
SELECTED PORTFOLIO SSMother Holdings, KB company, Sanwa Paint, JAM Trading, ZENSIN, HOPE INTERNATIONAL WORKS, YOLO JAPAN
WHO SHOULD APPLY Managers of venture companies (companies that have already developed business plans and have an annual turnover of more than ¥100 million) that create new value in the world. Applicants should aim for rapid expansion and seek to represent Osaka on the global stage
APPLY Applications open once a year around springtime. Please check the Osaka website for details.
WEB **pref.osaka.lg.jp/shogyoshien/hattenshien**

Startupbootcamp Scale Osaka

Startupbootcamp Scale Osaka is a matchmaking program with a difference: it aims to open up Japan to mature startups that are dedicated to entering new, large markets and to help Osaka become a leader in global open innovation. "Japan is often thought of as too difficult for startups," says Meghan Bridges, marketing director. "We help to break down cultural and language barriers and to execute truly cross-border, cross-cultural innovation." Unsurprisingly, it's a competitive entry process, and startups must demonstrate that they are the best fit for the program's Japanese corporate partners' needs. The program is semi-remote, taking into account the busy schedules of founders, and offers coworking space and discounted accommodation. Crucially, the program provides a pathway to making large Japanese corporations a customer through matchmaking and proof-of-concept project support.

SECTOR smart cities
SELECTED PORTFOLIO SoundPays, Oovvu, Genoplan, Chinafy, Enroute, FraSen
WHO SHOULD APPLY Mature startups with significant traction in their home markets and revenue or investment allowing for resources to be dedicated to overseas market expansion. Smart-cities-themed startups including mobility, proptech, health and sportstech, media and advertising.
WEB **startupbootcamp.org/accelerator/scale-osaka**

The DECK

Located in the heart of Osaka's manufacturing business district, The DECK is home to a melting pot of startups, creators and corporates and serves four main functions: it provides a coworking space, an event venue, a makerspace and shared offices. The interior design is a combination of modern and cozy, with tabletops created in its own makerspace. Projects and prototypes from companies based in The DECK are also on display as a source of inspiration. The space offers free drinks and a salad bar and hosts Takoyaki night, a well-attended monthly meetup. Founded as a base of open innovation for local organizations, The DECK is expanding to become internationally focused, holding regular events for foreign entrepreneurs and cross-border businesses and fostering introductions to business leaders and like-minded entrepreneurs.

ADDRESS 2-1-1 Minamihonmachi, Chuo-ku, Osaka-city, Osaka
OPENING HOURS Mon–Fri: 9 AM–10 PM; Sat, Sun and public holidays: 9 AM–7 PM.
USP Multiple uses, offering a coworking space, an event space, a makerspace and shared offices.
PRICE RANGE Drop-in: ¥300 per thirty minutes. Day: ¥3,000. Monthly membership: ¥12,800 per month. Corporate use options also available.
WEB thedeck.jp

Global Venture Habitat Osaka

Though housed in a commercial complex (Umeda's bustling Grand Front Osaka), Global Venture Habitat manages to pull off a homey atmosphere, utilizing an open-plan layout with a lack of partitions. It was one of the earliest coworking offices in Osaka, with an occupancy typically made up of local and foreign startups and students. It offers on-site events and seminars covering topics ranging from patent information, marketing and promotion to overseas expansion.

The well-connected space is located in the same tower as Osaka's Knowledge Capital, which showcases products and services using cutting-edge technology. Occupants can take advantage of the multitudinous restaurants and bars that stay open until 4 AM or even try out a bit of bouldering on the tower's sixth floor.

ADDRESS Tower C 7F Grand Front Osaka 3-1 Ofuka-cho, Kita-ku, Osaka 530-0011
OPENING HOURS Reception: Mon–Fri: 10 AM–6 PM; Members: 24/7
USP Not only a convenient and comfortable working space but also offers mentoring, seminars and a network for startups.
PRICE RANGE Not open to the public. Visit the website to view the membership application process.
WEB gvh-osaka.com

GVH#5

The abundance of plant life and natural lighting in GVH#5 gives the space a zen-like ambiance, particularly in the communal areas. GVH#5 is in the heart of Umeda's business and commercial district and surrounded by cafes, bars and restaurants. It's also serviced by three overground and two metro stations nearby. Established in 2014, GVH#5 hosts growth-oriented IT startups in seed to early stages and offers coworking and project spaces, private offices, meeting and seminar rooms, and a support network of investors, consultants and accountants as well as a resident community manager. GVH#5 is a Startupbootcamp Scale Osaka venue and serves as a gateway for overseas startups and a hub for open innovation, with regular events on the calendar.

ADDRESS 1-12 Kakuta-cho, Kita-ku, Osaka 530-0017
OPENING HOURS Members: 24/7. Staff on-site: Mon–Fri, 10 AM–12 PM and 1 PM–5 PM.
USP A startup-support facility operated by Hankyu Hanshin Holdings Group, leveraging a strong network of companies, universities, local government and support organizations in Osaka.
PRICE RANGE Not open to the public. Visit the website to view the membership application process.
WEB gvh-5.com/en

Kansai University

Kansai University (KU), founded in 1886 as Kansai Law School, celebrated its 130th anniversary in 2016. Its founding principle, to "protect justice from power," has helped to inform the school's transformation into a large university with more than 420,000 graduates and 35,000 current students. More than 20 percent of KU undergraduates are hired by the top four hundred companies in Japan, and KU alumni include executives of listed companies. In opening the Umeda campus (and its attached incubation facility, KANDAI Me Rise), the university is developing its own "philosophy of thinking," one that emphasizes thinking and acting positively. KANDAI Me Rise functions to not only educate but also provide a coworking facility to boost connections among different people and create a new image of a university campus.

LOCATION The main campus is located in Senriyama, northern Osaka. The Umeda Campus is located in Umeda, in the center of Osaka.

CLOSE TRANSIT CONNECTIONS Train access to Kansai University is from Hankyu Kanda-mae Station. The Umeda campus is a five-minute walk from the Hankyu Umeda Station.

PRICE OF TUITION Refer to the university website for up-to-date tuition information. Courses at the Umeda campus are free.

ENTRY REQUIREMENTS Students must pass an entrance exam given by the university, and there are no entry requirements for the program at the Umeda campus.

WEB kansai-u.ac.jp/umeda
kansai-u.ac.jp

Osaka-Umeda Landscape

Kindai University

Kindai University is one of the largest private universities in Japan. As of 2019, the school has more than 33,000 undergraduate and 1,000 graduate students. It has been ranked among the top 4 percent of universities by Britain's Times Higher Education (THE) World University Rankings 2020. The university's ideology reflects a progressive understanding of the challenges society must overcome in the near future, placing added importance on real-world learning and emotional intelligence. In 2017, the university established the Academic Theater. This new hub for innovation and entrepreneurship offers an incubation program, presenting students with opportunities to learn, gain experience and acquire funding and support to start a company. One of the courses offered is based on serial entrepreneur and Stanford professor Steve Blank's Lean Launchpad class.

LOCATION Higashiosaka City
CLOSE TRANSIT CONNECTIONS Kintetsu Nagase Station, Kintetsu Yaenosato Station
PRICE OF TUITION ¥726,500 per year
ENTRY REQUIREMENTS Japanese proficiency level N2 or higher for students who wish to take classes in Japanese. All applicants must take an entrance exam.
WEB **kindai.ac.jp/english**

Osaka City University

Osaka City University was founded in 1880 and is committed to upholding the local culture of Osaka while also contributing to the international community. The school achieves this by promoting free and creative education, by working with the city's citizens to improve urban culture and economy, and by sharing educational discoveries and research. At the university's Umeda satellite campus, the Graduate School of Urban Management offers a degree for working adults in entrepreneurship and problem solving with courses in urban business, policy, administration, and medical- and welfare-innovation management. In addition to undergraduate and graduate education, the university offers public lectures for citizens on subjects from culture to medical science. To further strengthen the city of Osaka, the university has an incubator close to campus that supports new industries and startup activities (including university-originated ventures) with the university's research and professors.

LOCATION The university's main campus is located at the southern end of Osaka, next to the Yamato River. There is also an innovation base in Umeda, in central Osaka.
CLOSE TRANSIT CONNECTIONS The main campus is accessible by train, from the JR Sugimoto-cho Station and by subway from the Abiko Station.
PRICE OF TUITION The average undergraduate tuition is ¥535,800 per year.
ENTRY REQUIREMENTS Students are mainly selected based on the National Centre Test (a common test in Japan) and the school's own Individual Assessment Test.
WEB **osaka-cu.ac.jp/en**

Hack Ventures

Hack Ventures supports Osaka- and Kansai-based startups in order to combine their technology and manufacturing expertise with Silicon Valley–style innovation and cutting-edge IT. Its goal is to grow the region into a globally connected startup ecosystem and fuel greater entrepreneurship.

SECTOR IoT, Internet of Everything, IT, IT services, healthcare

EMAIL info@hack-ventures.com

WEB hack-ventures.com

Hack Ventures was born partly out of fortuitous timing. Takashi Kanazawa had twenty years' experience working for the largest venture capital firm in Japan but felt there was a lack of fresh, innovative ideas. In 2013, the City of Osaka marked five years of recovery since the financial crisis and launched an initiative to promote innovation and entrepreneurship. Hailing from Osaka himself, Takashi joined forces with two other partners based in Silicon Valley to contribute to the city's goal. Together, they founded Hack Ventures with the vision of combining local expertise in manufacturing and technology with global knowledge and emerging business models. They raised approximately $45 million and were selected as the Osaka City Global Innovation Fund. Supported by both the city and by large corporations, the fund also has the unusual distinction of being backed by all three Japanese megabanks.

Hack Ventures' goal is to develop a broad startup ecosystem in the Kansai region through investing in passionate people who are dedicated to realizing this vision and manifesting meaningful change in society. Before making an investment decision, the Hack Ventures team strives to develop a strong connection on a personal basis with the startup founder, familiarizing itself with his or her values, vision and motivations. They spend a good deal of time together, sharing thoughts, ideas and perspectives on both business and life. Operating out of the Grand Front Osaka building (home to Osaka Innovation Hub), the fund also supports networking events, mentoring and an acceleration program. Currently, it cohosts three hundred events annually with startups and major corporations. While the aim of connecting Osaka startups globally is still at an early stage, Takashi says that entrepreneurship has greatly increased in the region, with many students and women getting involved. He hopes to see Kansai startups forging international collaborations in the near future.

HHP Co-creation Fund

HHP Co-creation Fund's mission is
to create reliable, comfortable spaces
by investing in tech startups that enrich
the urban environment.

SECTOR real estate, smart city

EMAIL info-sg@gvh-5.com

WEB hhp.co.jp/en

Real estate developer Hankyu Hanshin Properties (HHP) focuses on boosting the prosperity of the area around Osaka's Hankyu-Hanshin train line, which is its main business target area. With extensive expertise in the real estate business, the company understands that living and working spaces are critical to people's quality of life. Japan's aging and declining population, however, presents challenges to how people live and work.

This situation has inspired HHP to collaborate with startups whose cutting-edge technology and innovative approaches can revolutionize the urban environment. In 2015, HHP set up its Angel Fund to revitalize the local startup ecosystem. Since 2019, the company has been investing in startups in the proptech, smart city and smarthome sectors via its HHP Co-creation Fund No.1 LPS. Its goal is twofold: to support startups and to get exposure to, and expertise on, advanced technology in real estate and redevelopment. The startups' areas of expertise include AI, IoT, VR/AR, digital marketing, mobility as a service, image analysis, blockchain and the sharing economy. Successful investees have a product or service that makes people feel safer and more comfortable or encourages them to spend more time in a smart city.

Chikara Takagishi, senior general manager in the Urban Management Division at Hankyu Hanshin Properties, is passionate about how investing in these startups helps not only the community and the startup ecosystem in Osaka but also the company. "I have met amazing startups from all over the world that have cutting-edge technologies and disruptive ideas that I could never have imagined," he says. "By collaborating with them, we – as a company – can learn more and at a much faster pace. We are cocreating innovations with startups by using our CVC. This kind of collaboration is necessary for growth of the ecosystem and us." Chikara says that previously offered angel funding has allowed the company to gain knowledge about cocreation of business interests with external partners and organizations while boosting Osaka's startup ecosystem.

SENDAI

A youthful, bustling city with a large and highly educated workforce, Sendai brings together a vibrant mix of individuals and industries. From risk management to IT, startups have found their niche in Sendai. Here, in a city filled with natural beauty, they are able to take advantage of the city's resources while also remaining just a couple of hours by train from Tokyo or a short flight to Shanghai.

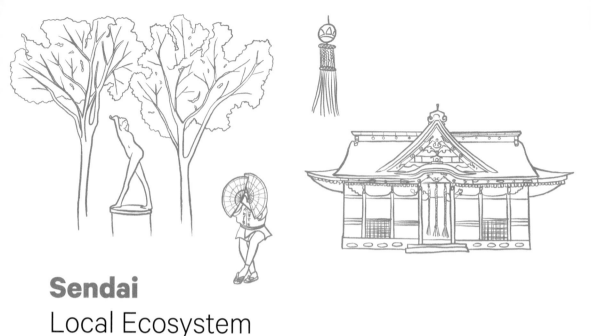

Sendai
Local Ecosystem

In a country known for its high-tech cities, skyscrapers rising into the air, ubiquitous screens and flashing lights, Sendai is a breath of fresh air. Nicknamed the "City of Trees," the northern Japanese city of Sendai has an abundance of parks, waterfalls and cherry blossoms, helping to make it one of Japan's most livable cities. From its tree-lined streets to the Hirose River, which runs through the center of the city, and Matsushima Bay, one of Japan's top scenic sites, Sendai offers a number of opportunities for residents and foreigners alike to get out and about.

Sendai, with its more than eighty thousand students and about one hundred universities, trade schools and other higher education institutions, has earned a reputation as a college town. This youth and level of education has also made it one of the best places in Japan to start up a business. Rent costs are low, and the international exchanges are bustling. Residents of Sendai can take advantage of the six-month startup visa program as well as a number of accelerator programs and opportunities; for example, Ignite Sendai and the Tohoku Growth Accelerator Demo Day. The city has a strong IT sector as well as programs such as GLOBAL Lab SENDAI aimed at developing the international reach of Sendai-based companies. The city has also become a global leader in disaster management after multiple earthquakes shook the city. In 2015, it hosted the United Nations World Conference on Disaster Risk Reduction. Resilience, along with youth and revitalization, is truly part of Sendai's core.

FACTS & FIGURES

– Sendai has a young, highly productive population, with more than 25% of the population between the ages of 20 and 30 and a workforce of more than 650,000 people.

– Between 2014 and 2016, the startup rate for Sendai was 7%, the second highest in Japan during that time.

– In 2023, the world's most advanced next-generation synchrotron radiation facility will open on the Aobayama campus of Tohoku University, supporting startups in various fields such as new material development and drug discovery.

– Sendai City is designated as one of the ten National Strategic Special Zones nationwide, focused on innovation across five fields: social entrepreneurship, women's empowerment, near-future technology demonstration, medical care and public space utilization.

– There are more than 100 higher-education institutions in the Sendai metropolitan area and more than 80,000 students. In particular, there are a large number of science and engineering universities and vocational schools.

– Tohoku University Venture Partners (THVP, Sendai) has invested a total of ¥3.18 billion in 13 Tohoku University venture companies in about three years (as of the end of August 2018).

– Sendai was ranked first among Japanese cities in the *issue+design* Creative City INDEX 2015.

– In 2017, Sendai City launched the country's first two area-wide acceleration programs in six Tohoku prefectures focused on building a community and ecosystem of diverse entrepreneurs.

NOTABLE STARTUP ACTIVITY

– Founded in 2016, Manaby, a provider of employment matching services and online employment training for persons with disabilities, has raised ¥101 million.

– TESS, established in 2008, manufactures and sells a pedal-operated wheelchair called Cogy. The startup has raised more than ¥200 million so far and sells more than 1,000 units a year.

– Ball Wave, a spinoff company of Tohoku University established in 2015, raised ¥830 million. Ball Wave has developed a small and highly sensitive sensor that aims to solve environmental problems, predict disasters and aid in space exploration.

– Hyakusen Renma established a reservation site called "STAY JAPAN" in 2012, with the aim of revitalizing the Tohoku region following the Great East Japan Earthquake. The startup provides lodging facilities across various regions. The company has raised a total of ¥2.2 billion and is raising its Series C round.

The Power and Potential of Innovation for Change

仙台市
SENDAI CITY

An interview with
Kazuko Kohri / Mayor, City of Sendai

In the city of Sendai and in the wider Tohoku region, individuals have a strong drive to contribute to local communities and society in general. This compulsion was in part triggered by the Great East Japan Earthquake that shook the area in 2011. The local government, aided by country-wide initiatives and a growing roster of international investment, has dedicated a lot of resources and time to bolstering the startup ecosystem to meet this passion for purpose.

"A once-in-a-thousand-year scale disaster brought about a once-in-a-thousand-year scale of change," says Kazuko Kohri, mayor of Sendai. "In such an environment, diverse entrepreneurs emerged, and the community's commitment to supporting those entrepreneurs is stronger than ever."

Kazuko is the thirty-fifth mayor of Sendai, a role she took on in 2017 after serving as the Parliamentary Secretary of the Cabinet Office and Parliamentary Secretary of Minister of Reconstruction for several years. Kazuko is a Sendai native who, prior to entering civil service, served as the director for a broadcast news production bureau in town.

" In such an environment, diverse entrepreneurs emerged, and the community's commitment to supporting those entrepreneurs is stronger than ever "

As a community leader, one of Kazuko's goals is to develop the startup ecosystem and to involve stakeholders such as corporates, universities and members of the public. She believes that the role of government in this ongoing mission is to provide opportunities and present to the entire region a vision of the importance of having a thriving startup ecosystem.

Since the earthquake in 2011, Sendai has rapidly grown its startup ecosystem, utilizing its diverse knowledge and accumulations of industry, academia, government and financial bodies. As the ecosystem has developed, Kazuko and her office have noticed that students, young people and especially female entrepreneurs have begun moving to

and starting up in Sendai, indicating that the efforts to spark ecosystem growth has garnered success. Startups are especially drawn to the research and cutting-edge technology coming out of Sendai's excellent universities.

In Sendai, there is a strong balance in the mindset between business success and making a positive impact. Business owners and entrepreneurs run their enterprises to do societal good while ensuring profit for their stakeholders. Sendai's universities have accumulated a wealth of cutting-edge technology and research, ready to be leveraged by innovative new startups hoping to create real and lasting change.

Sendai, known as the "City of Trees" for its abundant greenery and balance of modernity and nature, is the political and economic center of the Tohoku Region and has a busy downtown, residential suburbs, mountain communities and farming communities that have retained their traditions. "This diversity is ideal for startups who want to conduct validation experiments," says Kazuko. Outside the city limits, you also have six

prefectures of Tohoku nearby, so entrepreneurs can easily apply their ideas to challenges being faced outside Sendai's city limits. Sendai excels at impact entrepreneurship, as evidenced by public and private programs created to support purpose-driven entrepreneurs and companies. Sendai Future Creation Companies is the city's flagship program and is unique even on a national scale. Manaby Inc, which provides employment and online education support for people with disabilities, is one of the companies supported by the initiative.

"One of Sendai's strengths is that small and medium businesses, as well as startups, are strongly inclined to tackle social or community challenges," she says. "Startups and social entrepreneurs aiming to tackle social issues are important contributors to making the city an even better place."

Despite its many advantages, Sendai is only at the beginning of its journey to becoming a startup hub. When compared to ecosystems like Tokyo, for instance, it's apparent that Sendai still has to bring more startups, VCs and other initiatives to the region. Recognizing the work that has yet to be done has helped Kazuko and her team to create ecosystem-enrichment projects for the city and region.

In January 2014, the city created the Sendai Startup Support Center, and a year later it established the Exchange Salon, a hub complete with work and meeting spaces for seminars and events. The Sendai Future Creation Companies has been bolstering the city and region's purpose-driven companies, and, in December 2019, the Sendai Startup Ecosystem Promotion Council was established as a place where academia, government, finance and other industry leaders could come together to discuss how to grow the ecosystem. "By identifying what we lack and what can be done to change the situation, we are all committed to a collaborative effort to move forward," says Kazuko.

Despite its challenges, Sendai has laid the groundwork for a remarkable startup ecosystem as a testament to how far it's come and the importance of innovating for change. "From such soil, we believe startups can change the world, going beyond the dichotomy of business and social needs, eventually transforming the city into the Capital of Social Innovation where social innovators gather from all over the world," Kazuko says.

" From such soil, we believe startups can change the world, going beyond the dichotomy of business and social needs, eventually transforming the city into the Capital of Social Innovation where social innovators gather from all over the world "

[ABOUT]

The City of Sendai Startup Support Office, one of the City of Sendai Economic Affairs
Bureau departments, plans and coordinates support for small businesses, startups,
entrepreneurs and social enterprises. In cooperation with universities, financial
institutions, entrepreneurs and the local business community, the Startup Support
Office has implemented many support initiatives, including the event "SENDAI for
Startups!" and several acceleration programs. The vision is to create an entrepreneurial
ecosystem in line with the concept of *"Ohu no Mori"* – "Ohu" being the old name
for Tohoku's six prefectures and *"Mori"* meaning a rich entrepreneurial ecosystem.

[CONTACT]

WEB   sendai-startups.org   FACEBOOK **ohunomori**

EMAIL kei008030@city.sendai.jp

Adansons

ELEVATOR PITCH

" We research and develop technology using our original technology, reference AI, which provides anomaly detection by analyzing time-series data including vibration, voice and other biological metrics. "

SECTOR AI

WEB adansons.co.jp

MILESTONES

Forming a highly skilled and experienced team.

Securing investment of ¥10 million.

Identifying issues that can be addressed using our technology and carrying out our first projects relating to these issues.

Developing a range of products that can be downloaded from the cloud.

Haruki Ishii, Yushi Nakaya and Yoshitaka Kimura, MD PhD saw that using traditional AI can be expensive and time-consuming due to its high data needs, so they founded Adansons in 2019 to offer safe new-generation AI. Their idea was to support the medical and manufacturing fields by utilizing Yoshitaka's invention: reference AI, a white-box form of AI that learns using forward propagation. "Reference AI is faster, lighter and more resistant to noise than conventional deep learning, making it particularly efficient in analyzing vital data and manufacturing data," says Haruki, CEO. Adansons has developed reference-AI packages for different needs and put them in the cloud so clients can download them for a fee. Hospitals, for example, can choose the package that helps detect whether eye disease will develop in patients, while construction companies can choose the package that helps detect the likelihood of accidents.

TEAM

The members of Adansons' team all share the same vision: to help revolutionize the world of AI. They are all extremely motivated by the goal of creating the world's best AI system. When the cofounders started hiring, they were looking for people who were highly skilled in their fields. From Tohoku University's community of one hundred and fifty specialists, they recruited eight engineers, two designers and three medics. All employees are encouraged to approach their work with curiosity and to show initiative. Most are self-driven and self-sufficient individuals who don't need intensive management during tasks. The cofounders encourage this work ethic by never saying no to any employee's business idea. The team enjoys a fun workplace. Staff members get together at the office, at hackathons for professional and personal development, and at hot springs.

In establishing Adansons, the cofounders started out by obtaining an exclusive license to use reference AI and then recruiting ten engineers with experience in mathematics and information processing. They secured ¥10 million in seed money from a VC and began contacting companies that might be experiencing project setbacks due to the limitations of AI. After learning that few companies have a clear AI strategy, Adansons has expanded into consulting, advising on the kind of algorithm that should be used to analyze data so solutions can be offered. Haruki says Sendai has a growing startup community and events, which help the cofounders to develop their business acumen and interpersonal skills.

AI Silk

ELEVATOR PITCH

" We use an innovative dyeing technique to turn silk and other fibers into conductive materials, with wide application potential from medical wearables to IoT development in various fields. "

SECTOR materials, medical, IT

WEB ai-silk.com/english

MILESTONES

Being selected for a NEDO (New Energy and Industrial Technology Development Organization) grant, enabling us to establish mass-production technology.

Receiving investment by global venture capital firm Draper Nexus and subsequently participating in a Silicon Valley acceleration program.

Conducting joint product development with Japanese sports company ASICS and completing a design for commercialization.

Obtaining key patents for our technology, products and software solutions.

AI Silk founder Hideo Okano was originally based in Tokyo, working for the large manufacturer Olympus. He became R&D manager on a collaborative project between industry, government and academia, and began working with the University of Tohoku, researching medical technology. Sadly, this came to an abrupt halt with the 2011 earthquake and tsunami. However, he later heard about a government-funded program calling for experts to aid medical-research business development at the University of Tohoku. In 2013, he took the plunge, moved north and began acting as a coordinator between university startups and private businesses. New to the region, he felt the scale of depopulation and recognized the need for job creation, particularly through the growth of companies with technologies that can be applied across a range of industries. He happened across research into conductive fibers that could be used to monitor body data and immediately saw their potential for commercialization in the fields of medical and sports wearables and beyond. Leveraging a network of investors he had developed during a stint in the VC department at Olympus, Hideo launched AI Silk in 2015.

The business model is twofold: the company licenses the technology to manufacture conductive fibers to other businesses and then uses this revenue to develop software for measuring and processing the data gained from body movements and brain signals. While R&D is still in the early stages, Hideo sees great future potential for the automobile industry, such as being able to monitor a driver's physical condition and emotional state.

TEAM

AI Silk now has a team of ten full-time employees, including high-level researchers in chemistry, two senior electronic circuit designers, a senior AI software developer and a 3D CAD mechanical design engineer. The team is based in a coworking space near the university, where it often uses the facilities. AI Silk also has its own lab and is able to support university research through providing access to advanced measuring instruments at low cost. Hideo values an approach to R&D that involves constantly pursuing new ideas, making hypotheses and testing them thoroughly. With this in mind, he values open and free communication among team members and keeps a US venture-style in mind. They hold a weekly meeting that maintains a relaxed atmosphere, encouraging members to throw out ideas about research as well as discuss other topics. Of course, they socialize too – every month they head out for team drinks and dinner.

Brain Innovation

ELEVATOR PITCH

" We develop and produce innovative
new medicines and other intellectual
property that treat brain diseases
and improve brain health for people
all over the world. "

SECTOR **pharmaceuticals**

WEB **brain-innov.com**

MILESTONES

Completing two rounds of
fundraising in our early stage.

Getting an international patent
for our Alzheimer's medicine.

Entering the preclinical trial phase
for our Alzheimer's medicine.

Setting up our research institute,
which enables us to do research
independently.

Shigeki Moriguchi (CTO) and Hiroyasu Togo (CEO) cofounded Brain Innovation in 2018. The startup, a biotech venture run in partnership with Tohoku University, utilizes intellectual property for the development of medicine specialized in treating brain-related illness. Its business model involves evaluating the safety and effectiveness of medicines by carrying out clinical trials in order to file patents. With a patent, medicines can be licensed to pharmaceutical companies. Brain Innovation's first medicine, which treats the symptoms of Alzheimer's disease, is in the preclinical trial phase at locations overseas. The company is also working on its second pipeline as well as on the development of its own independent research institute.

Shigeki, a pharmaceutical scientist, has been working in the field of Alzheimer's disease treatment for more than twenty years. He learned about the molecular mechanisms of Alzheimer's disease at Northwestern University, Illinois, before returning to Tohoku University. He got the idea for Brain Innovation while working on Alzheimer's disease therapies and decided to start the venture with Hiroyasu, an experienced entrepreneur. Within six months of founding the company, the pair had secured a lead venture capital to fund the startup. Six months later, additional venture capital and private companies invested. So far, the startup has received about ¥400 million in funding. Hiroyasu attributes their success to luck and good relationships with key people who could support them. Brain Innovation's headquarters is in Sendai, so the team can work closely with Tohoku University and Miyagi Prefecture, and it has an office in Tokyo, enabling the team to focus on business development and attendance at pharma-related conferences and events.

TEAM

Brain Innovation's cofounders put together their early team from their personal and professional network. As the startup grew, they recruited staff. For the Sendai headquarters, they sought out people with a background in medicine and/or research as well as experience in pharmaceutical companies. The team members are highly dedicated to their work, which they say is their *ikigai*, a Japanese concept that means "reason for living" or "purpose in life." Across the two locations, most staff members are in their thirties, with a few in their twenties or forties. The team is a fifty/fifty split in terms of gender, and all members are Japanese. Brain Innovation's people are cheerful, positive and constructive in their approach to work. They enjoy spending time together over dinners of delicious local sushi, talking late into the night about science.

Co-LABO MAKER

ELEVATOR PITCH

" We provide a one-stop service for searching for equipment, facilities and technology for research purposes, available for rental on an hourly basis as and when needed. "

SECTOR R&D, rental services

WEB co-labo-maker.com

MILESTONES

Receiving ¥20 million in investment from Primal Capital in August 2017.

Launching the beta version of Co-LABO MAKER's research facilities and equipment-search service in early 2018.

Being chosen by the Ministry of Economy, Trade and Industry (METI)'s Startup Factory, receiving support tailored for hardware-focused startups.

Establishing our own liability insurance for laboratory equipment and facilities sharing.

The idea for Co-LABO MAKER came about when Yuki Furuya was undertaking semiconductor research for a large chemical and electronics manufacturer. He was becoming increasingly frustrated with the process, as he wanted to try out various experiments and new research methods, but the facilities and equipment were simply not available. Buying them would be too expensive, and getting permission from clients to try anything new would take too much time. "Wouldn't it be great if facilities could be rented, just briefly, for experimental research?" he thought. Moreover, he realized that many university laboratories were just sitting idle when university researchers were not using them. Having studied at Tohoku University previously, he consulted with Prof. Akira Yoshikawa, head of Open Innovation at the Institute for Materials Research, on how best to establish a business – only for Prof. Yoshikawa to invite him to join the team. He'd already been considering undertaking a PhD and his wife was originally from Sendai, so he moved back to Tohoku in 2017 and, while starting a doctorate, he launched Co-LABO MAKER.

In Sendai, Yuki joined the incubation space TECK LAB PAAK, where he received regular mentoring, and he soon had the opportunity to join a pitch event and present his concept in front of venture capitalists. He received an investment of ¥20 million, enabling him to transform his concept into an actual service. Co-LABO MAKER rents facilities and equipment to researchers by the hour. Currently, the company has more than three hundred organizations on board.

TEAM

"I was talking to entrepreneurs in Sendai about my idea, and asked them if they knew anyone who might be interested," says Yuki of his word-of-mouth recruitment strategy. The result has been a diverse team with employees not only from the Tohoku Region but also based in Tokyo, Chiba and the US. They are united behind the company goal of working towards improving the R&D ecosystem and are not afraid to try out new approaches. While the company uses the Enspace coworking space in Sendai as its office, the team members have yet to all meet in person. They work remotely, with core time between 10 AM and 12 PM for team meetings via Zoom and with flexible hours outside of that. Yuki has recently become a specially appointed associate professor at Tohoku University, and so the company is working more closely with the university to promote the use of its research facilities.

IoT.Run

ELEVATOR PITCH

" We develop and provide IoT devices and platforms, for rent or sale, as part of a sharing economy to help address the demographic challenges facing Japan. We also offer education and product-development services related to IoT. "

SECTOR IoT

WEB iot-run.co.jp

MILESTONES

Deciding the motto of the company: "To tackle demographic challenges."

Securing seed funding.

Attending Slush Tokyo where we were motivated by many other entrepreneurs.

Receiving an award from KDDI at the Tohoku Growth Accelerator in 2020.

IoT.Run is a carve-out from CO-works, an IT-focused manufacturing company founded by Yoshikazu Awaji in 2009. Yoshikazu, seeing people struggle financially because of Japan's declining population and worried about this trend continuing, decided to set up IoT.Run, launching in April 2019. His idea was to make a sharing economy platform for IoT so that people could continue the same level of business output even if facing a shortage of workers. "The fewer people there are, the less work can be done, meaning lower salaries," he says. "IoT can boost efficiency and productivity or even do the work of people, keeping sales high and increasing salaries. With higher salaries, the birth rate might even increase because people can afford to have children." IoT.Run's goals are to help people lead financially secure lives and to boost opportunities for startups in Tohoku, which was devastated by the Great East Japan Earthquake and Tsunami of 2011. Its cheap, time-saving technology helps people to develop their businesses.

TEAM

The startup's five staff members were recruited from the carve-out from CO-works. Most of them were previously involved in system development and engineering. However, IoT.Run was set up to focus on developing a new market and serving new kinds of customers, so when Yoshikazu was hiring, he chose employees based on their skills in these areas too. People in IoT.Run are skilled in creating something from scratch and knowledgeable about many aspects of entrepreneurship. They're also driven to help provide solutions to Japan's demographic problems and, as all are from the Tohoku area, they're passionate about supporting the revitalization of Tohoku. The team members often get together to cook curry and spend time talking while indulging in their culinary creations. They also like going out to have lunch in restaurants near their office.

The business model is centered around the renting and sale of Tibbo-Pi, an IoT device that allows users to develop their own apps or software. The startup also has a subscription-based IoT platform called IoT OneBox where users can access other users' apps and software for their own use. The concept is to make these products as easy to use as a family computer or an app store. Yoshikazu set up and ran IoT.Run with his own money before securing ¥20 million in seed funding.

Kenji Suzuki

**Founder and
Representative Director
/ TESS**

After graduating with a degree in education, Kenji Suzuki worked for six years as an elementary school teacher before joining a Tohoku University venture specializing in electrical stimulation of the body. With the goal of improving mobility so people can live more active lives, he set up TESS in 2008. The startup's main product is Cogy, a wheelchair powered by the pedaling of the user.

ABOUT THE COMPANY

TESS Co., Ltd. develops, produces and distributes nursing, medical and transport equipment. Its main product is the pedal wheelchair Cogy, which is used as a rehabilitation and training device at medical institutions and welfare facilities in Japan.

WEB **h-tess.com**

What was the inspiration for moving into the field of mobility?

When I was a teacher, one of my students was in a wheelchair. He couldn't take part in important school events like athletic festivals and had to stay with a teacher rather than mingle with the other kids. I thought that there had to be a way to improve the situation. Around the same time, I encountered some technologies at Tohoku University that might address the problem. I joined one of their venture companies to work on electronic stimulation of the body and later, thinking of my former student in the wheelchair, set up TESS.

Why are you so passionate about your work?

All of us will get weaker as we get older. People who start using walking sticks may eventually need to use a wheelchair. From there, they may have to move on to an electric wheelchair, which supplements functionalities rather than brings back functionalities. Eventually, electric wheelchair users may be confined to bed. Our pedal wheelchair can reverse this process of weakening. In Sendai, there is a 103-year-old person who was confined to bed before using Cogy. Now he can now walk inside using sticks. Our product is not designed to be used forever, so it's maybe not the best for business, but it gives people a better way of life.

*" Our product is not
designed to be used
forever, so it's maybe
not the best for business,
but it gives people
a better way of life. "*

**What were your early struggles while starting up
and how did you overcome them?**

Our wheelchair, Cogy, is powered by the pedaling
of the user. The idea of someone peddling their own
wheelchair was very strange to people at the start.
The history of the wheelchair goes back 2,600 years,
but it's always been powered by the user's arms or an
electric motor. People were very skeptical about our
new idea. They thought that people in a wheelchair
couldn't move their legs at all, but Cogy is for people
with some mobility in their legs. Pedaling is a form
of rehabilitation. It's hard, but they have to endure the
process. As everybody knows, once you have some
difficulty in your legs, no matter how much you work,
it's very difficult to move them again. People affected
in this way need to keep moving.

We struggled with the medical profession. In the case
of a man injuring his spine in a traffic accident, for
example, his doctor would tell him that he is going
to be in a wheelchair for the rest of his life. But, in
our pedal wheelchair, he can move his legs again
and can have some rehabilitation. Doctors don't like
that because patients become skeptical about what
the doctors say. The doctors' pride is hurt. That was
the obstacle we had in spreading this product. It was
easier to get compassion from the funders. It seemed
every one of them had a family member, friend or
colleague who would benefit from our wheelchair,
so they wanted to support us in order to help them.

**How did you find your team and what qualities
were you looking for in them?**

I'm not an engineer, manufacturer or a salesperson,
so I didn't have any of the most important elements
of the business at the beginning. I looked for
collaborators and partners. I found a sales professional
at the university venture I worked at before. He was
skeptical at first, but, after a demonstration of our
wheelchair, he joined the company. Finance was the
most difficult area to recruit for. I was reading a book
about an entrepreneur called Miki Watanabe, in which
there was a story about an excellent consultant.
Luckily, I was able to meet the consultant and show
him Cogy's design. He was moved and joined us.

After that, I tackled manufacturing by listing hundreds
of possible companies. I made calls, sent emails.
Wheelchair makers said they couldn't help because
wheelchairs had to be powered by a motor or
hands. Bicycle makers said bicycles are for healthy
people who have no physical problems. If people
with disabilities or elderly people were to use one
of their products and have an accident, there would
be a liability risk. Other small factories needed
funds up front, and I didn't have any. Finally, I found
one company that manufactures wheelchairs for
Paralympic athletes and was willing to help.
They made Cogy within three months, even though
a wheelchair usually takes three years from design
to manufacture.

**What do you wish you'd know before or what would
you have done differently?**

People see Cogy as a product for people who cannot
move, who gave up on mobility, but it can also be used
for people who have less serious issues, such as
pre-frail or frail people who can still move but have
some pains in their knees. If they could use our
product, their symptoms would not worsen; it could
help them live a longer and healthier life. We want
more people, particularly the elderly, to participate
in society, so we wish we'd promoted the wider use
of the wheelchair from the start.

What is the business model, and what are the challenges of making the business profitable?

Rather than one person using Cogy forever, we want lots of people to use Cogy. Once the person is better, they will stop using Cogy and we'll find other people who want the product. People all over the world will develop problems with their legs at some point in their lives. We want to make the slope to immobility as slow as possible.

Also, wheelchairs have different classifications around the world. In the US, they are medical equipment, so users need a prescription from their doctor. In Japan, they are welfare equipment, so anyone can use one. In Europe, wheelchairs are bought and distributed by local governments. Each region has a different political system, so that's the biggest challenge for the business. If we make Cogy only for Japanese standards, we confine our sales to Japan. We now have certification for the US, the EU and Vietnam, so we are preparing for distribution overseas.

Why did you choose Sendai as the location for the business?

There might be few advantages to setting up the business in Sendai. In Japan, new things and new ideas tend to come into the country from the West. They start in Kyushu or Osaka, then come to Tokyo and lastly Tohoku. It's mysterious, but it has always been the case. I wanted to change that. Another reason for choosing Sendai was our connection to Tohoku University. Its intellectual property is part of our product.

But Sendai has other advantages, too. It is a very compact city. If I had started this project in Tokyo, I wouldn't have been noticed, as there are so many talents and ideas popping up in there. In Sendai, there aren't so many new startups, so if you offer something new, you can easily get attention. Once you get attention, you can find people who are sympathetic to your product or service. Local communities are the biggest advantage for startups.

How do you manage your work hours, and do you follow any routines for self-discipline to separate your professional and private time?

I don't have any specific techniques for work–life balance. Since I was an elementary school teacher, I've learned to separate my time between professional and private. I'm still successful at doing that as I don't see a huge difference in my work then and now. I always have weekends off, for example.

What is your team culture like?

We have a larger ratio of female to male staff, but only four staff. We're very close, so we see each other and talk to each other all the time.

What professional advice would you give someone in the early stages of starting up?

Making something completely new can be the biggest obstacle. Universally, people tend to reject new things in their field, which can make it very hard for ventures to secure funding, human resources and so on. I advise introducing your product or service to people around you. Get more people to understand it, even those outside your industry. The more people who like your product, the easier your business will become, especially if you are creating something entirely new.

What are the biggest challenges you face now?

In Japan, Cogy can be accessed using social insurance. There are also subsidies to buy it and grants to rent it. But I think there is a limit. Social security is not stable. At some point, the Japanese government will no longer have the funds to offer this system. We will need to find another way to finance Cogy so we can continue to distribute it. We want to let people rent or purchase it using installments. The concept of renting a car has been around for a long time, so we're working on adding Cogy to such existing schemes. I'm talking to people in the car and airplane industries to see how we can do that. •

What are your top work essentials?
Not setting limits on what is possible.

At what age did you start your company?
Thirty-five.

What's your most used app?
Schedule management.

What's the most valuable piece of advice you've been given?
Don't set limits.

What's your greatest skill?
Staying positive.

What do you do every morning (or night before) to prepare for the day ahead?
Nothing in particular as every day is different.

What book has most influenced your career?
Books by Kenji Miyazawa.

What favorite positive habit have you cultivated?
I always think positively.

Miho Koike

CEO
/ Material Concept

Miho Koike worked for fourteen years at a government agency, where she cofounded a patent-licensing company called Advanced Interconnect Materials LLC in 2006. In 2010, she accepted the role of board member at a startup in the field of photovoltaic systems. The startup was affiliated with the University of Tokyo. She oversaw business collaboration, corporate planning and sales. Inspired to make a difference in the Tohoku region following the Great East Japan Earthquake and Tsunami of 2011, she founded Material Concept, Inc. in 2013 with the goal of promoting low-cost and easily accessible renewable energy by developing new materials.

ABOUT THE COMPANY

Material Concept, Inc. produces advanced interconnect materials that enable electronic equipment to perform better and more reliably at lower cost. It is the creator of the world's first mass-producible copper paste for forming wires and electrodes for solar cells and electronic equipment.

WEB mat-concept.com

What sparked your interest in becoming an entrepreneur?

I wanted to become a role model that would inspire people and make them feel like they could start a venture business. In Japan, there are not so many women running companies or in positions of leadership, so I wanted to change that too. Also, I was really passionate about establishing the ideal research institution, and I thought I could do that in my startup.

What was the inspiration for the business?

Having lived in Japan during the time of the earthquake, tsunami and resultant accident at the Fukushima Nuclear Power Plant, I realized the importance of renewable energy. Solar cells are one of the most popular sources of renewable energy, but they require the use of silver conductive lines. These lines draw out electrical power generated within the cells. When we compared the price of raw metals, silver was one hundred times more expensive than copper. In paste form, silver had hit the highest price in recent history.

We thought we could make copper paste at between one-tenth and one-fifth the price of silver paste, thereby reducing the cost of solar cells, so we started to develop copper paste technology to make conductive lines for solar cells. However, as Chinese solar cells began to spread worldwide, especially to

*" Never compromise,
no matter how difficult
your challenges are;
otherwise, you will
suffer more later. "*

Japan under a generous feed-in-tariff policy, the cell price plunged quickly. There was not much difference in price between the Chinese solar cells and our copper paste cells. Because of this unexpected event, our clients' interest in copper paste had dissipated.

In response, we moved on to find new applications for our copper paste technology in various electronic components, such as the electrical conductive lines on flexible films and rigid ceramics, as well as the heat-conductive layer of automobile parts. Unlike in forming copper lines by electroplating or chemical etching, our copper paste technology does not produce waste chemicals. It's environmentally friendly and cheaper than other materials. Because of these advantages, it has been attracting much attention from a number of companies.

What is your business model, and what are the challenges to make it profitable?

We focus on the development and sale of copper paste for various engineering applications. Since copper paste is used on a sheet of polymer, metal or ceramic, we also develop an interface layer to bond copper with the sheet material. We customize the copper paste and the interface materials to meet diverse client needs. This is our strength.

In the early days of the company, we relied on government funding. We were granted funding from START (Startups from Advanced Research and Technology) by the Ministry of Education, Culture, Sports, Science and Technology. That allowed us to operate up to the proof-of-concept phase of the business. Utilizing the proof-of-concept results, we moved on to the fundraising stage. Though funding is considered very difficult, especially for startups in the field of materials, we secured generous funding from VCs. One was a joint government–corporate

fund, and the other was a corporate fund related to the reconstruction of Tohoku. With this capital, we did R&D and found many potential customers. The next stage will be to make sufficient profit to become self-reliant.

What were your early challenges while starting up, and how did you overcome them?

In the early stages, the development of original products was the first priority, so the company was made up solely of researchers. When we faced problems in other areas of the business, we outsourced activity in those areas to professionals and collaborated with external experts. Tohoku University was an important resource for us, because it is where knowledge, know-how and technologies are accumulated.

What skills, qualities or experience do you draw on to help overcome challenges?

Thanks to my career so far at the Japan Science Technology Agency and the startup affiliated with the University of Tokyo, I have established a wide personal network. It includes business executives and academic researchers who help me without delay. They assist me in running the company and steering it in the right direction. In terms of skills, I think that my quick insight really helps me overcome challenges.

How have you approached the management and development of the startup so far?

As founder and CEO, I have always aimed to act as efficiently as possible. I've implemented the necessary changes in the business quickly and smoothly. I've also been trying to manage the entire team – and the corporate environment in general – with agility and flexibility.

Why did you choose Sendai as the location for the business?

Sendai is perhaps not as stimulating a city as Tokyo, but it has its advantages. It's only ninety minutes away from Tokyo by Shinkansen, so access is good. It's the home of Tohoku University, which is very important

because it has so much accumulated knowledge and expertise that supports the business. Sendai is such a good environment for setting up a company that I wonder why there is such a concentration of new ventures in Tokyo.

Aside from these practical reasons, I chose Sendai as the location because I wanted Material Concept to base its R&D, manufacturing, personnel development and jobs in Tohoku to help the region achieve sustainable development and growth. The Great East Japan Earthquake and Tsunami, which devastated large parts of Tohoku, exacerbated the demographic problems already facing the region: steep population decline, a super-aging population and shrinking communities. By being based in Sendai, we can help address these problems and make a positive contribution to the region.

Can you share a little about your team, both in the early days and today?

When I started up the company, most of the team members came from the university research laboratory. Also, as we launched the company not long after the Great East Japan Earthquake and Tsunami, there was a large pool of people in Sendai who had returned home because they wanted to contribute to their community and the Tohoku region. We recruited

some people from this pool. Back then, the company was entirely research-based and in the R&D phase, so I was looking for people with clear abilities and expertise in materials such as metals and chemistry.

Today, we've grown to eleven permanent employees, including four women – a higher ratio than most companies in the Tohoku region – and one non-Japanese staff member. Because of the nature of the company, I still look for high-quality researchers, but recently I've also been looking for people to work in production and sales. We used to receive external support for these functions, but now we take care of these functions by ourselves.

What's your company culture like and what do you do as a team?

Our culture values freedom and flexibility. We're a compact organization that fosters open discussion and creative ideas and has rapid and responsive decision making. Our people are honest and moderate, and never give up on anything.

Before our daily morning meeting, all staff, including me, clean our laboratory and production rooms as part of our routine. We believe this activity is connected to maintaining the quality of the products that we make; it helps us perform better as a team for the benefit of our clients.

All staff also enjoy spending time together socially, for example going out for lunch or after work.

Looking to the future, what are your biggest challenges?

The company is scheduled to move to the InterConnect Advanced Technology Center on the engineering campus of Tohoku University in September 2020. This new building will be inaugurated as a collaboration center between our company and the university. In this new center, we will develop new materials and process technology that is from nano to millimeter in scale. I hope it will result in new applications for the business.

What professional advice would you give people in the early stages of starting up?

I would say, never compromise, no matter how difficult your challenges are; otherwise, you will suffer more later.

How do you manage your time? And do you have any habits that make you work better?

I take real care with my time. I try not to make too many appointments or to waste time on useless things or redundant work. I aim to be efficient, so I use my time wisely. I always secure sufficient time in my diary to think about the various aspects of the business and to visit our various labs and production facility, to keep an eye on activity on the ground as well as in the office.

How do you separate your professional and personal life to try to have work–life balance?

At the moment, I see no distinction between my professional and personal life, but I'm OK with that; my work is exciting and fun. It gives me great opportunities, including meeting people in different fields and exchanging ideas, which I particularly enjoy. •

At what age did you found your company?
Fifty-four.

What's your most used app?
Navitime.

What's the most valuable piece of advice you've been given?
If not now, when?

What do you do every morning to prepare for the day ahead?
I look at a photo of my late mother and say, "I've got to do my best today."

What book has most influenced your career?
The biography of Albert Schweitzer that I read in childhood.

What favorite positive habit have you cultivated?
Exercise at the gym.

DA-TE APPs!

DA-TE APPs! is an app-creation contest aimed at producing new services and companies that will contribute to the Sendai IT market. It also aims to provide a platform that connects students to local businesses. The name "DA-TE" represents the Date clan who built Sendai Castle and were responsible for the area's prosperity in the seventeenth century. The DA-TE APPs! contest is divided into a game-creation contest and an IT-development contest, the most recent winners of which are "Building Crash," a game with high profitability ratings, and a team from Tohoku University that developed an IT system for customer engagement and employee evaluation that has good potential for commercialization. The contest, during which students test their skills by presenting their app ideas, provides a networking opportunity for local students and local companies and attracts over two hundred spectators.

SECTOR IT services and games
PAST WINNERS Human Academy Colleges, Sendai Campus; Tohoku Computer College, Tohoku University.
WHO SHOULD APPLY Any students from the Tohoku region may enter. Sendai City has an agreement with Oulu, Finland and students of the Oulu Game Lab may participate with the students in Sendai.
APPLY globallab.sendai@nttdocomo.com
WEB globallab-sendai.com

Sendai X-Tech Innovation Project

X-Tech Innovation aims to pair IT talent and startups with companies and organizations looking for innovative, cutting-edge technological solutions, and to create new businesses that solve problems as diverse as population decline and diversification of consumer behavior. In partnership with Sendai City, X-Tech Innovation is focused on technologies such as AI, augmented reality, 5G and IoT. Participants receive access to resources, facilities, equipment provided by Sendai City and the possibility of developing partnerships with Tohoku University. The city's relatively compact nature lends itself to an agile way of working, and the networking opportunities are enhanced by the feeling of a tight-knit professional community. Ultimately, the goal of the program is to update and enhance the urban experience through the promotion of open innovation and projects with a positive social impact.

SECTOR sector-agnostic
SELECTED PORTFOLIO Rakuten Baseball Team, Fujisaki Department Store
WHO SHOULD APPLY IT talent aimed at developing creative products and services, such as local companies or large companies that aim to create new industries by combining advanced IT technologies (such as AI and IoT) with local industries.
WEB techplay.jp/sendaixtech

Tohoku Growth Accelerator

Tohoku Growth Accelerator is a six-month accelerator focused on startups that combine innovation with social impact and are committed to growth. Participants receive mentoring and attend lectures and workshops. Participating startups are typically in the pre-seed or seed phase and are based (or plan to be based) in the Tohoku region. Coworking spaces in Sendai are made available free of charge during the program. Sendai has many advantages: it has the second-highest rate of new startups in Japan, yet its relatively compact size lends itself to establishing networks easily, something the accelerator fosters through a series of annual events. It also offers the Studio Course aimed at young and intrepid entrepreneurs looking to launch a business.

SECTOR sector-agnostic
SELECTED PORTFOLIO HERALBONY, Adansons, IoT.RUN, Co-LABO MAKER, ZIG.
WHO SHOULD APPLY Startups that primarily address the following themes: research seeds from universities, ICT, existing industries' innovations and businesses that make the most of the Tohoku region's strengths.
WEB **tohoku-growth-ap.jp**

Tohoku Social Innovation Accelerator

The Tohoku Social Innovation Accelerator fosters socially conscious entrepreneurs who have a passion for developing sustainable solutions to societal challenges in the Tohoku region. The core function of the program is to help budding entrepreneurs learn to effectively communicate their vision in a way that appeals to potential supporters. Participants attend workshops, lectures and presentations and will complete the program with a business plan, mission statement, professional profile photo and a short video explaining their idea. Expats living in Japan are welcome to apply, though written and spoken Japanese ability is required. At the completion of the program's 2019 round, twelve participating entrepreneurs presented their ideas at the "SENDAI for Startups!" event with over one thousand people in attendance.

SECTOR social innovation, sustainability
WHO SHOULD APPLY Entrepreneurs who are passionate about developing solutions to social challenges in Tohoku.
APPLY Email **info@intilaq.jp** for information about how to apply.
WEB **social-ignition.net**

cocolin

cocolin coworking space has a relaxing, almost spa-like atmosphere and is designed to boost concentration and productivity. Seated at the window-facing desks, users can enjoy the view of a beautiful Japanese garden. The coworking space offers two membership types: fixed desk, which grants users twenty-four-hour access to the space 365 days a year, and flex desk. Unlike many coworking spaces, the use of the two meeting rooms is provided at no charge. The space also offers a range of services for small companies such as phone lines, mailboxes, company registration and accounting services. cocolin is managed by LASSIC, an IT company that aims to drive new industry growth locally and create employment opportunities for tech workers migrating away from Japan's major cities.

ADDRESS Shimizukoji, 6-1 Higashi Nihon Fudousan Sendai First Building 1F, Wakabayashi-ku, Sendai 984-0075
OPENING HOURS Flex-desk member hours: Mon–Fri: 9 AM–9 PM; Saturdays: 9 AM–6 PM. Fixed-desk member hours: 24/7.
USP A practical coworking space with a soothing atmosphere.
PRICE RANGE Flex-desk membership: ¥12,000 per month + ¥10,000 registration fee. Fixed-desk membership: ¥32,000 per month + ¥10,000 registration fee.
WEB cocolin.jp

enspace

enspace is an impressively large, seven-story coworking space thoughtfully designed to facilitate growth and connection for entrepreneurs and businesses. Flex seating, personal desks and private offices are available in a range of sizes to meet members' business needs. This comprehensive coworking space also features sofa seating, conference rooms, classrooms, a nap room, a shower, a kitchen, a rooftop balcony and even an oxygen chamber. The basic membership level starts at ¥15,000 per month and includes twenty-four-hour access to all communal spaces, plus unlimited use of the oxygen chamber. Various back-office and secretarial services, such as invoice and document creation, flight and hotel reservations, and business-card printing, are available to members for a fee. Events are organized monthly, giving members frequent opportunities to learn and network.

ADDRESS 1–4–9, Kokubun-cho, Aoba-ku, Sendai 980-0803
OPENING HOURS 24/7
USP A seven-story, fully equipped coworking space with an oxygen chamber.
PRICE RANGE Flex-desk membership: ¥15,000 + ¥3,000 common-area fee per month. Fixed-desk membership: ¥36,000 + ¥6,000 common-area fee per month. Private-office membership: ¥68,000 to ¥128,000 + ¥12,000 to ¥20,000 common-area fee per month
WEB enspace.work

INTILAQ Tohoku Innovation Center

INTILAQ Tohoku Innovation Center opened its doors to budding entrepreneurs in 2016. Funded by the Qatar Friendship Fund as part of an initiative to help the Tohoku region recover from the devastating 2011 tsunami, the center aims to foster innovation and creativity through its unique design, facilities and programs. It offers coworking areas, office spaces, a lecture theatre, digital fabrication equipment, a Qatari-themed room and even a broadcast studio. The building was designed by award-winning architect Dr. Hitoshi Abe and incorporates his trademark design features, being spatially complex and structurally innovative. There are many programs and events to help entrepreneurs, with a focus on promoting sustainable growth in the region, connecting with other regions and globally through INTILAQ's network. There are even workshops for children.

ADDRESS 2-9-1 Oroshimachi, Wakabayashi-ku, Sendai 984-0015
OPENING HOURS Mon–Fri: 9 AM–9 PM; Sat: 9 AM–6 PM; Sun and national holidays: Closed.
USP INTILAQ supports all types of entrepreneurs and future entrepreneurs of all ages.
PRICE RANGE Coworking space: ¥10,000 per month. Residence space: ¥30,000 per month. Office space: ¥200,000 per month. Rental space: ¥1,000–¥20,000 per hour.
WEB intilaq.jp

THE6

THE6 is a coworking space and coliving facility designed for creative professionals. The third-floor coworking space features flex desks for up to twenty-six people, four private desks, two private offices, two meeting rooms and a shared kitchen. Desks, kitchen usage and rooftop access come standard at all membership levels, while mailboxes, lockers and other perks can be unlocked for an added fee. Apartments for rent are located on the fourth, fifth and sixth floors, and basic-level coworking membership is granted to all residents at no additional charge. Events focused on social, professional and design-related topics are held several times a month. THE6 is managed by ECOLA, a real estate company whose focus is on renovating and repurposing aging apartment buildings in Sendai.

ADDRESS 9-15 Kasugamachi, Aoba-ku, Sendai 980-0821
OPENING HOURS Access hours vary by membership level.
USP A coworking space and coliving facility for creative professionals
PRICE RANGE Drop-in: ¥500 per two hours or ¥1,000 per day (9 AM–6 PM). Flex desk: ¥8,000 + ¥2,000 common-area fee per month (9 AM–11 PM). Fixed desk: ¥32,000 + ¥3,000 common-area fee per month (24/7). Private offices and apartments are also available, starting from ¥25,000 + common-area fees.
WEB the6.jp

Miyagi Gakuin Women's University (MGU)

Founded 130 years ago as Miyagi Girl's School, at a time when women in Japan were not represented in higher education, Miyagi Gakuin Women's University is still blazing trails for women. "It is rather unusual for women's universities in Japan to have business departments," says Jun-Ichi Watanabe, professor of Contemporary Business. "We're continuing the mission to empower women by helping them get better positions in business, and even starting their own." The university has four faculties and two graduate schools. Among its offerings is the Program for Women's Entrepreneurship, whose curriculum is based on fostering new ideas while learning the flow of a company through a process of simulated investment, launch, commercialization and selling the business. Support is provided by organizations such as the Tokyo Stock Exchange and Sendai City. The Contemporary Business faculty boasted a near 100 percent success rate of graduates going on to find permanent employment in 2020.

LOCATION The university is the principal feature of this suburban neighborhood, though there is the Branch Sendai shopping area a short distance away.

CLOSE TRANSIT CONNECTIONS Bus from Sendai Station. Taxi from Sendai Station or Asahi-ga-oka subway station

PRICE OF TUITION 2019 Academic Year (Contemporary Business), approximately ¥4,260,000 JPY over four years.

ENTRY REQUIREMENTS To qualify for admission as international students, applicants must have completed a total of twelve years of school education and be of non-Japanese citizenship. Applicants whose native language is not English are required to have studied English as a foreign language during high school.

WEB
mgu.ac.jp/main/english/index.html (English)
mgu.ac.jp (Japanese)

Tohoku Gakuin University

Tohoku Gakuin University (TGU), founded in 1886 as Sendai Theological Seminary, became an officially accredited university in 1949. With over eleven thousand students, three libraries and thirteen research institutes, it is one of the largest private universities in northern Japan. The school's fundamentals are centered on academic freedom, global perspectives and intercultural understanding, and it offers a variety of extra-curricular athletic and cultural activities, such as kendo, a type of martial arts, and kyūdō, a traditional form of archery. From the impact of natural disasters to an aging population, the Tohoku region has significant challenges to overcome, and TGU welcomes and offers support to international students who desire to work together on solutions to these and other problems. Tuition reduction is available to full-time international students.

LOCATION Aoba-ku, Sendai City
CLOSE TRANSIT CONNECTIONS Atagobashi subway station and Itsutsubashi subway station (Namboku Line).
PRICE OF TUITION ¥1,259,217 (average)
ENTRY REQUIREMENTS
Varies depending on course.
Please see **tohoku-gakuin.ac.jp/en/inquiries** for more detailed information.
WEB **tohoku-gakuin.ac.jp/en**

Tohoku University

Since its establishment in 1907, Tohoku University has championed a policy of practice-oriented research. The university, which ranked first in the Times Higher Education Japan awards, provides programs through its Exploration and Development of Global Entrepreneurship for NEXT generation (EDGE-NEXT) initiative. Programs range from introductory entrepreneurial courses to design-led programs seeking to identify and tackle business and community problems. The Japan Biodesign Program Tohoku accepts fellows with diverse backgrounds from medicine, engineering and business. They are challenged with identifying unmet clinical needs and developing solution concepts, culminating in business plans. Founders then seek to launch startups with the support of the global Biodesign community including Japan Biodesign alumni. Tohoku University Startup Garage (TUSG) is the university's all-in-one platform for students and faculty members to connect with entrepreneurs, investors and accelerators. It provides a mentoring platform, startup consultation and entrepreneurial courses and hosts events like pitch contests and seminars.

LOCATION The four main campuses are in Sendai city, ninety minutes from Tokyo by bullet train.
CLOSE TRANSIT CONNECTIONS Sendai Station
PRICE OF TUITION ¥535,800 per year. The law school and accounting school cost ¥804,000 and ¥589,300, respectively.
ENTRY REQUIREMENTS Tohoku University is proud of its open-door policy. Entry requirements vary depending on faculty, undergraduate or graduate, and may include interviews and examinations.
WEB **tohoku.ac.jp/en**

Makoto Capital

Makoto Capital aims to establish a startup ecosystem in Tohoku that not only revitalizes the region but expands to have a global impact. Its vision is to create a better society by supporting startups with strong business potential.

SECTOR Tohoku startups
EMAIL info@mkto.org
WEB mkto.org/capital

It was only four months after the 2011 Tohoku earthquake and tsunami when Tomohiro Takei decided to establish his own company as part of a regional recovery strategy. Having graduated from the life science department at Tohoku University and later working at Tohoku Innovation Capital Co., he felt strongly about the region and its potential for innovation. He set about offering consulting to startups and working on government projects supporting entrepreneurship, including running startup school classes. Finally, in 2015, he managed to build up enough of a reputation to convince Fukushima Bank to invest $10 million in Makoto Capital's first fund. And this was no ordinary fund: it was only for founders who were establishing a business in Fukushima and had tried and failed before. "Japan is really harsh towards anyone who has gone bankrupt, but I think these founders can still have a lot of potential," says Takei, who was inspired by Silicon

Valley and Bay Area culture, which often treats failure as a positive or necessary stage in entrepreneurship.

Takei's unusual fund attracted a lot of media attention in Japan. This helped draw attention to his vision of establishing a Tohoku ecosystem and his goal of attracting many people from Tohoku back to the region, including those who had been displaced by the 2011 tsunami and earthquake or had moved to Tokyo for work. "I want to create many exciting jobs in the area. That is the challenge I'm working towards." In 2018, he established a second fund to support all promising startups in the Tohoku region. Takei says that his fund prioritizes the startup founder's potential, business skill and passion when making investment decisions. Its portfolio includes companies operating in a range of sectors, such as biotech, IT, AI, IoT and agritech.

Tohoku University Venture Partners

Tohoku University Venture Partners aims
to bridge the gap between excellent academic
research and business by providing key
investment and mentoring for startups.
The team envisions a Tohoku-wide network
that has a positive economic and social impact
on the region.

SECTOR IT services, materials,
chemicals, medical devices, bio/
pharma, electronics, machinery

EMAIL info@thvp.co.jp

WEB thvp.co.jp

"Our goal is to see Tohoku University research implemented in society," says Daisuke Katagiri, deputy director of the investment department at Tohoku University Venture Partners (THVP). University research is traditionally not seen as attractive by venture capital firms due to the long lead time needed to get results and develop a profitable business. To foster these kinds of ventures, THVP provides early-stage investment as well as business-development support. Tohoku University was one of four universities to be permitted to establish its own venture capital firms following a legal change in 2014, and the fund was established early the following year.

Daisuke, who worked as a researcher in pharmaceuticals and established his own bioventure before joining THVP as a venture capitalist, says there is a lack of people who have experience in both the academic and business worlds. In the US, many people with PhDs go on to launch businesses, but

Japan still lags behind in this field. As a result, THVP is focused on not only providing capital for university ventures but also growing the ecosystem from the bottom up, changing both teachers' and students' mindsets so that entrepreneurship is seen as a natural option after leaving academia. THVP works with Tohoku University to oversee a business-incubation program, through which they provide mentoring in addition to an annual "gap fund" for five to ten researchers who are developing projects. THVP may then subsequently invest in a venture. Moreover, some researchers are even undertaking internships at THVP to learn more about venture capital. THVP's future mission is to establish a second fund that invests in university research across Tohoku and surrounding regions. "I believe the Tohoku ecosystem can be really important," says Daisuke, "as it has the potential to become a role model for innovation in smaller cities and rural areas nationwide."

TOKYO

Behind the glitz and glamor of Tokyo's flashing lights and neon signs sits a diverse and evolving startup world. Life sciences, robotics and fintech are the drivers of Japan's biggest city's startup ecosystem, which is supported by the Tokyo Metropolitan Government and increasingly looks to bring in new and diverse populations. Investors and foreign entrepreneurs alike are flocking to Tokyo, excited to take part in its startup revolution.

Impact HUB Tokyo

**Impact HUB Tokyo is a collaborative community
for the people who want to make an impact.
We have space for work, programs and events
to boost your entrepreneurial journeys.**

It has been seven years since we founded Impact HUB Tokyo as a pioneer of new concepts with coworking space and community. We continue to develop and innovate in an "organic community" together with numerous members, including impact-driven entrepreneurs within or outside of Tokyo's startup ecosystem.

It's hard to ignore that there are many startups and people in Tokyo who address issues unique to Japan and are trying to make such an impact on a global scale. Yet until now, the context of "impact" has not been well understood, which we have acknowledged through the curation process for this Tokyo chapter. There is still a misconception that making "impact" must be something enormous. This trivializes the actual work of people who are making an impact in society. To represent an authentic ecosystem map in Tokyo, we put extra effort into bringing up the names of people and businesses who could be marginalized otherwise. When working with the global community, it became apparent that the understanding of impact investment in Japan is not only still shallow but also based on the unique circumstances built upon the culture and startup history of Japan and Asia.

"Democratization of Innovation" is our core vision; hence, we have joined this project to help expose uniquely impact-driven communities and people to the global community. As a community partner, it was very interesting to work with this specific theme. It is surprising to see the scale of development in recent years with startup industries pursuing everything that combines the impact and business mindset. We are very excited about seeing this innovation expand explosively. This guide book could be the first map to show this development, and, hopefully, it encourages you to take action.

Shino Tsuchiya,
Cofounder, CEO

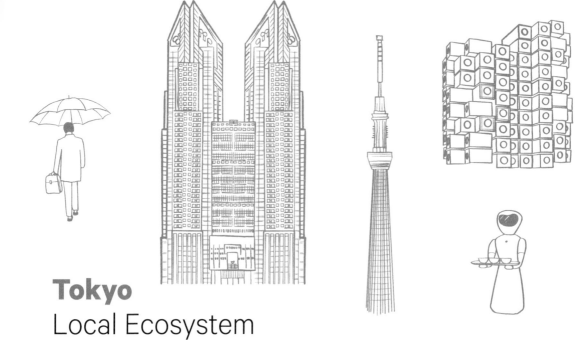

Tokyo
Local Ecosystem

Tokyo is now known as one of the world's biggest and most vibrant cities, but this wasn't always the case. In fact, it's a relatively new urban center. Tokyo was founded just four hundred years ago as a small fishing village, and it has changed a great deal since. Today's metropolis is home to more than thirty million people and an advanced technological infrastructure. The capital of Japan since 1868, Tokyo has long attracted diverse populations and international influences that live in harmony with traditional Japanese culture.

As a startup city, Tokyo leads Japan in terms of investment and startup creation – there are more than 1,200 startups worth more than $10 billion in the city. Along with Fukuoka, it was one of the first two cities in Japan to pilot a six-month startup-visa program. The Tokyo Metropolitan Government has gone out of its way to support startups, implementing a one-stop shop for early-stage startups, an innovative coworking project that aims to bring on twenty thousand members, and a government-led training program for managers and emerging leaders in entrepreneurship. Increasingly, healthcare and medicine are playing an important role in Tokyo, with a number of accelerator programs like Beyond Next Ventures focusing on turning out startups aimed at reshaping these industries. The Tokyo Startup Gateway contest is a case in point for how the ecosystem has shifted: its most recent contest title was "DREAM or NEVER."

FACTS &
FIGURES

– There are approximately 1,200 startups in Tokyo, representing a net value of $14 billion.

– More than three-quarters of investment in Japan's startup ecosystem (77%)
  is in Tokyo.

– The University of Tokyo is the top university for spinoff companies,
  with businesses started by students and graduates of the institution surpassing
  $200 million in investment.

– On average, early-stage startups in Tokyo raise $336,000.

– Tokyo is a top city for advanced manufacturing and robotics, ranking in the
  top 20 worldwide.

– Tokyo is actively developing its life sciences sector. The 2019 Beyond Next Ventures
  accelerator cohort featured 15 startups in medicine or healthcare (out of 23 total).

– Tokyo was named the fifth best city worldwide for fintech, according to Deloitte.

– Tokyo is the epicenter of Japan's Society 5.0 plan, which aims to use robotics
  to solve human problems.

NOTABLE
STARTUP
ACTIVITY

– Beyond Next Ventures has spun out more than 20 medical and life sciences
  companies that have gone on to a successful IPO, including several notable
  Tokyo-based companies: Oncotherapy Science (a therapeutic cancer drug),
  Terra (a vaccine that strengthens dendritic cells) and CellSeed (a technology
  enabling cell-seed engineering for regenerative medicine).

– Japan's top startup in 2019, Preferred Networks, has raised more than $1 billion in
  investment and is working to develop self-driving technologies with Toyota Motor.

– LPixel, which uses image analysis to help researchers in life sciences fields, received
  more than $25 million in investment from Fujifilm, Olympus and CYBERDYNE.

Behind Tokyo's plan to attract foreign startups to Japan

An interview with

Masafumi Yonazu / Senior Director of Special Zone Promotion

Tokyo, as one of the first Japanese cities to offer a startup visa for entrepreneurs and with emerging industries in life sciences, fintech and mobility and a number of world-class universities, is setting the bar high for startup creation in Japan. The effort to support foreign and domestic startups is spearheaded on a national scale by the Japanese government and also relies heavily on local players such as The Tokyo Metropolitan Government.

Growing a strong startup ecosystem is a two-way street. Although it's often thought of as an organic, private-sector–focused activity, the process of starting up a company can also benefit from national and local investment aimed at attracting and supporting innovative businesses that shape the world for the better. The city of Tokyo is out to show that such a partnership between the startup world and local governments can have impressive results.

" We think what is required is the ideas and technology provided from startups, so we're trying to get large companies and universities to be involved to receive their help. "

Between 2016 and 2017, investment in the Japan startup ecosystem increased by one-third. According to Startup Genome, in 2019 Tokyo alone accounted for more than 1,200 startups valued at around $14 billion in total. City officials see this growth as just the beginning. "Tokyo is a big city, and there are lots of people and resources and money, but we haven't seen much innovation," says Masafumi Yonazu, the senior director for Special Zone Promotion, Tokyo Metropolitan Government's office for Strategic Policy and ICT Promotion. "We think what is required is the ideas and technology provided from startups, so we're trying to get large companies and universities to be involved to receive their help."

Japan still ranks relatively low in the World Bank's Ease of Doing Business ranking, but in recent years, the Japanese government has opened up its business regulations to foreign companies and startups. The Tokyo Metropolitan Government has taken a number of additional steps to bring foreign startups into the ecosystem and to grow its reach internationally.

Perhaps most importantly, the city was one of the first two Japanese ecosystems (along with Fukuoka) to introduce a startup visa for foreign entrepreneurs. The visa, Masafumi explains, includes a six-month incubation period for startup founders, during which time they can build their business. It allows founders to stay for up to six months if they've submitted a business plan to the Tokyo Metropolitan Government and the proposal is admitted by Immigration Bureau, Ministry of Justice. Potential entrepreneurs can learn more about starting up in Tokyo by visiting one of the government's official overseas consultation offices around the world. There are locations in London, Paris, San Francisco and Singapore.

For companies that are already installed in Tokyo, the Tokyo Metropolitan Government has endeavored to promote new startup investment through its Global Financial City: Tokyo plan, which includes, among other measures, the creation of an organization called FinCity.Tokyo to promote Tokyo as a global financial center.

Tokyo Metropolitan Government sees a number of fields as potential growth sectors in the ecosystem. Among these are life sciences, fintech, robotics and creative-contents, Masafumi says. Japan has long led the world in robotics, having created the first robotics-focused trade association in the early 1970s. But now, Masafumi says, the goal is to expand to other fields and bring more diversity – in terms of gender, ethnicity and nationality – into the startup scene. "Now, the rules are becoming different and we believe that the field is becoming broader as well," he says.

Masafumi recognizes that starting up in a new country is not easy. As such, the city launched the Business Development Center TOKYO as a one-stop shop for startups looking to understand the regulations and red tape that might be involved and to seek Japan-based business partners. "What we can say about Tokyo is it is safe for business and also to live," Masafumi says. "However, I also understand that it might not be fully comfortable to live in a new city at first." To help ease any culture shock and build community, startup founders can gather at the Tokyo Startup Station, a government-sponsored coworking space that aims to bring a diverse mix of entrepreneurs together under one roof.

Masafumi believes that an increasingly diverse mix of startup founders from abroad and across Japan, as well as established multinational businesses and world-class universities, has the potential to lead Tokyo to rapid ecosystem growth. Increased government support, he acknowledges, will continue to play a key role in ensuring that this growth is equally distributed. "There are a lot of people in Tokyo, and there are a lot of businesses as well, and these businesses are supported very well, not only from Tokyo but from the Japanese government," he says. "They are welcoming this movement, and we would like to provide more chances for these startup businesses to join the ecosystem of Tokyo."

[ABOUT]

The Tokyo Metropolitan Government is creating an international center
of business and attracting foreign companies by utilizing the National Strategic
Special Zone system and other approaches. With the goal of making Tokyo
the most business-friendly city in the world, it also stimulates innovation
by promoting the formation of ecosystems, creating initiatives based on the
"Global Financial City: Tokyo" Vision and developing new businesses that utilize
the latest technologies, such as autonomous driving.

[CONTACT]

WEB investtokyo.metro.tokyo.lg.jp/en

EMAIL ml-office-ahq@section.metro.tokyo.jp

LINKEDIN bdc-tokyo

FACEBOOK Invest-Tokyo-736266616582601

Crono

ELEVATOR PITCH

" We enable students to pursue educational opportunities and career goals without worrying about finances and the burden of student loans by matching them with companies that invest in talent. We also provide a comprehensive search platform for scholarships. "

SECTOR **social impact, education**

WEB **crono.network**

MILESTONES

Receiving first investment of close to ¥25 million in May 2019.

Meeting all requirements to be officially certified as an employment-placement service.

Launching the company and graduate-matching service in November 2019.

Launching the scholarship search platform for students to easily search for financial support.

"I didn't come from a wealthy family," says Yinglong Gao, CEO and cofounder of Crono. "My dad worked a lot but we always struggled, so I thought I could find happiness by joining a large foreign firm and earning a good salary. But I wasn't working towards something I wanted to do as an individual, and I wasn't satisfied." This was the beginning of the idea for Crono. Even with a good salary as a strategy consultant, Yinglong's student loans placed a heavy burden on him. He wondered whether it would be possible to create a system where people could pursue their goals without worrying financially.

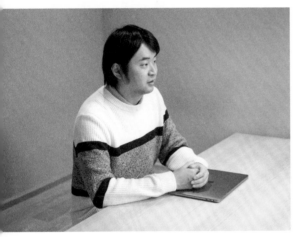

In July 2018, he launched Crono with a university friend, Takayoshi Araki, who had also struggled financially. Their plan was to match students with companies who would pay off the students' loans in return for the acquisition of excellent and loyal talent. The idea was so revolutionary that he spent months pitching to confused investors who didn't understand his vision and doubted whether he could ever get companies on board. "'Can you really do it?' was the most common reaction," says Yinglong. Yet he didn't waver and, finally, in May 2019, an angel investor took a leap of faith. Three months later, two venture capital firms also invested. Crono now offers a further service that collates information on scholarships and funding in a large database, allowing students to search easily for funding. They are hoping to acquire enough data to offer loans with greater flexibility to meet students' needs.

TEAM

Crono has a small team of only three members. Two of them work remotely, while Yinglong bases himself in a coworking space in Kasumigaseki. While he initially tried recruitment websites to find collaborators, he found utilizing his network has been the best way to meet people who truly understand Crono's vision, and this, for him, is the most important part of building a successful team. All three are focused on the goal of enabling young people to pursue their educational and career goals without financial worries, and they often discuss future ideas for the business together. They have a fair amount of freedom to choose how and when they work, but of course they respond to clients within normal working hours. When they get together, it's not just the team; they also get together with the students and sometimes they organize study groups too. Through this, they are aiming to build a Crono community.

Heralbony

ELEVATOR PITCH

" We promote the creativity and skill
of people with intellectual and lifelong
developmental disabilities by placing
their art in the public domain:
in apparel, interior design and
building decorations. "

SECTOR licensing

WEB heralbony.jp

MILESTONES

Securing finance and a great team
in Hanamaki and Tokyo.

Accumulating one thousand pieces
of art created by one hundred
artists.

Collaborating with corporations
and renowned art galleries.

Wrapping a site in Tokyo's
fashionable Marunouchi district
and JR Kichijoji Station.

Twin brothers Takaya and Fumito Matsuda, twenty-eight, set up Heralbony in 2018 to change society's perception of people with intellectual and lifelong developmental disabilities. Their inspiration came from close to home. Growing up, they saw that their older brother, Shota, who has autism, often wasn't accepted or valued by others. After graduating from university, Takaya joined an advertising agency while Fumito worked for a construction company. They got the idea for Heralbony after seeing pictures painted by a mentally impaired artist. "We wanted to show that people with intellectual disabilities have colorful personalities and individual skills, like greater sensibility, delicate hands, bold ideas and sharpened concentration," says Takaya. The name of the startup was a nod to Shota; it was one of combinations of letters that he had written repeatedly as a child.

TEAM

Cofounders Takaya and Fumito Matsuda say that being based in Hanamaki with an office in Tokyo allows their team to utilize the best of both locations. Staff in Hanamaki are tapped into local knowledge and contacts, while staff in Tokyo are focused on information gathering and on making national and international contacts, as well as attending events and searching for investors. When hiring, the cofounders were looking for people seeking long-term positions and a passion to use their work to help improve social welfare for people with intellectual disabilities. Few staff members have an academic background in social welfare; instead, their experience is mainly in business. Their backgrounds range from advertising and editing to IT and construction. Almost all team members have been found via referral. Employees in each location enjoy having lunch together on weekdays, and the whole team gets together regularly via video call.

Takaya and Fumito began by gathering art created by people with intellectual disabilities and selling the license to produce the art on neckties and handkerchiefs. Next, they licensed the use of the art in interior design for items like wallpaper and cushions, securing contracts with large corporations such as Panasonic and Mitsui, which saw the efforts as a way of helping to support the UN's SDGs. Heralbony's next step was selling licenses for use of the art on the exterior of buildings. The startup has received no investment to date. It operates two offices – one in Hanamaki and the other in Tokyo – using finances from a loan secured by the cofounders.

Holoeyes

ELEVATOR PITCH

" We are revolutionizing healthcare
communication and surgical procedures
through cutting-edge virtual reality
and mixed-reality technology. "

SECTOR virtual reality, mixed reality, healthcare

WEB holoeyes.jp/en

MILESTONES

Being selected for a seed
accelerator and receiving our
first funding from a VC firm.

Launching our VR service in 2019.

Building a nationwide network
of sales partners to introduce our
products to more remote hospitals
and clients.

Getting certified as Class II
medical-device software by
the regulatory Pharmaceuticals
and Medical Devices Agency.

Holoeyes CEO Naoji Taniguchi was working as a freelance software engineer and planner when he was asked to help digitize a healthcare dictionary. Half a day of internet searching led him to his cofounder, Maki Sugimoto (COO), who had written an article on the potential in the healthcare field for new technologies, such as 8K resolution and motion sensors. It wasn't long before the two were swapping ideas. They first set about 3D-printing a liver from CT-scan data, but then Naoji began to consider how this data could be combined with a video game engine to explore inside the human body. "I think I was the first person to have the idea to go inside a human skull using virtual reality," he says. When comparing the low cost of virtual reality (VR) headsets to internal cameras, the pair realized they had found a gap in the market, and Holoeyes was born in October 2016.

TEAM

"The best thing is we're a group of professionals," says Naoji. Holoeyes has a small team sourced mainly through Naoji's network that he built while freelancing. Everyone works on a part-time basis and has other professional commitments, meaning that hours are flexible. Almost all team members are based in Tokyo, but they primarily work remotely. "Most employees are in their forties," says Naoji, "so almost everyone has a family. That's why we want to go home at a reasonable time or work from home." Thursday is a meeting day where the team will come into the office to discuss projects and progress face-to-face and head out for a team lunch. They might also be spotted trying out the headsets and making various gestures as they explore VR medical worlds.

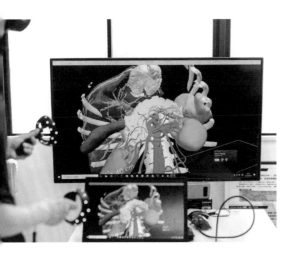

The company was selected for a science-and-technology seed accelerator. This led to ¥10 million in seed funding from a venture capital firm, allowing it to push forward with software development and marketing. Maki, who is a surgeon by profession, began demonstrating how VR could be used to plan out operations on real patients. The pair also introduced their software and its potential for communicating medical and surgical knowledge at several healthcare conferences. Holoeyes has subsequently received significant investment from two other VC firms and is currently developing software for three different headsets.

Infostellar

ELEVATOR PITCH

" We are creating a global network
of ground stations that satellite
operators can connect to through
our cloud-based system StellarStation.
Our vision is to reach the point where
satellites can be operated with the
same ease as ground-based IoT
devices. "

SECTOR space

WEB infostellar.net

MILESTONES

Closing our seed financing round
in October 2016.

Reaching ten employees and
closing our Series A financing
round in September 2017.

Launching StellarStation's
commercial platform in
October 2018.

Opening our first overseas office
in the UK in May 2019.

Infostellar CEO and cofounder Naomi Kurahara was a postdoctoral researcher at the University of Tokyo, working on a large-scale satellite project, when she identified a problem she wanted to solve – one that led her to refocus her gaze from the stars to the earth. The problem was that there were insufficient services on the ground to communicate with the satellites. Starting from scratch, it took Naomi and her colleagues nearly two years to design and develop a ground system for their satellite operations. She began to consider how to make this more efficient. She joined forces with Kazuo Ishigame (COO), who had startup experience, and with Toshio Totsuka (board member), who led a radio communications company, and together they launched Infostellar to provide a global network of ground stations.

Through Infostellar, satellite operators need only connect to the cloud-based StellarStation system and use the simple interface to find a ground station that matches their requirements, saving time and energy in searching for a vendor and setting up a connection. This gives fast, convenient and affordable access to antennas around the world to download data. Equally, ground station operators are able to easily monetize surplus capacity. After successfully closing two rounds of funding and launching the StellarStation platform at the end of 2018, they gained their first customers in 2019 and are now focused on growing their clientbase. The team is based in Tokyo and expanded to London in 2019, reflecting both a drive within the UK to develop its space industry and also Infostellar's goal to be recognized within the international industry.

TEAM

Infostellar's team of sixteen is very international – around half the members are Japanese, with others hailing from North America and Europe, and around one-third are women. "It really is quite diverse, without wanting to sound cliché," says Melissa Molseed, who hails from the UK and helps with everything from people operations and business development to communications and marketing. Their workstyle, with flexible hours, is more typical of a North American or European office than a Japanese company. On Fridays, the Tokyo team finishes earlier so they can get together for food and drink, and Infostellar also holds occasional offsites. With such diversity, there is an emphasis on building strong relationships between team members from very different backgrounds. While around two-thirds of their team speaks Japanese, English is the working language, reflecting the standard across the space industry, and Infostellar's clientbase, which is primarily based overseas.

JobRainbow

ELEVATOR PITCH

" We provide a platform through
which the LGBTQ community can
find employment opportunities at
companies that offer diverse and
friendly work environments. We strive
to build a better society where
everyone can be proud of themselves
regardless of differences. "

SECTOR **employment, social impact**

WEB **jobrainbow.jp**

MILESTONES

- Pivoting the business model from
  a website reviewing LGBTQ-friendly
  companies to a recruitment tool.

- Hitting 100,000 users
  in September 2017.

- Receiving ¥50 million in investment
  and taking on our first employee.

- Reaching 400,000 monthly active
  users in the summer of 2019.

Kento Hoshi was no stranger to discrimination due to his sexuality. He was bullied so badly at middle school that he dropped out for one-and-a-half years. Through an online gaming community, he came to feel accepted for who he was and regained his confidence, eventually entering university and founding an LGBTQ group. However, he again witnessed discrimination when his close friend was rejected multiple times during job hunting due to her identity, causing her to become depressed and drop out. Wanting to take action, Kento initially founded a website where people could review LGBTQ-friendly companies, but he soon realized there was demand for a job-search tool. In 2015, he won a pitch contest, receiving mentoring from former McKinsey consultant Yuji Akabane, who helped him formulate his business model.

TEAM

Kento established JobRainbow with his older sister, Mariko, who's JobRainbow's COO and a law graduate. Together, they have grown the team into eleven full-time staff with around fourteen interns and freelancers. Roughly 80 percent of their employees are LGBTQ, and their very first employee was a professional female soccer player who transitioned to male and was the crucial sales talent they needed during their early growth phase. For Kento, psychological safety in the workplace is paramount. One employee, who transitioned to female and has a female partner and children, says she did not ever envision finding a work environment where she could be herself and didn't need to lie about her identity, and many of the team feel similarly. Hours are flexible, and several members choose to work from home. Those who head into the coworking-space office often go out for lunch together, and every quarter they hold a BBQ event.

During his final two years at university, Kento ran JobRainbow on the side, but, upon graduation, he made a snap decision to pursue it full time. A friend who worked at successful startup Sukedachi introduced him to the CEO, who was impressed and in turn introduced him to Genesia Ventures. In a relatively short space of time, he received ¥50 million in investment, allowing him to recruit his first employee. Having undertaken summer internships at large firms, he leveraged his connections to bring big names on board; Microsoft Japan was among the first, which helped attract tech companies such as Rakuten, IBM and Facebook. JobRainbow now offers training and consulting services for companies who want to be more LGBTQ-friendly.

WOTA

ELEVATOR PITCH

" We make autonomous, decentralized
water-recycling systems with the goal
of clean and sustainable water use
for everyone, everywhere. "

SECTOR manufacture and
development of water treatment
equipment, algorithm research

WEB wota.co.jp

MILESTONES

Choosing to use biological treatment
and filtration in our water-recycling
products.

Developing multiple prototypes
for portable showers.

Providing showers on the ground
following the Kumamoto Earthquake
2016 and subsequent natural
disasters in Japan since then.

Launching our first water-recycling
system, the WOTA BOX and Outdoor
Shower Kit.

Founded in 2014, WOTA Corp. aims to address water scarcity around the world. The idea came after the three founders learned of Japan's problematic water infrastructure. The system, which includes dams, water-treatment plants and pipelines, was built following WWII. Today, its running cost is about ¥10 trillion annually, but it generates only about ¥4 trillion of revenue. With the country's aging population, revenue is expected to decrease, making the infrastructure's future viability uncertain. "We have a very big water issue in Japan," says Yosuke Maeda, COO of WOTA, "which we hope to solve with our technology and then make that technology available to people anywhere in the world. We have an opportunity to provide an alternative to the existing model."

In 2015, WOTA started work on a compact, portable, off-grid water-recycling system that would be affordable for families and communities to own. After many trials and prototypes, the company developed a system that uses multiple filters to recycle gray water (from showers and washing machines). Its first target was the disaster-relief and disaster-preparedness market. Since 2016, WOTA has provided its technology to support local communities following natural disasters in Japan. After extensive R&D, WOTA launched the WOTA BOX and Outdoor Shower Kit in 2019. It recycles 98 percent of used water and can be set up anywhere in fifteen minutes. WOTA is targeting growth in Japan, followed by developing countries.

TEAM

Most people at WOTA are graduates of the University of Tokyo, but their specialties are diverse. Some are experienced in water equipment and water treatment or have an academic background in biology, chemistry, electrical engineering or mechanical engineering. Others have studied architecture, computer science or data science. It's a deliberate recruitment measure, as the startup wanted a team whose members could solve all types of problems and be ready for the future of water treatment. The water industry in Japan has nascent levels of digitalization, with a lag in use of IoT, but WOTA foresees development in this area. Having water-treatment specialists and data engineers on the same team is an asset. The office has a culture of curiosity, with active engagement, discussion and collaboration among the diverse team (40 percent are women and a number of nationalities are represented).

Emi Takemura, Naofumi Iwai & Yuji Fujita

Cofounders
/ Peatix

Before cofounding Peatix, Emi Takemura, Naofumi Iwai and Yuji Fujita were working at Amazon Japan alongside fellow New York–based Peatix cofounder Taku Harada. Taku was in charge of DVDs and music, Emi was leading the marketing department, and Naofumi and Yuji were working on the marketplace. Bringing together their various skills and experience, they brainstormed ideas for a business they could set up and run together. The result was Peatix. Today, Naofumi is responsible for platform management and product development while Yuji takes care of sales, marketing and community management. Emi acts as an adviser, introducing opportunities and advising on business strategy.

ABOUT THE COMPANY

Peatix is an event-registration platform that provides organizers with the tools to create, promote and sell out events. After launching in Japan in 2011, it expanded into the US and Singapore in 2013. Peatix's mobile-centric solution for event management has served more than forty thousand events to date, from concerts to conferences.

WEB **peatix.com**

What was the inspiration behind setting up?

EMI We wanted to offer people something different to what we had seen at Amazon. We wanted to connect the people who create content (the artists) and the consumers (the audience). Our idea was to create a direct-to-consumer platform for creative people. Initially, it was a digital-content site, offering books and so on, and then we pivoted to become an event community platform.

What early difficulties did you face in the business? And how did you overcome them?

EMI The Great East Japan Earthquake on March 11, 2011, was the first big hiccup. We were due to launch Peatix that month but couldn't. All of us fled from Tokyo with our development team to my parents' house in Osaka. While there, about six of us shared one big tatami mat room and spent a few weeks finishing the product.

NAOFUMI When we launched in May, no entertainment events were being held because of the aftermath of the earthquake. We had thought that Peatix would be used mostly by indie artists and musicians, but, after the disaster, mainly nonprofit organizations wanted to use it. That made monetization really difficult. As most of the clients were nonprofits or volunteers, it was pretty hard to ask for money.

" Don't start a business without personal passion. It takes a lot longer to build a successful business than you think. "

EMI In Japan – and globally – there is a big shift away from seeing event ticketing as a transactional business; i.e., making money from the commission of selling tickets for a concert. With a database business like ours, every customer is registered under an account. That allows us to see their journey on Peatix, transforming a one-time, transactional relationship into a lifelong relationship. That's the best thing we've done for the company.

What do you wish you'd known before starting up? What would you have done differently?

NAOFUMI This is our first startup experience. I'd heard from a lot of friends that fundraising for a business can be tricky. You raise money by selling some shares, which involves losing some control of the business. If we had known that we'd lose so much control by fundraising from VCs and others, we would have self-funded. If we could manage the business one hundred percent, that would be amazing.

EMI There should have been a trade-off between someone else investing in the business and us investing in the business with our own money. Before we started Peatix, we were thinking up other entrepreneurial ideas and funding ourselves for a while. For Peatix, we saw promise compared to the other products we'd thought up in the past, so we felt we should raise external funding to go big and grow fast. In hindsight, because we didn't know every nut and bolt about fundraising strategies, we made some mistakes.

YUJI Although it was a really tough time for us, it turned out to be a really good thing because we decided to support the community's social activities.

EMI Yes, we saw a surge of events in the social community and social-good area. People were really trying to roll up their sleeves to help out people in need. We decided to actively help out these people by giving them discounted service and other support.

What was the best decision you made with the business?

NAOFUMI In the early days, many of the clients saw us as a ticket service, a tool service. We tried to shift away from that to a database or network business. We had a feature that allowed event organizers to sell tickets without account registration, but we decided to kill that feature and made it mandatory for every user to register with a Peatix account so we could engage with them. Once they joined a Peatix event, we could accumulate data on the kind of events they were interested in. We gradually transformed Peatix from a ticketing business to a database business. The benefit has been that we can look at the data and leverage it for other services. For example, if an event attendee goes to a gourmet event, they might be interested in other food-related products like Amazon Fresh.

Why did you choose Tokyo as the startup location, and why is Tokyo good for your business?

NAOFUMI The market was the deciding factor: Greater Tokyo has more than half of the total market here in Japan.

EMI The venture capital was in Tokyo as well. When we started ten years ago, there was almost no venture capital for seed funding in Japan, and what was available was in Tokyo. It was the beginning of the startup boom in Japan, and it made sense to choose Tokyo.

YUJI Being based in Tokyo has enabled us to build up a lot of collaboration with other startups in the city. Lots of companies are interested in building a business community. Since we started up, we've been running community events for event organizers and sharing tips on how to create their communities around events, for example.

NAOFUMI Also, lots of Japan's big companies are good with technology but lack experience in the software business. And the software-as-a-service business sector – our sector – is where they are most behind. Because they haven't grown internal talent, they need to look externally, so there are a lot of innovation programs between big companies and startups nowadays. It's a win-win situation and it offers opportunities for us.

How did you hire your team in the early days of the business?

EMI Referrals were vital to help us find a good team in the first five years of the business. We also found good people at startup events. When we expanded into Singapore in 2013, we relied on support from the government. We were part of its entrepreneurship program; the government helped us find candidates

to fill our positions, provided we helped those candidates in their professional development by letting them attend entrepreneurship classes during their workday. Those classes were once a week for about a year.

How do you hire now, and what have you learned along the way?

EMI We prefer to hire people we know or have worked with in the past. If that isn't possible, we look for strong, multiple referrals as we've found that works quite well.

NAOFUMI We also use recruitment tools like Wantedly and Indeed to help us find the right person.

EMI We've found that, when considering people from outside our network, it's very important to know them as much as possible, to ensure they will fit well in the position and organizational culture.

What qualities are you looking for in your people?

NAOFUMI Above all, we value leadership and ownership.

EMI Yes, leadership qualities are definitely important, as is passion for what Peatix is trying to achieve.

How would you describe your team culture? And what makes your team special?

YUJI I would say the culture is open and flat. We make efforts to facilitate communication amongst the team, because that's important. Everyone enjoys chatting together socially, too.

NAOFUMI Yes, we communicate very openly, often via Slack, Zoom and GitHub. Our team likes to use Zoom and Slack, as it helps them get better connected with each other, especially among the staff who work remotely. We have a very casual culture.

Do you have any personal work habits that have proved helpful for your work? What steps do you take to help you achieve work–life balance?

NAOFUMI I make sure I go to the office every day. Also, every morning I look at key metrics to help me grasp the health of our platform, because that reflects the health of the business. I try to manage my work–life balance by not staying at the office for long hours and leveraging remote working where I can.

YUJI I find that having a coffee every morning and spending time listing what I need to do within that day is really helpful. My work life and private life are quite mixed together, but I think each is well balanced.

What professional advice would you give someone in the early stages of starting up a company?

NAOFUMI I would say, don't raise too much money before building a robust business model.

EMI My advice would be don't start a business without personal passion. It takes a lot longer to build a successful business than you think. •

What are your top work essentials?

EMI iPhone, wifi and laptop.
NAOFUMI Data, to make data-driven decisions.
YUJI Design communication with users and clients. Communication with team members.

At what age did you found your company?

EMI Forty.
NAOFUMI Thirty-four.
YUJI Twenty-nine.

What's your most used app?

EMI Facebook Messenger.
NAOFUMI Slack.
YUJI Slack.

What book has most influenced your career?

EMI *The Borderless World* by Kenichi Ohmae.
NAOFUMI *The Mind of the Strategist* by Kenichi Ohmae.
YUJI *Amazon.Com: Get Big Fast* by Robert Spector.

What's your greatest skill?

EMI Developing new services and businesses.
NAOFUMI Data analysis.
YUJI Communication.

What do you do every morning to prepare for the day ahead?

EMI Short stretch and meditation.
NAOFUMI Download metrics data for analysis.
YUJI Create and prioritize to-do lists.

What is your favorite positive habit you've cultivated?

EMI Treat everyone with respect, regardless of their background.
NAOFUMI Walking, even during conference calls on Zoom.
YUJI Cycling.

Toshiki Abe

Founder and CEO
/ Ridilover

Born in Kyoto and raised in Yokohama, Toshiki Abe had an impoverished childhood. When he was thirteen, his father left and the relationship with his mother worsened, so he moved out and ended up living on the street. During this time, he was unmotivated in his studies and rarely did any homework; however, after reading a book about a boy in a similar situation who made it to university, he was inspired to study hard. He moved to Tokyo to attend the University of Tokyo. In 2008, while still a student, he founded a volunteer organization called Ridilover to address social issues. In 2013, he transformed the organization into a for-profit company.

ABOUT THE COMPANY

Ridilover is a travel agency offering the planning, management and arrangement of study trips about social issues for schools and companies. It also develops and operates a web platform for identifying and addressing social issues.

WEB en.ridilover.jp

What was your inspiration to address social issues?

When I lived on the street, I hung out with people who had experienced terrible things. … These people had problems, but they were also smart and quick-witted. I realized that what had happened to us wasn't our fault. I also became angry at the adults who didn't help us when we needed them, and angry at society for not taking enough notice of the problems we faced.

When I started university, I heard from individuals involved in the areas of human rights and social issues that the general public was too busy in their daily lives to think about the social problems around them. I wanted to change that, to help solve that problem. I started the volunteer organization Ridilover with the mission of helping us say farewell to the ignorance of society.

It was difficult to run as a volunteer organization, so I later set it up as a company. I thought it could work as a business because we could offer something that no other company has. We could offer people the chance to go on tours to engage in social issues for themselves, in the hope that they could help solve those issues.

" A company is a tool to make a better society. "

issues. Participants pay us to go on them. We offer tours for education (junior and high school students), for training (companies), for business development (companies), and for information (bureaucrats). We also get revenue from think tanks and other organizations for the research that we carry out in preparation for the trips.

We define tourism as a tool for users to learn about social issues. We also have online media by subscription for consumers, and we invest some money in businesses that help solve social issues, which gives us a return.

What were the early challenges with starting up and how did you overcome them?

As a volunteer organization, it was easy for us to attract more and more volunteers, and we expanded to a seven-hundred-member group, but the members didn't all share the same ideals, methodology or culture. Our biggest challenge was how to define a social problem. Making that definition and addressing social issues requires expertise. Also, none of the volunteers had any money or incentive to carry out the work that needed to be done to help achieve our goals.

Shifting Ridilover from a volunteer group to a business helped us to overcome these challenges. It was a critical step in our history. The volunteers had simply wanted to belong to a community, to have fun or to learn about some social issues. By becoming a business, I could demand that the team receive training in relevant areas and work to achieve the business' goals.

What is your business model and how did you start making a profit?

As part of our mission, "Farewell to the ignorance of society," our core activity is "engagement tourism." We research, manage and arrange four kinds of trips that are designed to be like fact-finding missions for participants who might be able to solve some social

What was your best decision?

Turning Ridilover from a voluntary organization into a business. It was critical to our success as it allowed me to make demands on the team and it gave people incentives to work hard.

What professional advice would you give people in the early stages of starting up?

Define the future you want to make.

Why did you choose Tokyo as the location for the business and how does being in Tokyo benefit the business?

As I was living in Tokyo and the volunteer organization was made up of students at the University of Tokyo, it made sense to base the business there. When I started the business, I won an award for businesses run by students from the Tokyo Metropolitan Government, which included money and other support. Tokyo is a very efficient and practical location for us because it has a wide variety of social issues. In rural areas, for example, it's rare to see homeless people, but we can see them in Tokyo. This makes it easy for us to do research, carry out interviews and learn more about social issues in Japan. We want to understand social issues in both urban and local areas.

In the early days, how did you hire your team?

Because so many people were involved in the organization, it wasn't difficult to recruit staff when we made the switch to becoming a company. We had plenty of people to choose from and a lot of our team were once volunteers. However, we couldn't hire all the staff we needed from this base. As our company vision and business model were very unique at that time, it was hard to acquire people who had the required skills, so I hired people who had compassion for our mission and the potential to learn and develop their skills on the job. I spent time training them to do the roles that we needed. In the early days of Ridilover being a company, I did nearly everything that had to be done for the business until this training phase was completed and the staff could work at full capacity.

How do you hire now and what skills are you looking for in your staff now?

I still hire people who have compassion for our mission. I think that people's attitude to what we're doing as a company is still the most important consideration when we hire staff. Aside from that, what we want for people in all our positions is culture fit. Whether the person will be working in the department of editing, writing, marketing, research or sales, it's vital that they are suited to the culture of our team and of our company.

What is the culture like in your office?

It's friendly and casual. Our people have a purpose and feel like their job is their lifework. In terms of company structure, we're very flat and all staff love to discuss things. In Japan, there's a famous movie character called Tora-san. I'm sure almost all Japanese people know him, as he has been in more than fifty movies in Japan. He doesn't have logic but he has humanity. Our staff are encouraged to become scientists who can communicate to Tora-san about social issues. To succeed in this task, they need to be logical and even controversial in their approach, but the most important requirement is humanity.

As we have about fifty staff, some of the newer recruits don't know the longer-term members. To help overcome this, we have icebreakers at our all-staff meeting, which is held once a week. By having this fun time together, all staff can know more about each other and feel more relaxed when working with each other. Four times a year, we have a company trip to promote mutual understanding. Staff also love having lunch together on weekdays.

What's the next step for you and the business?

I believe that a company is a tool to make a better society. I want to think about what makes an ideal society and then assess the gap between that ideal and the present situation. I want to be a visionary and make a concrete action plan to help bridge that gap. As I'm a PhD student majoring in the field of complex systems at the University of Tokyo, I apply my studies to my work, as our business model is connected to complex systems. I'm interested in using complex systems to help discover the truth about how social issues can be better recognized.

Regarding business development, we offer about three hundred trips all over Japan. Some trips are even to Myanmar. As our mission is about creating a marketplace for social issues around the world, we want to expand globally.

How do you manage your professional and personal time?

I love my work. It is my lifework and gives me a strong purpose. I would be happy to spend all my time managing and developing the company, but I have other responsibilities as well, including writing my PhD thesis. I also want to use my time to contribute to my local community, as I think that's important. I'm a director of my local kindergarten's softball team, which I enjoy as a way of giving back. •

At what age did you found your company?
Twenty-six.

What's the most valuable piece of advice you've been given?
Practice *sapere aude* (the Latin phrase meaning "Dare to know").

What's your most used app?
Slack.

What's your greatest skill?
Vision-making.

What do you do every morning to prepare for the day ahead?
Take a bath to help me wake up.

What book has most influenced your career?
Shippai no honshitsu.

ETIC

ETIC is a startup-mentorship program strengthened by a network of partner organizations and business leaders, who provide support to entrepreneurs taking their first steps toward starting a business. This support comes primarily in the form of mentorship, networking assistance and business-plan coaching. Participants are typically between the ages of fifteen and thirty-nine and passionate about solving societal challenges. Expats living in Japan are welcome to apply, though at least a basic level of Japanese language ability is encouraged. ETIC also offers an entry-level entrepreneurship program geared toward non-Japanese participants called Tokyo Startup Gateway. Many graduates of this program go on to join ETIC. In the twenty-six years that ETIC has been running, it has supported 1,500 entrepreneurs and another 12,500 business leaders.

SECTOR sector-agnostic
SELECTED PORTFOLIO freee, Litalico, Life is Tech!
WHO SHOULD APPLY Passionate entrepreneurs focused on solving social challenges.
APPLY info@etic.or.jp for information about how to apply, or visit tokyo-startup.jp/english for the Tokyo Startup Gateway program.
WEB etic.or.jp

FoundX

FoundX is a free acceleration program offered exclusively to current students, alumni and researchers at the University of Tokyo. Applications are open to individuals with an idea for a company or small teams in the early stages of founding a startup. Participants receive support in the form of office space, mentoring, networking and access to potential customers. The program is divided into three tracks: the Fellows Program, which is designed to help students come up with an idea for their startup; the Pre-Founders Program, which helps startups prepare to commit full-time, and the Founder's Program, which is for startups that are already established and ready to focus on product- and customer-development, fundraising and pitching. FoundX also hosts internal demo days and a variety of theme-based luncheon lectures.

SECTOR sector-agnostic
SELECTED PORTFOLIO The program launched in 2019 and is hosting its first batches in 2020.
WHO SHOULD APPLY Currently enrolled students, alumni and researchers at the University of Tokyo.
APPLY **foundx.jp/founders**
WEB **foundx.jp**

Team 360

Team360 is an accelerator program hosted by Impact HUB Tokyo focused on helping participants realize their business ideas and on making their business models more sustainable. The name "Team360" represents the complete view that participants, as a team of entrepreneurs, should have of their own and each other's business models. "The core purpose and mission is to train the ability to think in order to brush up business models through team learning," says Shino Tsuchiya, program director. "Instead of learning passively or competing with each other, the program supports and facilitates dialogue for shared learning." Participants first concentrate on refining their business models by analyzing their vision of starting a business. By combining that with customer analysis based on value proposition, they find the base on which to build their business. Participants are encouraged to continue the proactive discussions and carry on their entrepreneurial journey after the program.

SECTOR sector-agnostic
SELECTED PORTFOLIO Kokoruku, Encourage, Mago Channel, Moff
WHO SHOULD APPLY Entrepreneurs with an impact-driven business who are, or would like to be, part of the Impact HUB Tokyo community.
APPLY **hubtokyo.com/contact**
WEB **hubtokyo.com/programmes/team360**

J-Startup

J-Startup concentrates public and private resources to support Japan's roughly one hundred high-potential startups selected from the ten thousand in the country.

SECTOR
sector-agnostic

J-Startup was set up by the Ministry of Economy Trade and Industry (METI), Japan External Trade Organization (JETRO), and New Energy and Industrial Technology Development Organization (NEDO) to create cutting-edge Japanese startups that can succeed in the global market. These startups are expected to empower Japan's startup ecosystem and offer value to the world via their innovative products or services. The program offers startups support from both private and public organizations. The main supporters are VCs, accelerators, large corporations and government organizations, including JETRO and NEDO. Startups are selected into the program by an external judging committee appointed by the secretariat and METI. The selection is based on each committee member's experience and achievements in supporting ventures.

From the private sector, startups in the program receive office space and training facilities, opportunities to collaborate on experimental studies with robots and access to acceleration programs. They also receive advice from specialists and referrals to customers who may be interested in the startup. Startups can connect with the VCs, accelerators and corporations involved to receive mentoring by management and relevant sector experts. The government provides the startups with easy access to public support programs (such as regulatory sandboxes) and with expertise on intellectual property strategy and overseas expansion. To support overseas expansion, the government welcomes the startups on missions abroad led by government officials and publicizes the companies through a dedicated website and news releases to foreign media. It also helps startups to exhibit at large-scale overseas and domestic events.

J-Startup is open to any kind of startup at any stage of its development. One notable example is Sansan, a company offering business-card-based contact-management solutions, which went public in June 2019 after receiving strong support from J-Startup.

MOST IMPORTANT TIPS

Have a mission.
We're looking for startups with a clear goal
of what they want to achieve and why, as well
as how and with whom they can achieve it.

Value diversity with originality.
We value diversity as well as originality.
That means we're focusing on startups
with original ideas that have various
backgrounds (such as in SDGs) or are
located in regional areas.

Show relevant background.
Team members should demonstrate they
have the potential to become a "unicorn"
by showing their relevant skills, education,
experience and expertise to set them apart
during our rigorous selection process.

Have the potential to grow.
We're interested in startups that can lead
the startup ecosystem in Japan and succeed
on the world stage, so the team should be
able to demonstrate a willingness and ability
to develop the business globally.

[CONTACT]

WEB j-startup.go.jp
FACEBOOK JStartup.goj

Anchorstar

The Anchorstar Lounge is a startup space that creates a community of support for mission-driven companies looking to establish themselves in Japan. This support includes both the physical space and guidance from in-house advisors on how to best enter the Japanese market. The Lounge is designed like a modern startup space with distinct areas for privacy, working quietly and connecting with other members. Being mindful of the daily challenges that foreign startups face, it provides its members with a kitchen and even a barber within the facility. Anchorstar is located in Toranomon, a developing area of Tokyo that is expected to become a global business center with a mix of old and new companies. The space overlooks a small park that blooms with sakura every year.

ADDRESS Daiichi Nan'o Building 6F,
2-21-2 Nishi-Shinbashi, Minato-ku,
Tokyo 105-0003
OPENING HOURS Members: 24/7;
Reception: 9 AM–5PM
USP The space features a barbershop and kitchen, helping entrepreneurs with their daily challenges.
PRICE RANGE Lounge membership: ¥50,000 per person per month.
WEB anchorstar.com

The National Art Center, Minato-ku, Tokyo

Impact HUB Tokyo

Impact HUB Tokyo is a community with coworking space for entrepreneurs and startups who want to question current paradigms and take action to effect change. "People with different ideas, businesses and solutions shape the community together," says Yuko Mishio, a community builder at IHT. Community builders are a feature of IHT as they communicate with members daily in order to understand their struggles and needs. Based on what they learn, they propose, organize and host various events for members; for example, workshops on refocusing or polishing their business model, or practicing pitches with feedback from the community. They also host bigger events like FuckUp Nights Tokyo, a global movement breaking away from the stigmas surrounding failure, where entrepreneurs share lessons learned from business failures.

ADDRESS 1st Floor, Insatsu Kojo 2-11-3, Meguro, Meguro-ku, Tokyo 153-0063
OPENING HOURS Mon–Fri: 9 AM–10 PM; Sat, Sun, and holidays: 10 AM–8 PM. Those with an unlimited membership, fixed desk or private office have access 24/7.
USP Located in a calmer part of the city with local cafes and restaurants and a river with cherry blossom trees alongside.
PRICE RANGE Visit the website for more details about membership fees.
WEB en.hubtokyo.com

Ryozan Park

The Takezawa family, who have lived in Sugamo for more than a century, founded Ryozan Park in 2012 as a share house, but the community quickly grew to meet its members' needs to include coworking offices, event spaces and a preschool. "It made sense to build the community here since it really is a family project," says Rachel Ferguson, co-owner. Ryozan Park attracts companies that appreciate the family-oriented, quieter, more traditional corner of Tokyo. "It has its own pull for people looking for the unique combination of services we offer: integrated accommodation, coworking and childcare," says Rachel. Members can access all three coworking spaces (ANNEX, LOUNGE and CORE) as well as the rooftop garden and tatami kitchen in Otsuka, and the gym and shower facilities in Sugamo.

ADDRESS Sugamo, 1–7–6, Toshima-ku, Tokyo 170-0002
OPENING HOURS Reception: Mon–Fri, 10 AM–4 PM; Members spaces: 6 AM–12 AM.
USP A complex spread across four buildings, including three coworking spaces, shared living and a preschool. Parents who enroll their child in the school can use the CORE coworking space in that same building for free.
PRICE RANGE Full membership is ¥15,000 per month, part-time membership is ¥10,000 per month (not including tax).
WEB ryozanpark.com/en

205

Imperial Palace Gardens, Tokyo

Eirene University

Cofounded by Takanori Kashino in 2012 as an informal, independent study group, Eirene University was created to fill a need for innovation and entrepreneurship education. In 2013, the study group became the nonprofit organization Design Thinking Institute and later began offering professional executive education in 2018 as the Eirene Management School. Since then, the organization has become Eirene University. The school's two main programs are the Innovation Management Course and the Design Thinking Masterclass. The Innovation Management Course spans three months and covers innovation mindset, mission statement composition, organizational strategy, idea development and go-to-market strategy. The Design Thinking Masterclass focuses on design-thinking tools and consists of an intensive four-day program. The school also launched a six-week online design thinking course in 2020 in response to the COVID-19 work-from-home environment.

LOCATION Minato-Ku
(Minato City neighborhood)
CLOSE TRANSIT CONNECTIONS Hamamatsucho JR/Tokyo Monorail stop (JK23, JY28, MO01); Daimon Toei Oedo/Asakusa subway stop (A09, E20). JR/Tokyo Monorail, (JK23, JY28, MO01), Toei Oedo/Asakusa Line, "Daimon" subway stop (A09, E20).
PRICE OF TUITION Innovation Management Course: $14,400; Design Thinking Masterclass: $3,100.
ENTRY REQUIREMENTS Prospective students of the management course must send a purpose statement and summary of experience to qualify. The masterclass has no specific requirements for enrollment.
WEB ems.eireneuniversity.org

Graduate School of Management, GLOBIS University

With a commitment to developing visionary leaders, the Graduate School of Management at GLOBIS University offers unique full- and part-time MBAs. The school, originally named GLOBIS Corporation, started in 1992 as a small classroom led by entrepreneur and venture capitalist Yoshito Hori. It has since grown into Japan's largest business school. With its background as a startup venture, the school's MBA includes practical coursework such as entrepreneurial leadership, venture capital and venture strategy, and a curriculum that gives students the chance to develop their own business plans. Focusing on management education, the MBA puts an emphasis on technology and innovation, and it features an evolving Technovate course series on AI, IoT, big data and robotics. Many of the GLOBIS lecturers are successful entrepreneurs and venture capitalists, and it even has its own VC, GLOBIS Capital Partners. Students round off their studies with internships, job opportunities and research projects.

LOCATION Central Tokyo, near Kojimachi Station and ten minutes from Tokyo Imperial Palace by foot.
CLOSE TRANSIT CONNECTIONS Kojimachi Station.
PRICE OF TUITION Full-time MBA: ¥4.1 million. Part-time/Online MBA: ¥3.1 million.
ENTRY REQUIREMENTS Be at least twenty-two years old, with two years of work experience (minimum), English proficiency and a Bachelor's or equivalent degree. Preliminary screening in some cases.
WEB globis.ac.jp

i.school

Formed in 2009, i.school is a year-long program focused on generating innovative solutions for social issues. It's designed to foster creativity and ideation methods. "We take a human-centered approach," says project assistant Ryoko Suzuki, "though technology is, of course, an important means to an end to help solve social issues." Students can participate in nine types of workshops that foster novel approaches to solving social issues. The school uses many methods, such as analogical thinking and extreme-user and bias-breaking approaches. Students come from diverse academic backgrounds but share a desire to make an impact. While most workshops are in Japanese, the summer program is in English and attracts international students. "The school's focus is on raising future innovators," says Ryoko, "not just entrepreneurs but also intrapreneurs."

LOCATION The school is located just in front of the University of Tokyo's Red Gate.
CLOSE TRANSIT CONNECTIONS Hongo-sanchome Station (subway).
PRICE OF TUITION Free for students.
ENTRY REQUIREMENTS Students apply with a short essay followed by a series of interviews.
WEB ischool.or.jp

D4V (Design for Ventures)

In partnership with global design firm IDEO, D4V enables early-stage Japanese ventures to create impact in the world through design, mentorship, connections, insights and capital.

SECTOR sector-agnostic

EMAIL info@d4v.com

WEB d4v.com

D4V (Design for Ventures) is a venture capital firm in partnership with global design company IDEO. D4V was launched in 2016 after Makoto Takano (CEO of D4V, chairman of Linkties Co., Ltd. and chairman and publisher of *Forbes JAPAN*), Tom Kelley (IDEO partner) and Mamoru Taniya (CEO of Asuka Asset Management) came together with the vision to create a design-oriented venture fund. For its first fund, D4V raised approximately $50 million. The firm's aim is to help Japanese startups create a positive impact in the world by combining hands-on support from venture capitalists and design expertise from IDEO in order to help grow and accelerate startups with a human-centered lens. The concept is based on D4V's beliefs that great design creates great businesses and that design is a powerful enabler and differentiator across all industries and at all stages of a venture's life cycle.

D4V is industry agnostic, funding startups in the fintech, entertainment, AI and lifestyle sectors, among others. The key component across most of the startups it funds is global scalability and synergy with design. The current fund was raised in Japan and most of D4V's portfolio companies operate in Japan.

D4V seeks to provide the bridge for startups to expand globally. The startups are typically early-stage or pre–Series A, though there are a few notable exceptions in the mid-to-late stages. Investments have ranged from $100,000 to $3 million, with typical investments averaging around $500,000. There are about forty startups in D4V's portfolio. Notable examples include ExaWizards, a startup focused on tackling social issues using AI; and airCloset, a startup that launched a subscription service to deliver boutique Japanese clothing brands directly to customers' doors.

DEEPCORE

DEEPCORE is an AI-focused incubator that cultivates entrepreneurs who aspire to change the world with technology.

SECTOR AI

EMAIL deepcore.jp/en/contact-form

WEB deepcore.jp/en

DEEPCORE is an incubator and VC working to create more AI-related startups by supporting visionaries in the technology sector. With a focus on disruptive innovation in AI, particularly deep learning, its goals are to provide community, business opportunities, people exchange and problem solving. DEEPCORE was created in 2018 in collaboration with the University of Tokyo and other educational research institutions, including the Okinawa Institute of Science and Technology Graduate University. Its investment fund, DEEPCORE TOKYO, has support from limited partners including Mizuho, Dentsu, Mistletoe, Development Bank of Japan, Japan Business Systems and KSK Angel Fund. Since launching in April 2018, it has invested in thirty-six startups (as of March 2020). Investment is offered to startups in the seed through early stages. Though startups can contact the firm to apply for investment, many startups are connected via referral.

DEEPCORE also offers an incubation community and coworking space called KERNEL, which launched in August 2018. Here, researchers and entrepreneurs can come together in the coworking space to launch startups. The space is equipped with high-tech computer resources for research as well as office facilities. KERNEL's four-hundred-strong membership consists of AI engineers and businesspeople from fields in which AI has an impact. These range from finance, IT and retail to agriculture, healthcare and leisure. Some members are serial entrepreneurs. DEEPCORE provides KERNEL members with opportunities to do joint projects involving companies and other organizations. Projects typically last several months and involve working on a proof of concept for a product or service with the potential to tackle social issues. By supporting these fledgling innovators, DEEPCORE's goal is to create startups within KERNEL that have long-term potential and are suitable for investment.

SEA Fund

SEA Fund is committed to solving social
issues through innovative business by
investing in social entrepreneurs alongside
supporting social-impact startups to scale.

SECTOR social impact, social innovation
EMAIL **info-ea@social-ea.org**
WEB **social-ea.org**

During his university days, Kunihiro Ogiwara was
studying at the height of Japan's economic bubble.
Despite the country's flourishing wealth, he noticed
that many people were struggling emotionally and
mentally. This led him to establish Peacemind,
an organization that supports mental health in the
workplace. After nearly twenty years managing the
business, he turned his focus to supporting other
startups and entrepreneurs. "When I first started out,
social problems were seen as things to be tackled
through NGOs, NPOs or by going into politics," says
Kunihiro. "They were quite separate from business.
But now business is seen as a more natural way of
improving society. I believe that today's generation
of young people can really make a difference in this
field." With large companies pursuing corporate social
responsibility (CSR) and working towards supporting
the Sustainable Development Goals (SDGs), Kunihiro
saw a way to connect both sides. He teamed up with
Hitoshi Shindo, founder of General Partners, an

organization that supports those with disabilities in
the workplace, and founded the Social Entrepreneur
Association (SEA) in August 2018, establishing the
fund three months later.

SEA has three goals: supporting and mentoring social
entrepreneurs, investing in seed-stage startups and
creating a general community of social entrepreneurs
working towards having a positive impact. Before
investing, the fund considers several aspects, such as
how much social impact a business can have, whether
the CEO has the skills and talent to manage the
company and whether the business has feasibility.
Since it invests at a very early stage, SEA Fund also
looks for a CEO who demonstrates commitment to
its vision and who has the flexibility to adapt the
business model as needed. The support SEA Fund
provides goes beyond initial funding: the team works
hard to ensure that startups get the right mentoring
and connections to move forward and scale up.

Tokyo Skytree, Sumida-ku, Japan

EXPERTS

Collaboration in the Age of Digital Transformation

Fujitsu Accelerator

[SECTOR]
startup acceleration
and incubation

[LOCATION] Tokyo

Hirofumi Ukita / Head of Accelerator Program

Fujitsu Accelerator, Fujitsu's internal startup acceleration program, brings startups in as partners and integrates their technologies with the company's products and services. The accelerator began as a grassroots movement at first, with only four startups selected in the first batch of the program. After a few iterations of the program, many business units within Fujitsu group joined in, hoping to leverage the accelerator's growing experience working with startups to enhance their existing portfolios of solutions.

After nearly twenty years at Fujitsu, Hirofumi Ukita, head of the Fujitsu Accelerator, is confident in his assertion that "we need to start collaborating with startups or we won't be around in the future." Hirofumi has led the Fujitsu Accelerator since April 2019. Prior to taking on this role, he was a founding member of Fujitsu's cloud business and helped the company expand into the cloud-computing market around the world. As his main sector is cloud computing, he had the chance to work with startups before taking on the mantle of accelerator lead.

" We need to start collaborating with startups or we won't be around in the future. "

Over the course of five years, comprising seven cohorts, the Fujitsu Accelerator has gone through over 120 business collaboration trials, taking startups through product development and giving them access to Fujitsu's sales channels. Hirofumi says that the program is seeking international startups ready and willing to drive business in the Japanese market, especially those that work in sectors that match Fujitsu's business units.

Startups outside of Japan may feel daunted at the prospect of entering the Japanese market, which is why Hirofumi believes international startups should use Fujitsu Accelerator as a stepping stone into the market and ecosystem.

On top of this, Fujitsu is currently in the process of pivoting its business around digital transformation. This being the case, the corporate is gaining a better understanding of the value provided by collaboration with startups. "Our team understands that the best way to become a digital transformation company is to work with startups," says Hirofumi. "We need to have the speed and cutting edge technology that they offer."

Hirofumi recommends that founders who think their startup would be a good fit in Japan should simply apply for the Fujitsu Accelerator. If you believe you have a strong technology offering, then joining the program opens you up to a huge segment of the Japanese market.

" We want to work with startups so we can solve problems together. "

Fujitsu is a responsible enterprise, so startups should understand that the expectation set for them is to innovate towards purpose and positive impact. Startups hoping to apply to the accelerator should also look to align with Fujitsu's commitment to the UN's Sustainable Development Goals (SDGs). Fujitsu's wide stakeholder reach includes key players in social entrepreneurship and innovation, so startups should leverage this to address social challenges. "We want to work with startups so we can solve problems together," says Hirofumi.

The next batch of the program is scheduled to open in Summer 2020, with more batches on the way, so keep checking the accelerator's website for your own chance to join Fujitsu. Once selected, startups team up with the relevant business divisions within the Fujitsu group. For example, from October 2019 to July 2020, twenty-five business units specializing in various sectors from AI to manufacturing and retail are participating in batch eight of the accelerator. "We have commitments from the business unit heads to the accelerator," says Hirofumi. "The business units are aligned with our program, and they are eager to learn new ideas and adopt the latest technologies from startups." To ensure that startups and Fujitsu collaborate smoothly, the accelerator team works diligently to match each startup with the right business unit.

Fujitsu promotes the startups via their internal and external media outlets, with other benefits including a customer reach of over 170,000 corporations in the Japanese market and access to distribution channels. The program also provides investment by the Fujitsu Corporate Venture Fund, to further deepen the collaboration between startups and Fujitsu.

Fujitsu Accelerator is communicating to internal stakeholders about how technologies coming from entrepreneurs may be better than what Fujitsu itself is developing. The Japanese market is unique, and decision making within Japanese corporates can be quite slow. Startups, especially those coming from abroad for acceleration, should learn as much as they can about the Japanese market and business culture.

✳ MOST IMPORTANT TIPS FOR STARTUPS

Be adaptable. As willing as corporates are to work with startups, their operational and decision-making speed is still likely slower than that of startups. Be ready to adapt to slower processes and know when to get behind your own technologies when you receive pushback.

Learn all you can about the Japanese market. The business culture and markets in Japan are unique. If you understand how Japanese markets operate, you're better positioned to bring your technology solutions to Japan. Companies like Fujitsu have very established ways of doing things based on their home culture.

Commit to the SDGs. Startups applying for the Fujitsu Accelerator should align with the corporate's commitment to the SDGs. As a potential player in a responsible enterprise, your startup and technology should further social and/or sustainable development initiatives.

If you have good technology, it will work in Japan. Although the business culture and markets in Japan are likely different from startups coming from abroad, you should trust in your technology and apply to the accelerator. If your ideas are sound, Fujitsu will help introduce them into the Japanese market.

[ABOUT]

Fujitsu Accelerator, launched in 2015, aims to provide new values to the world by combining ideas and technologies from innovative startups with existing products and solution services from Fujitsu Group. The accelerator creates new business opportunities by matching startups with Fujitsu business divisions that may benefit from collaboration and cocreation.

[CONTACT]

WEB
fujitsu.com/jp/innovation/
venture/en/index.html

EMAIL
contact-fap@cs.jp.fujitsu.com

Helpful Parallels: Entrepreneurship and Tea Ceremonies

Hankyu Hanshin Properties Corp.

[SECTOR]
Real Estate

[LOCATION] Osaka

Chikara Takagishi / Senior General Manager,
Urban Management Division

Entrepreneurial wisdom often comes from unlikely sources. In the case of Chikara Takagishi, a senior leader driving startup acceleration and collaboration initiatives at Hankyu, his core advice comes from traditional Japanese tea ceremonies. "You have to treasure every encounter as if it's a once-in-a-lifetime thing," he says.

For entrepreneurs and startups, this translates to the importance of taking chances on potentially beneficial collaborations. If you meet a corporate or investment leader or are able to join an accelerator or incubator, take that chance and cherish the opportunity. "All successful startups I have seen at Hankyu have done this," says Chikara.

Chikara is the senior general manager for Hankyu Hanshin Properties' Urban Management Division, a role he has held since 2018. He first joined the corporate in 1991 with the desire to make a positive impact on the world and then spent more than fifteen years managing large-scale urban development projects. In 2011, he helped establish the GVH Osaka incubator, and three years later he launched another startup-support program in HHP and opened the GVH#5 coworking space. In 2019, he launched Startupbootcamp Scale Osaka in cooperation with Rainmaking Innovation Japan.

Hankyu Hanshin Holdings Group was founded over one hundred years ago and has always worked to create and sustain prosperity along its railway lines and connected real estate. Against the backdrop of the age of digital transformation, it shifted to providing products and solutions for a future-oriented client base and society. Chikara noticed that the company's resources were not enough to provide and maintain solutions for their customers in this present context, especially in the face of socioeconomic challenges such as the declining and aging population, diversification of values and rapid globalization.

This is precisely why he dedicated more than a decade to integrating startups (and the cutting edge, quick-paced knowledge they bring with them) into HHP. Of course, this hasn't always been easy. Prior to many of Chikara's initiatives, Osaka's ecosystem was very closed and domestically oriented, and few corporates were collaborating with startups. However, as local and international startups were increasingly drawn to

> *" I strongly believe that it is essential for corporates to collaborate with startups, so that we will be exposed to their advanced technology and innovative ideas. "*

HHP's entrepreneurial offerings, HHP distinguished itself as a potential collaborator, and Chikara was able to bring corporate partners on board for his support programs.

"I felt there was a need for corporations to gain insight from entrepreneurs and startups with global perspectives," says Chikara. "I strongly believe that it is essential for corporates to collaborate with startups, so that we will be exposed to their advanced technology and innovative ideas." Through working together with startups, Hankyu has gained insight into how to recognize the needs of customers, how to track changes in the market, and how to use new technologies from their collaborators.

In terms of impact, Chikara believes that collaborating with startups helps HHP contribute to many of the UN's Sustainable Development Goals (SDGs), most notably Goal 9 (Industry, Innovation and Infrastructure) and Goal 11 (Sustainable Cities and Communities). Hankyu's main impact initiative is to provide solutions for urban development and town management; and with Chikara leading the charge, the company accelerates startups in order to take innovative ideas and bolster their offerings in support of the SDGs. "Working hand in hand with startups, we have a chance to face big changes and future socioeconomic trends," he says.

Despite Chikara's drive to open up and bring aboard startups to HHP and to the Osaka ecosystem, entrepreneurs should be aware that entering the Japanese market is rather difficult. The speed of decision-making is different than in most markets, and the systems behind Japanese corporates are unique. One thing to focus on is creating strong, sustainable relationships with local startup supporters and corporate leaders. Treat each new interaction and meeting with the same attentiveness as in a tea ceremony: as if it's a once-in-a-lifetime opportunity.

This means knowing who to approach. Chikara recommends entrepreneurs and startups visit the city government's Osaka Innovation Hub, which is considered to be an excellent landing pad for new startups in the region. Entrepreneurs should also stop by the coworking spaces GVH#5, where community managers can connect you to advisers and industry experts. Chikara also urges entrepreneurs to join one of Hankyu's programs. "It's a good shortcut to becoming part of the ecosystem," he says.

✳ MOST IMPORTANT TIPS FOR STARTUPS

Foster strong relationships. Person-to-person relationships go a very long way in Osaka and in the Japanese market in general. The country's business culture moves quite slowly and runs on its own unique system, so make sure to learn the culture and then foster relationships aligning with cultural norms and values. It may take a while, but well-cultivated relationships pay off.

Find your landing pad. New startups should approach support initiatives to get the financial, technical and networking help required. In Osaka, you should take time to visit the Osaka Innovation Hub and GVH#5 and join Hankyu's own initiatives, such as Startupbootcamp Scale Osaka.

Be oriented toward a better future. Hankyu and other corporates want to work with startups for their perspectives and technology. What you're offering should further purpose-oriented goals and align with the SDGs.

Treat every chance like it's once in a lifetime. You never know which opportunity or relationship will launch your venture toward success, so you should treat every event, meeting, chance and connection like it's a once-in-a-lifetime opportunity.

[ABOUT]

Hankyu Hanshin Properties (HHP) develops, leases and administers commercial facilities, office buildings and residential properties to create lively communities and provide quality work environments and residences that match the individual needs of every customer. HHP is one of the core companies within the railroad-based conglomerate Hankyu Hanshin Holdings Group and operates in Japan as well as the ASEAN region.

[CONTACT]

WEB
hhp.co.jp/en

EMAIL
info-sg@gvh-5.com

New Ideas and Ventures Through Diversity

Japan External Trade Organization (JETRO)

[SECTOR]
investment and trade development

[LOCATION] Tokyo

Kiyoshi Nakazawa
/ Director, Information Technology Department

Perspectives on entrepreneurship and innovation and on being active in the global ecosystem in Japan are broadening and changing. More and more people are adopting the mantle of entrepreneur, and larger firms are welcoming intrapreneurship into their operations. The cultural practice of remaining in one company for nearly a lifetime, which is common in Japan's professional environment, is slowly dissolving in favor of entrepreneurship and change.

However, Japan's ecosystem still lacks some knowledge about how the rest of the world is practicing innovation. This can make it both tricky for Japanese entrepreneurs to expand outside their country, market or company-stage scope and challenging for foreign companies who wish to scale up in Japan.

Kiyoshi Nakazawa, director of the IT Department for the Japanese External Trade Organization (JETRO), advises that it's vital for entrepreneurs, corporations and others in the Japanese ecosystem to start connecting and collaborating with their peers abroad. "We have to start working with global players now," he says. In his role, Kiyoshi is dedicated to forging meaningful relationships between local and international players to boost the ecosystem. "I try to be the contact point in Japan," he says.

Established in 1958, JETRO is a government-supported organization that helps Japanese startups expand internationally and aids foreign companies in connecting with the Japanese market. Kiyoshi has been working with JETRO in New York City since 2017 to help grow the startup ecosystem in Japan. Additionally, he is the founder of Innovation Collective Japan (ICJ), a nonprofit platform he created in 2019 to connect entrepreneurs and innovators to universities, corporations, government entities and other startups both inside and outside of Japan. Kiyoshi is set to return to Japan in 2020 and will continue growing ICJ after his arrival in Tokyo.

For Kiyoshi, the benefits of creating connections between Japanese and international startups and other organizations is quite clear. Japanese companies that build networks outside their home country learn new ways to pitch, seek investment, innovate, network and more. Firms from outside Japan that put in the effort to learn the Japanese market and work with local people widen the potential they have to succeed as new members of the ecosystem. Overall, it helps tremendously to learn the business culture and expectations of other countries and ecosystems. "This is a universal principle," he says.

Kiyoshi's advice to connect with ecosystems outside your own directly correlates with one of the challenges Japan is facing: diversity in the ecosystem. "My favorite thing about living and working in NYC has been the diversity," says Kiyoshi, who believes that Japan's startup community could benefit from the same. "If we connect with more foreign entrepreneurs, we achieve better diversity, which will lead to new ideas and ventures."

In his experience, people in other countries and ecosystems tend to understand what makes them unique in the workforce better than those who work in Japan. "In Japan, if you work in a company for a long time, you won't think about your specific skills or strengths," he says. One change he'd like to see in Japan's entrepreneurial and corporate communities is more people understanding their particular competencies and individual selling points. In order to change this facet of the working culture, Japan "needs to promote the tendency toward entrepreneurship and intrapreneurship."

This circles back to the need to connect Japanese players to global players. Entrepreneurs abroad may have specific skills or know-how with the potential to solve challenges in the local ecosystem. "In Japan, we need to know the 'who' more than the 'how' to be agile," says Kiyoshi. If neither you nor your company has the necessary expertise, it's important to foster a big international network of partners, mentors and peers. The business and cultural knowledge coming from this network will invariably afford you new perspectives and opinions on what you're hoping to build. It's who you know on a global scale.

" In Japan, we need to know the 'who' more than the 'how' to be agile. "

Of course, networking to build these connections saps your time and energy. This is where Kiyoshi and JETRO come in. "JETRO and I can help you get connected to the appropriate people domestically and globally," says Kiyoshi. "I want to be the global contact point."

So whether you're a local Japanese startup looking to receive the benefits of connecting with the global ecosystem or an international team excited to dig into the Japanese market, your first course of action should be to contact Kiyoshi. Being open to networking support from JETRO and Kiyoshi will bring you into contact with potential team members, advisors, investors and collaborators, giving you the "who" that your business needs.

MOST IMPORTANT TIPS FOR STARTUPS

Build a solid, trustworthy team. Having a great team is essential if you want your startup to survive. As entrepreneurs, you'll face many difficult challenges, and having a strong team of people who understand their roles will ensure that you can overcome those challenges.

Learn to be flexible. It's important to learn to be flexible as an entrepreneur, as sticking to your original plans may decrease your chances at success, especially if those plans aren't working as quickly as you'd like. Being flexible and listening to others in the ecosystem is crucial

Network, network, network. Networking is absolutely crucial. Sometimes, knowing people who have solved problems you are facing is more important than having the requisite know-how.

[ABOUT]

The Japan External Trade Organization (JETRO) is a government-affiliated organization that promotes mutual trade and investment opportunities between Japan and the rest of the world. Founded in 1958, JETRO focuses on promoting foreign direct investment into Japan and aiding SMEs in Japan to improve the potential of their global exports.

[CONTACT]

WEB
jetro.go.jp/en

EMAIL
knakazawa@innovationcollectivejapan.org

FACEBOOK
jetroinnovation

TWITTER
@JETRO_info

225

The Velocity of Collaboration

Koichi Noguchi
/ Partner, Global Innovation Factory

PwC Japan Group

[SECTOR]
assurance, tax, deal advisory, consulting, legal

[LOCATION] Tokyo

For Koichi Noguchi, who leads PwC Japan's Global Innovation Factory, the path toward new business success depends on startups and corporates fostering meaningful, collaborative partnerships. With the advent of the digital age, large companies are trying to keep up with dramatic changes in the business world but also struggling to transform to meet the needs of their clients. "We need to transform ourselves and our organizations," says Koichi, "otherwise, we cannot be successful in terms of new business and selling new services." Closely working with startups and adapting to speed, technological innovations, business models and disruptive ideas is vital to this transformation.

> "We need to transform ourselves and our organizations; otherwise, we cannot be successful in terms of new business and selling new services."

In response to the developing needs of clients and customers, PwC launched the global initiative PwC Global New Ventures. The initiative, officially launched in July 2016, works with startups to accelerate their development to leverage their technology for the corporate and opens up sales and network channels for these startups.

Koichi leads the Global Innovation Factory (GIF), a consulting team within PwC Japan Group responsible for startup partnerships. With his team, Koichi builds powerful partnerships between PwC and startups that have developed great tech products. "We can support startups by bringing their product into the market and help them gain visibility as quickly as possible," he says. "Collaboration brings startups into the light."

One complication to forging powerful partnerships, however, is that as a large-scale corporate, PwC has tough internal regulations, which makes leveraging partnerships with startups difficult. "This is a big barrier to overcome," says Koichi. One way GIF tackles this issue is by having team members dedicated to learning as much as they can about each of PwC's business units and creating strong collaborative bonds so that when startups do come in, they integrate well.

On top of this, there's the challenge of relative work styles. "I've learned that one of the biggest gaps between startups and major companies is speed," says Koichi. Startups and corporates vary greatly in how quickly they make and adapt to decisions and changes, as corporates often have deeply rooted internal regulations, and startups are still finding their regulatory footing.

In Koichi's opinion, major corporates and startups should find ways to adapt to each other's speeds. Larger companies should catch up with startups in terms of overall pace when they can, and startups should keep in mind that corporates take more time, both strategically and operationally. Koichi believes that when it comes to these kinds of changes, corporates share the responsibility with startups. To foster excellent collaborations between PwC and startups, Koichi and company work toward having an equal, win/win relationship with the startups they partner up with.

Koichi believes that any new startup, whether it's hoping to collaborate with GIF or not, should innovate toward purpose and impact. "New businesses need to be useful in terms of addressing social issues, especially in Japan," he says. Specifically, if you want to collaborate as a startup with Koichi and GIF, you must be working to tackle a societal challenge.

He also advises startups to be able to clearly define the benefits and advantages of future collaborations with every stakeholder and collaborator. This is crucial when working with major companies and academic institutions. "In many cases, the benefits are not clearly defined enough," he says. Be sure to define the benefits at the start of the collaboration and know that they may change during the lifetime of your work together.

It's also important to know that you don't always have to stick with your original idea. "In my experience, the second good idea we come up with through collaborations can be commercialized earlier than the first idea," he says. To get the best products and technologies out of your collaborative efforts, you should be flexible with your ideas.

Finally, Koichi urges startups to attend events hosted by PwC, as the company brings together organizations and initiatives from all over the world to network, pitch to one another and learn from each other's processes. "We host and sponsor various events so me and my team and all the startups have opportunities to interface with stakeholders from across the world," he says. With Koichi at the helm, PwC is poised to learn a lot from their startup partners, so it's recommended that you introduce yourself and your innovations to a corporate that is committed to changing positively with the times.

[ABOUT]

PwC Global New Ventures is PwC's internal SaaS incubator, which collaborates with leading tech companies worldwide to build software solutions that integrate into their existing systems, unlocking business value in real time. PwC Japan's Global Innovation Factory (GIF) team, in collaboration with the PwC Global New Ventures, offers a digital platform that leverages partnerships with startups, universities, research institutions and NPOs from all over the world.

[CONTACT]

WEB
pwc.com/jp/en

pwc.com/gx/en/services/
new-ventures.html

EMAIL
koichi.k.noguchi@pwc.com

✳ MOST IMPORTANT TIPS FOR STARTUPS

Be mindful of your pace. Startups and corporates move at very different speeds. As an entrepreneur, be mindful of the slower pace and stricter regulatory framework of your corporate partners, and adapt to that speed as best as possible. Also, be sure to help your corporate peers adapt to the agility of a startup.

Be ready to use your second idea. In working with a corporate, you should be flexible in your ideas, products and technologies. The second idea found via the partnership may be far stronger for solving the problem you're tackling than the first idea, so you want to be able to adopt this new concept swiftly.

Innovate toward social impact. To partner up with PwC New Ventures, you have to be working toward societal impact and positive change. Your products and technology should solve a real need in the market. This is a vital prerequisite for any startup (local or international) that wants to share their business with PwC in Japan.

Focusing on Problems that Matter

Keihanna Science City

[SECTOR]
science and technology innovation

[LOCATION] Kyoto

Hiroyuki Suzuki / PhD, Strategic Director and Leader of Innovation Hub Activity Keihanna Research Complex Project / Executive Vice President, Representative Director Advanced Telecommunications Research Institute International (ATR)

As a scientist and innovation leader, Hiroyuki Suzuki, PhD, understands both the importance of focusing on pressing challenges and the importance of connecting the Japanese and global markets to share the resulting innovations.

Hiroyuki is a strategic director and executive vice president of several projects within Keihanna Science City, a complex of research and business districts located between Kyoto, Osaka and Nara. In his role as a key leader within the complex, Hiroyuki drives innovation activities at many of its programs and hubs.

" You need to follow scientific criteria to select startups that are better for certain collaborations. "

Prior to joining Keihanna Science City, which comprises a research complex, several incubators, corporates, startups and more, Hiroyuki was a scientist working in both lab and corporate contexts, where he strove to bring innovations into the real world. His efforts to connect lab innovations to practical business applications brought him into the world of startups and venture capital, eventually landing him his current role at Keihanna Science City.

Keihanna Science City, which houses nearly 150 R&D and R&D-related organizations, universities and industry hubs, has grown to its current stature as a globally recognized tech hub in part because of Hiroyuki's early efforts to welcome startups and connect support networks from all over the world to the complex. "We're the best platform for Japanese and global startups who want to do business in Japan," says Hiroyuki. The complex has strong ties to academia and research, and it can match startups with professional support when needed.

Hiroyuki's advice to entrepreneurs and startups is layered, though at the heart of his message is the idea that startups should seek to collaborate as much as possible with academic and corporate entities, not only for the mutual business benefit but also for the resulting solutions to challenges in the local and global ecosystems. Innovation blossoms best from collaborative efforts.

" To use new technology, you need to achieve at least an entire order of magnitude of improvement. "

Hiroyuki advises innovators to understand their challenges first and then to figure out what scientific and tech knowledge to draw from in solving them. Innovation should rely more on solving problems rather than the science and tech itself. "Social demand should come first," he says. "If you start with the technology and try to find places to apply it, you likely won't achieve innovation."

Equipped with this mindset, entrepreneurs and startups should consider working with corporates, as these collaborations often spark more potent innovation than can be achieved by either party alone. "To make innovation happen in Japan, the best thing is to work with big companies," says Hiroyuki. "Most talents and technical outputs have been accumulated within these big companies." Keihanna Science City dedicates a lot of time matching the right startups with corporates looking to solve internal issues.

Being part of the Japanese ecosystem as a startup means working in some way with a corporate partner, as they have tons of talent and tech resources. Hiroyuki advises startups entering the Japanese market to be patient with the larger companies they'll likely be working with. To get the most out of those collaborative relationships, startups especially have to take their time in building that closeness, prior to gaining access to the assets they desire.

Startups that work with Keihanna Science City should also think globally. "If you only think within the Japanese market, you won't have the space to scale," says Hiroyuki. Working with stakeholders all over the world helps to accelerate innovation, as startups and corporates from outside the Japanese market may have ideas and technology you haven't thought of.

Some of the most exciting programs to look into at Keihanna Science City are the Keihanna Open Global Service Platform for Accelerated Co-Innovation (KOSAINN), a matching platform for big companies and global startups; the Keihanna Open Innovation Center (KICK); and the Keihanna Global Acceleration Program Plus (KGAP+), the complex's main acceleration initiative. These are just a few of the initiatives that are worth applying for as a startup. As a growing hub for entrepreneurial research and technology in the Kyoto prefecture, Keihanna Science City is a valuable resource, especially with its commitment to bridging the gap between the Japanese and global ecosystems to foster the best innovation possible.

☀ MOST IMPORTANT TIPS FOR STARTUPS

Start with the problem, not the technology.
As an entrepreneur working with high-level research and technology, you should make sure to first focus on the challenge that needs to be tackled and consider carefully whether you really need to build entirely new technology to solve the problem.

Think like a scientist. In fostering meaningful partnerships, Keihanna uses scientific methodology to find the best match-ups between startups and corporates. You should adopt this methodology as well, shaking off any biases you may have and looking at complete data sets when working with your partners.

Innovate on a global scale. To scale your business and innovation, you should seek to work on a global scale. Attempt to forge partnerships with stakeholders all over the world and look to far away markets to see if there are problems you can solve outside your local market.

Join Keihanna Science City. The best thing you can do is to become part of one of the complex's initiatives. Keihanna Science City has a staggering number of offerings, so there will definitely be an option that suits you.

[ABOUT]

Keihanna Science City, constructed in 1987 and maintained under the Kansai Science City Construction Act, is a national project and complex nestled in the Keihanna hills between Kyoto, Osaka and Nara prefectures. Taking up 15,000 ha (150 km²) of land, the city houses twelve research districts scattered about in a cluster, including 140 research and cultural facilities, universities, corporates and startups. The project has driven success in cultural and scientific research and has fostered collaborative partnerships between local and global startups, universities and big corporates in Japan.

[CONTACT]

WEB
kri.or.jp/en

EMAIL
kri.or.jp/en/contact

233

Taxi in Japan

directory

REGIONAL INITIATIVES

EDGEof, Inc.
edgeof.co

Le Wagon Japan - Coding Bootcamp
Meguro 2-11-3, Meguro-ku
Tokyo 153-0063
lewagon.com/tokyo

Open Network Lab
Digital Garage
DG Bldg., 3-5-7 Ebisu Minami,
Shibuya-ku
Tokyo 150-0022
onlab.jp/en

Venture Cafe Tokyo
CIC Tokyo
Toranomon Hills Business Tower
Toranomon 1-17-1, Minato-ku
Tokyo 105-0001
venturecafetokyo.org

FUKUOKA ▼

CITY PARTNER

Business Startup Support Section
Economy, Tourism & Culture Bureau
Fukuoka City Government
1-8-1 Tenjin, Chuo-ku
Fukuoka 810-8620
city.fukuoka.lg.jp/Keizai/r-support/
sougyou/index.html

STARTUPS

Doreming
1-15-35 Rengo Fukuoka Tenjin Bldg.
6F, Tenjin, Chuo-ku
Fukuoka 810-0001
doreming.com

Kids Code Club
Fukuoka Growth Next 207
2-6-11 Daimyo, Chuo-ku
Fukuoka 810-0041
kidscodeclub.jp

Kyulux, Inc.
Suite 227, FiaS Bldg. 2
4-1 Kyudai-shinmachi, Nishi-ku
Fukuoka 819-0388
kyulux.com

On Grit
Fukuoka Growth Next
2-6-11 Daimyo, Chuo-ku
Fukuoka 812-0024
on-grit.com

FOUNDERS

Groovenauts, Inc.
3F TenjinCLASS
1-19-22 Imaizumi, Chuo-ku
Fukuoka 810-0021
groovenauts.jp

Qurate Inc.
remix DAIMYO 3F
1-1-23 Daimyo, Chuo-ku
Fukuoka 810-0041
qurate.com

PROGRAMS

Co-necto
Toppan Printing Co., Ltd.
Kyushu Division
1-17-28 Yakuin, Chuo-ku
Fukuoka 810-0022
toppan-co-necto.com

Hirameki Sprint
GarrawayF
1-7-11-B1F
Tenjin, Chuo-ku
Fukuoka
garrawayf.com

Jump Start Program
Fukuoka Growth Next
2-6-11, Daimyo, Chuo-ku
Fukuoka 810-0041
growth-next.com/en/about

Updraft
GxPartners
2F, Tenjin Meiji-dori Bldg.
1-15-5 Tenjin, Chuo-ku
Fukuoka 810-0001
Updraft.asia

SPACES

The Company Canal City Front
1F, 2F Dai-ichi Prince Bldg.
8-13 Gionmachi, Hakata-ku
Fukuoka 812-0038
thecompany.jp/en

Engineer Cafe – Hacker Space Fukuoka
1-15-30 Tenjin, Chuo-ku
Fukuoka 810-0001
engineercafe.jp/en

fabbit Global Gateway "ACROS Fukuoka"
ACROS Fukuoka 1F
1-1-1 Tenjin, Chuo-ku
Fukuoka 810-0001
fabbit.co.jp/facility/
global-gateway-acros-fukuoka

Fukuoka Growth Next
Fukuoka City Startup Support
Facility Steering Committee LLP.
2-6-11 Daimyo, Chuo-ku
Fukuoka 810-0041
growth-next.com

SCHOOLS

Fukuoka University
8-19-1 Nanakuma, Jonan-ku
Fukuoka 814-0180
fukuoka-u.ac.j

Kyushu University
744 Motooka, Nishi-ku
Fukuoka 819-0395
kyushu-u.ac.jp/en

INVESTORS

Dogan beta, Inc.
Shin-Nihon Bldg. 3F
2-4-22 Daimyo, Chuo-ku
Fukuoka 810-0041
dogan.vc

FGN ABBALab
2-6-11 Daimyo, Chuo-ku
Fukuoka 810-0041
fgnabbalab.com

GxPartners
1-15-5 Tenjin, Chuo-ku
Fukuoka 810-0001
gxpartners.vc

KYOTO ▼

CITY PARTNER

Kyoto City Office
Industrial Tourism Bureau
488 Teramachi-Oike
Nagakyo-ku
Kyoto 630-8201
city.kyoto.lg.jp

STARTUPS

aceRNA Technologies
46-29 Yoshidashimoadachicho,
Sakyo-ku
Kyoto 606-8304
acernatec.com/en

Atomis
Creation Core Kyoto
Mikuruma #211
448-5 Kajii-cho, Kamigyo-ku
Kyoto 602-0841
atomis.co.jp/en

mui Lab, Inc.
2F, 294-1 Tawaraya-cho,
Nakagyo-ku
Kyoto 604-0966
Mui.jp

Space Power Technologies
Kyoto-University Katsura
Venture Plaza North Bldg.
1-36 Goryouoohara, Nishikyo-ku
Kyoto 615-8245
spacepowertech.com

Stroly Inc.
109-1 Kanegaecho, Shimogyo
Kyoto 600-8258
stroly.com

FOUNDERS

HACARUS Inc.
Dai 12 Hase Bldg. 5A
2-2-7 Hashibenkei-cho,
Nakagyo-ku
Kyoto 604-8151
hacarus.com

Nota Inc.
Kawamoto Bldg. 5F
110-16 Goshohachiman-cho,
Kamigyo-ku
Kyoto 602-0023
notainc.com

PROGRAMS

**KGAP+ (Keihanna Global
Acceleration Program Plus)**
ATR (Advanced
Telecommunications Research
Institute International)
2-2-2 Hikaridai, Seika-cho,
Soraku-gun
Kyoto 619-0288
keihanna-rc.jp/en/business/
business-support/#kgap

ME310/SUGAR
KYOTO Design Lab at the Kyoto
Institute of Technology
Matsugasaki Hashikamicho,
Sakyo-ku
Kyoto 606-8585
me310kyoto.org

Phoenixi
32 Yoshidatachibana-cho,
Sakyo-ku
Kyoto 606-8303
phoenixi.co.jp

SPACES

engawa KYOTO
Dentsu
647 Nijohanjikicho
Shimogyo-ku
600-8412 Kyoto
engawakyoto.com

Impact Hub Kyoto
Impact Hub
97 Kainokamicho, Kamigyo-ku
Kyoto 602-8061
kyoto.impacthub.net/en

Kyoto Makers Garage
Monozukuri Ventures
73-1 Sujakuhozocho, Shimogyo-ku
Kyoto 600-8846
kyotomakersgarage.com/en

SPACE KANTE at Co & Co KYOTO
Fukutoku Bldg. 2F
Tearaimizu-cho 670, Chukyo-ku
Kyoto 604-8152
space-kante.com/en/kyoto

SCHOOLS

Doshisha University
Kamigyo-ku
Kyoto 602-8580
doshisha.ac.jp/en

Kyoto Summer School
kyotostartupschool.org

**Kyoto University Graduate School
of Management**
Yoshida Honmachi
Sakyo-ku
Kyoto 606-8501
gsm.kyoto-u.ac.jp./en

INVESTORS

Kyoto iCAP
36-1 Yoshida Honmachi, Sakyo-ku
Kyoto 606-8317
kyoto-unicap.co.jp/en

Monozukuri Ventures
Kyoto Makers Garage
73-1 Sujakuhozocho, Shimogyo-ku
Kyoto-shi 600-8846
monozukuri.vc/en

OSAKA ▼

CITY PARTNER

**Osaka Innovation Hub
(Osaka City)**
7th Floor, Grand Front Osaka
Tower-C
3-1 Ofuka-cho, Kita-Ku
Osaka 530-0011
innovation-osaka.jp

STARTUPS

Gochiso Inc.
GVH#5 2F Hankyu Five Annex Bldg.
1-12 Kakuta-cho, Kita-ku
Osaka 530-0017
gochiso.jp

Next Innovation
Berni Minami Morimachi
3-6-5 Tenjinbashi, Kita-ku
Osaka 530-0041
Nextinnovation-inc.co.jp

Remohab
404 Yonezawa-Daigobiru
1-23-19 Esaka-cho, Suita-shi
Osaka 560-0003
remohab.com

Review
Ookini Midousuji-Kawaramachi
Bldg. 8F
4-4-7 Kawaramachi, Chuo-ku
Osaka 541-0048
macci.biz

Wefabrik
#701 Tatsuto Utsubo Park Bldg.
1-14-24 Kyomachibori, Nishi-ku
Osaka 550-0003
wefabrik.jp

FOUNDERS

akippa Inc.
Nanba Parks Tower, 14F
2-10-70 Nanbanaka, Naniwa-ku
Osaka 556-0011
akippa.co.jp

Beautiful Smile Co., Ltd.
Yotsubashi Center Bldg. 9F
1-1-21 Kitahorie, Nishi-ku
Osaka 530-0014
beautifulsmile.co.jp

PROGRAMS

AIDOR Acceleration
AIDOR Consortium
2 Chome-1-10 Nankokita,
Suminoe-ku
Osaka 559-0034
teqs.jp/acceleration

OIH Seed Acceleration Program
Osaka Innovation Hub
7th Floor, Grand Front Osaka
Tower-C
3-1 Ofuka-cho, Kita-ku
Osaka 530-0011
innovation-osaka.jp

RISING!
General Incorporated Association
EO Osaka
Bluek Nagahoribashi Bldg.
Minamisenba 1-6-12, Chuo-Ku
Osaka 542-0081
eoosaka.org

Startupbootcamp Scale Osaka
Rainmaking Innovation Japan
1-12 Kakudacho, Kita-ku
Osaka 530-0017
startupbootcamp.org/accelerator/
scale-osaka

SPACES

The DECK, Inc.
2-1-1, Minamihonmachi, Chuo-ku
Osaka 541-0054
thedeck.jp

**Global Venture Habitat Osaka
(GVH Osaka)**
Urban Innovation Institute
3-1 Ofuka-cho, Kita-ku
Osaka 530-0011
gvh-osaka.com

GVH#5
Hankyu Corporation
1-12 Kakuta-cho, Kita-ku
Osaka 530-0017
gvh-5.com/en

SCHOOLS

Kansai University
3-3-35 Yamate-cho, Suita-shi
Osaka 564-8680
kansai-u.ac.jp/umeda

Kindai University
3-4-1 Kowakae, Higashiosaka City
Osaka 577-8502
kindai.ac.jp/english

Osaka City University
3 Chome-3-138 Sugimoto,
Sumiyoshi-ku
Osaka 558-8585
osaka-cu.ac.jp/en

INVESTORS

Hack Ventures
Hankyu FIVE Annex Bldg. 5th Floor,
Kakuda-cho, Kita-ku
Osaka 530-0017
hack-ventures.com

HHP Co-creation Fund
Hankyu Hanshin Properties Corp
Hankyu Terminal Bldg.
1-1-4 Shibata, Kita-ku
Osaka 530-0012
hhp.co.jp/en

SENDAI ▼

CITY PARTNER

Startup Support Office
3-7-1 Kokubuncho, Aoba-ku,
Sendai 980-8671 Japan
sendai-startups.org

STARTUPS

Adansons
Enspace
1-4-9 Kokubuncho, Aoba-ku
Sendai 980-0803
adansons.co.jp

AI Silk Corporation
6-6-40 Aramaki, Aoba-ku
Sendai 980-8579
ai-silk.com/english

Brain Innovation Co., Inc.
308 T-biz
6-6-40 Aramaki, Aoba-ku
Sendai 980-8579
brain-innov.com

Co-LABO Maker
T Biz101
6-6-40 Aoba, Aramakai, Aoba-ku
Sendai 980-8579
co-labo-maker.com

IoT.Run
Ichibancho
1-8-10 Ichibancho, Aoba-ku
Sendai 980-0811
iot-run.co.jp

FOUNDERS

Material Concept, Inc.
Tohoku University Aobayama
Campus, T-Biz Room 410
6-6-40 Aoba, Aramaki, Aoba-ku
Sendai 980-0845
mat-concept.com

TESS Co., Ltd.
3-9-15-101 Tsutsujigaoka,
Miyagino-ku
Sendai 983-0852
h-tess.com

PROGRAMS

DA-TE APPs!
9F-3-6-1 Kokubuncho
Aoba-ku
Sendai 980-0803
globallab-sendai.com

Sendai X-Tech Innovation Project
City of Sendai Economic
Affairs Bureau
9th Floor, Sendai Park Bldg.
3-6-1 Kokuncho, Aoba-ku
Sendai 980-0803
techplay.jp/sendaixtech

Tohoku Growth Accelerator
9th Floor, Sendai Park Bldg.
3-6-1 Kokuncho, Aoba-ku
Sendai 980-0803
tohoku-growth-ap.jp

**Tohoku Social Innovation
Accelerator**
Organized by: Sendai City
Operated by: IMPACT
Foundation Japan
2 Chome-9-1 Oroshimachi,
Wakabayashi-ku
Sendai 984-0015
social-ignition.net

SPACES

cocolin
LASSIC
Higashi Nihon Fudousan Sendai
First Bldg. 1F
Shimizukoji, 6-1, Wakabayashi-ku
Sendai 984-0075
cocolin.jp

enspace
1–4–9 Kokuncho, Aoba-ku
Sendai 980-0803
enspace.work

**INTILAQ Tohoku Innovation
Center**
IMPACT Foundation Japan
2-9-1 Oroshimachi
Wakabayashi-ku
Sendai 984-0015
intilaq.jp

THE6
ECOLA
9-15 Kasugamachi, Aoba-ku
Sendai 980-0821
the6.jp

SCHOOLS

Miyagi Gakuin Women's University
9-1-1, Sakuragaoka, Aoba-ku
Sendai 981-8557
mgu.ac.jp/main/english/index.html

Tohuku Gakuin University
1-3-1 Tsuchitoi
Aoba-ku
Sendai 980-8511
tohoku-gakuin.ac.jp/en

Tohoku University
2-1-1 Katahira, Aoba-ku
Sendai 980-8577
tohoku.ac.jp/en

INVESTORS

Makoto Capital
East Japan Real Estate
Sendai First Bldg. 1F
6-1 Shimizukoji, Wakabayashi-ku
Sendai 984-0075
mkto.org/capital

**Tohoku University Venture
Partners**
Tohoku University Material
Solutions Center
2-1-1 Katahira, Aoba-ku
Sendai 980-8577
thvp.co.jp

TOKYO ▼

CITY PARTNER

Tokyo Metropolitan Government
2-8-1 Nishi-Shinjuku
Shinjukuku
Tokyo 163-8001
metro.tokyo.lg.jp

STARTUPS

Crono
1-4-1, Kasumigaseki, Chiyoda-ku
Tokyo 100-0013
crono.network

Heralbony
1-2 Higashimiyanome
Hanamaki City 025-0003
heralbony.jp

Holoeyes
#303 Mourin-building
2-17-3 Minami Aoyama, Minato-ku
Tokyo 107-0062
holoeyes.jp/en

Infostellar
3F Kearney Place Gotanda Bldg.
8-8-15 Nishi-Gotanda,
Shinagawa-ku
Tokyo 141-0031
infostellar.net

JobRainbow
2-16-8 Dogenzaka
Shibuya-ku, Tokyo 150-0043
jobrainbow.jp

WOTA Corporation
4-12-5 Hongo, Bunkyo-ku
Tokyo 113-0033
Wota.co.jp

FOUNDERS

Peatix Japan
4-6-1 Ebisu, Shibuya-ku
Tokyo 150-0013
peatix.com

Ridilover
Iguchi Bldg. 2F
3-9-1 Hongo, Bunkyo-ku
Tokyo 113-0033
en.ridilover.jp

PROGRAMS

ETIC
APPLE OHMI Building 4F
1–5–7, Jinnan, Shibuya-ku
Tokyo 150-0041
etic.or.jp

FoundX
University of Tokyo, DUCR
5-23-13 Hongo, Bunkyo-ku
Tokyo 113-0033
foundx.jp

J-Startup
1-3-1 Kasumigaseki, Chiyoda-ku
Tokyo 100-8901
j-startup.go.jp

Team360
Impact HUB Tokyo
1st Floor, Insatsu Kojo 2-11-3
Meguro, Meguro-ku
Tokyo 153-0063
hubtokyo.com/programmes/
team360

SPACES

Anchorstar
Daiichi Nan'o Bldg. 6F
2-21-2 Nishi-Shinbashi,
Minato-ku
Tokyo 105-0003
anchorstar.com

Impact HUB Tokyo
1st Floor, Insatsu Kojo 2-11-3
Meguro, Meguro-ku
Tokyo 153-0063
en.hubtokyo.com

Ryozan Park
1–7-6 Sugamo, Toshima-ku
Tokyo 170-0002
ryozanpark.com/en

SCHOOLS

Eirene Management School
Nihon-Kochiku 2nd Bldg. 8F
2-7-15 Hamamatsucho, Minato-ku
Tokyo 105-0013
mms.eireneuniversity.org

Graduate School of Management, GLOBIS University
Sumitomo Fudosan Kojimachi Bldg.
5-1 Niban-cho, Chiyoda-ku
Tokyo 102-0084
globis.ac.jp

i.school
i.school studio
Akamon-Higuchi Bldg.
5-27-8 Hongo, Bunkyo-ku
Tokyo 113-0023
ischool.or.jp

INVESTORS

D4V (Design for Ventures)
One Omotesando 7F
3-5-29 Kita Aoyama, Minato-ku
Tokyo 107-0061
d4v.com

DEEPCORE Inc.
Unizo Hongo 4-Chome Bldg. 3–4F
4-1-4 Hongo, Bunkyo-ku
Tokyo 113-0033
deepcore.jp/en

SEA Fund
Kyobashi Dai-ichi Life Bldg.
Kyobashi 2-4-12, Chuo-ku
Tokyo 104-0031
social-ea.org

EXPERTS

Fujitsu Accelerator
Shiodome City Center
1-5-2 Higashi Shimbashi, Minato-ku
Tokyo 105-7123
fujitsu.com/jp/innovation/venture/
en/index.html

Hankyu Hanshin Properties Corp.
Hankyu Terminal Bldg.
1-1-4 Shibata, Kita-ku
Osaka 530-0012
hhp.co.jp/en

Japan External Trade Organization
Ark Mori Bldg., 6F 12-32
Akasaka 1-Chome, Minato-Ku
Tokyo 107-6006
jetro.go.jp/en

Keihanna Science City
Keihanna Plaza
1-7 Hikariday, Seika, Soraku-gun
Kyoto 619-0237
kri.or.jp/en

PwC New Ventures
Global Innovation Factory
PwC Consulting LLC
2-6-1 Marunouchi, Chiyoda-ku
Tokyo 100-6921
pwc.com/jp/en

ECOSYSTEM PARTNERS

Business Startup Support Section
Economy, Tourism & Culture Bureau
Fukuoka City Government
1-8-1 Tenjin, Chuo-ku
Fukuoka 810-8620
city.fukuoka.lg.jp/Keizai/
r-support/sougyou/index.html

EDGEof, Inc.
edgeof.co

J-Startup
1-3-1 Kasumigaseki, Chiyoda-ku
Tokyo 100-8901
j-startup.go.jp

Startup Support Office
3-7-1 Kokuncho, Aoba-ku
Sendai 980-8671
sendai-startups.org

**Hub Tokyo Co., Ltd.
Impact HUB Tokyo**
1st Floor, Insatsu Kojo 2-11-3
Meguro, Meguro-ku
Tokyo 153-0063
hubtokyo.com

WeWork Japan G.K.
WeWork Nogizaka
1-24-3 Minami-Aoyama,
Minato-ku
Tokyo 107-0062
wework.com

Venture Café Tokyo / Cambridge Innovation Center Tokyo (CIC)
1-17-ban 1-go, Toranomon
Minato-ku
Tokyo 105-0001
venturecafetokyo.org
cic.com/tokyo

Social Impact Lab Japan
1–20–9-7F Jinnan
Shibuya-ku
Tokyo 150-0041
socialimpactlabjapan.org

Kyoto International Entrepreneurs Community - KIEC
facebook.com/Kyoto-
International-Entrepreneur-
Community-3050720867921193/

Startupbootcamp Scale Osaka
Rainmaking Innovation Japan
1-12 Kakudacho, Kita-ku
Osaka 530-0017
startupbootcamp.org/accelerator/
scale-osaka

BANKS ▼

Aozora Bank
aozorabank.co.jp/english

Japan Post Bank
jp-bank.japanpost.jp

Joyo Bank
joyobank.co.jp/eng

Mizuho Bank
mizuhobank.co.jp

MUFG Bank
bk.mufg.jp/global

Nishi-Nippon City Bank
ncbank.co.jp

Resona Bank, Ltd
resona-gr.co.jp/holdings/english

Seven bank
sevenbank.co.jp/english

Shinsei Bank
sp.shinseibank.com/english

**Sumitomo Mitsui Banking
Corporation (SMBC)**
smbc.co.jp/global

FUKUOKA
Bank of Fukuoka
fukuokabank.co.jp

Fukuoka Chuo Bank
fukuokachuo-bank.co.jp

KYOTO
Kyoto Bank
kyotobank.co.jp

OSAKA
Kansai Mirai Bank
kansaimiraibank.co.jp

The Senshu Ikeda Bank, Ltd
sihd-bk.jp/houjin

SENDAI
77 Bank
77bank.co.jp

Sendai Bank
sendaibank.co.jp

TOKYO
au Jibun Bank
jibunbank.co.jp

Sumishin SBI Net Bank
netbk.co.jp/contents/

COFFEE SHOPS & PLACES WITH WIFI ▼

FUKUOKA
Manu Coffee Daimyo
1-1-3 Daimyo, Chuo-ku
Fukuoka 810-0041
manucoffee.com

Robert's Coffee Fukuoka
1-12-5 Daimyo, Chuo-ku
Fukuoka 810-0041
robertscoffee.com

**Starbucks Coffee Fukuoka
Ohori Park**
1-8 Ohorikoen, Chuo-ku
Fukuoka 815-0041
starbucks.co.jp

KYOTO
Len Kawaramachi
709 Uematsucho, Shimogyo-ku
Kyoto 600-8028
backpackersjapan.co.jp/
kyotohostel/en

MTRL Kyoto (Fabcafe)
Motoshiogama-cho 554,
Shimogyo-ku
Kyoto 600-8119
mtrl.com/en/kyoto

Walden Woods Kyoto
508-1 Sakaecho, Shimogyo-ku
Kyoto 600-8194
eng.walden-woods.com

OSAKA
cafe labo
North Bldg., 3-1 Ofukacho,
Kita-ku
Osaka 530-0011
cafelabo.fun

Downstairs Cafe
North Bldg., 3-1 Ofukacho,
Kita-ku
Osaka 530-0011
mercedesme.jp/cafe_restaurant

Startup Cafe Osaka
Kansai University Umeda
Campus 2F
Tsuruno-cho 1-5, Kita-ku
Osaka 530-0014
startupcafe-ku.osaka

SENDAI
Blue Leaf Café
3-8-8 Ichibancho, Aoba-ku
Sendai 980-0811
instagram.com/blueleafcafe.sendai
blueleafcafe.jp

Darestore
Kanehachi Ichibancho Bldg. 3F,
3-11-27
Sendai 980-0811
instagram.com/darestore2017
darestore-sendai.com

Matsurica 1978
22-14 Nishi Park Mansion,
Aoba-ku
Sendai 980-0822
matsurica1978.jp

TOKYO
10°Cafe
3-12-8 Takada, Toshima-ku
Tokyo 171-0033
judecafe.com

Base Point
7-22-3 Nishi Shinjuku, Shinjuku-ku
Tokyo 160-0023
b-pt.jp

café 1886 at Bosh
3-6-7 Shibuya, Shibuya-ku
Tokyo 150-8360
bosch-cafe.jp/en

Cafe Asan
5-9-9 Ueno, Taito-ku
Tokyo 110-0005
cafeasan.jp

Editory
Yasutomi Bldg.
2-12-3 Kanda Jimbocho,
Chiyoda-ku
Tokyo 101-0051
editory.jp

Fab Cafe
1-22-7 1F, Dogenzaka, Shibuya-ku
Tokyo 150-0043
fabcafe.com/tokyo

the SNACK
7-5-4 Ginza, Chuo City
Tokyo 104-0061
the-snack.jp

EXPAT GROUPS, MEETUPS & STARTUP COMMUNITIES ▼

FUKUOKA
Global Startup Center
startup.fukuoka.jp

Startup Fukuoka
meetup.com/Startup-Fukuoka

KYOTO

Hacker News Kansai
hnkansai.org

Le Wagon Kyoto
lewagon.com/kyoto

PechaKucha Kyoto
pechakucha.com/cities/kyoto

OSAKA

Hacker News Kansai
hnkansai.org

JAPANESE CLASS & LANGUAGE EXCHANGE GROUP in Osaka
meetup.com/JAPANESE-CLASS-LANGUAGE-EXCHANGE-GROUP-in-Osaka

Osaka International Friends Meetup
meetup.com/Osaka-International-Friends-Meetup

SENDAI

Internations Sendai
internations.org/sendai-expats

Miyagi EU Association
sendaicci.or.jp/eu/Pages/index_e.html

Sendai English Conversation Cafe
meetup.com/Sendai-English-Conversation-Cafe/events/269547767

Sendai Tourism, Convention and International Association (SenTIA)
int.sentia-sendai.jp

TOKYO

International House of Japan
i-house.or.jp/eng

InterNations Tokyo
internations.org/tokyo-expats

Startup Lady Japan
startuplady.org

Tokyo International Communication Committee
tokyo-icc.jp/english/tonai/index.html

FINANCIAL CONSULTING SERVICES ▼

Actus
actus.co.jp/en

AKJ Partners
akj-partners.com

Grant Thornton Japan
grantthornton.jp/en

KPMG
home.kpmg/jp/en/home

PwC Japan
pwc.com/jp/en

Tokyo Consulting Group
kuno-cpa.co.jp/english-page

FUKUOKA

Fukuoka City Startup Cafe
2-6-11 Daimyo, Chuo-ku
Fukuoka 810-0041
startupcafe.jp

Yasunaga Accounting Firm
3 Jiroumaru, Sawara-ku
Fukuoka 814-0165
yasunaga-cpa.com

TOKYO

Archetype Co., Ltd.
Azabu Matsuya Bldg. 4F
2-8-10 Azabujuban, Minato-ku
Tokyo 106-0045
archetype.co.jp

Capital Tax
Place Canada 1F
7-3-37 Akasaka, Minato-ku
Tokyo 107-0052
capitaltaxltd.com/japan

Gaia Tax
Noguchi Bldg. 3F,
3-48-4 Nishihara, Kita-ku
Tokyo 114-0024
gaia-tax.com/foreigner-tax-service-english

Kaori Fuchi Tax and Consulting
Portal Point Shibuya 104
4-17 Sakuragaokacho, Shibuya-ku
Tokyo 150-0031
kaori-fuchi.com/en

KONO International Tax & Accounting Office
Nakagawa Bldg. 4F
1-14-8 Nishi-Shimbashi, Minato-ku
Tokyo 105-0003
kono-tax.jp/service/expat

Urushimatsu Tax Accounting Office
5-38-20-505 Narashinodai,
Funabashi
Tokyo 274-0063
urushimatsu-zeirishi.com

Yurakucho CPA Office
Ginza B Bldg.6F
1-6-5 Ginza, Chuo-ku
Tokyo 104-0061
yurakucho-cpa.jp

FLATS AND RENTAL ▼

FUKUOKA

Fukuoka Apartments
f-apartments.com

Miyoshi Real Estate
miyoshi-realestate.jp

Village House
villagehouse.jp

KYOTO

Elitz
elitz.co.jp

Flat Agency
flat-a.co.jp

House Navi
housenavi-jpm.com

OSAKA

YOLO JAPAN
yolo-base.com/en/hotel

SENDAI

Gaijin Pot
apartments.gaijinpot.com

Kimira House
kimirahouse.com

Real Estate Japan
realestate.co.jp/en

TOKYO

Arkios
arkios.co.jp

At Hearth
athearth.com

Balleggs
rent-apartment.tokyo

Housing Japan
housingjapan.com

IMPORTANT GOVERNMENT OFFICES ▾

FUKUOKA

Fukuoka City Hall
1-8-1, Tenjin, Chuo-ku
Fukuoka 810-0001
city.fukuoka.lg.jp

Fukuoka Regional Immigration Bureau
3-5-25, Maizuru, Chuo-ku
Fukuoka 810-0073
immi-moj.go.jp

Fukuoka Tax Office
4-8-28 Tenjin, Chuo-ku
Fukuoka 810-8689
nta.go.jp

Japan External Trade Organization Fukuoka
City Hall 14F, 1-8-1 Tenjin, Chuo-ku
Fukuoka 810-8620
jetro.go.jp/en/invest/region/fukuoka-city

KYOTO

Advanced Science, Technology & Management Research Institute of Kyoto (ASTEM)
134 Chudoji Minamimachi,
Shimogyo-ku
Kyoto 600-8813
astem.or.jp/en

Japan External Trade Organization Kyoto
Yabunouchi-cho,
Shimotachiuri-dori, Kamikyo-ku
Kyoto 602-8570
jetro.go.jp/en/invest/region/kyoto/

Kyoto Branch Immigration Office
34-12 Higashimarutacho,
Sakyo-ku
Kyoto 606-8395
immi-moj.go.jp/english

Kyoto Overseas Business Center
Kyoto Keizai Center 3rd Floor
78 Kankoboko-cho Shimogyo-ku
Kyoto 600-8009
kyoto-kc.jp

OSAKA

Osaka Business and Investment Center
C/O International Division
Osaka Chamber of Commerce and Industry
2-8 Hommachibashi, Chuo-ku
Osaka 540-0029
o-bic.net

Japan External Trade Organization Osaka
Osaka International Bldg. 29F
Azuchi-machi, Chuo-ku
Osaka 541-0052
jetro.go.jp/en

Sansokan
Osaka Sangyosouzokan 2F
1-4-5 Honmachi, Chuo-ku
Osaka 541-0053
sansokan.jp/startupvisa

SENDAI

City of Sendai
city.sendai.jp

Industry Promotion Section Industry Policy Dept
3-7-1 Kokubun-cho, Aoba-ku
Sendai 980-8671
jetro.go.jp/en/invest/region/sendai-city

Sendai International Center
1F, Conference Bldg.,
Aobayama, Aoba-ku
Sendai 980-0856
int.sentia-sendai.jp/e/exchange

Sendai Regional Immigration Bureau
Sendai Second Legal Affairs Joint Government Bldg.
1-3-20 Gorin, Miyagino-ku
Sendai 983-0842
immi-moj.go.jp/english/soshiki/kikou/sendai

TOKYO

Japan External Trade Organization Tokyo
Ark Mori Bldg., 6F 12-32
Akasaka 1, Minato-Ku
Tokyo 107-6006
jetro.go.jp/en

Tokyo Employment Consultation Centre
t-ecc.jp

Tokyo Metropolitan Government
senryaku.metro.tokyo.jp/tokku/english/index.html

Tokyo Metropolitan Industrial Location Support Centre
ilsc.tokyo/eng

INSURANCE COMPANIES ▾

AIG insurance
aig.co.jp/sonpo

Daido Life
daido-life.co.jp

Nippon Life
nissay.co.jp

Sumitomo Life
sumitomolife.co.jp

The National Health Insurance
city.fukuoka.lg.jp/hofuku/kokuho/hp/english

OSAKA

Healthone
healthone.jp

TOKYO

Frich
frich.co.jp

LANGUAGE SCHOOLS ▾

FUKUOKA

Fukuoka Japanese Language School
1-1-33 Hakataekihigashi,
Hakata-ku
Fukuoka 812-0013
fukuokaschool.com

Genki Japanese and Culture School
1-16-2 Hakataekihigashi,
Hakata-ku
Fukuoka 812-0013
genkijacs.com

Meiji Academy
5-1-26 Watanabedori, Chuo-ku
Fukuoka 810-0004
meijiacademy.com

KYOTO

Kyoto International Community House a.k.a. Kokoka (Kokusai Koryu Kaikan)
2-1 Torii-cho, Awataguchi,
Sakyo-ku
Kyoto 606-8536
kcif.or.jp/en

Kyoto JaLs - Japanese Language School
Co&Co Kyoto: 670
Tearaimizucho
Karasumadori-Nishikikojiagaru
Nakagyo-Ku
Kyoto 604-8152
japanese-languageschool.com/kyoto

Kyoto Language Classes
FVC Mesh: Hase Bldg. 2F
680-1 Omandokorocho,
Shimogyo-ku
Kyoto 600-8413
kyotolc.com

OSAKA
**Osaka International
House Foundation**
ih-osaka.or.jp/english

**Osaka YMCA Japanese
Language School**
osakaymca.ac.jp/nihongo

SENDAI
**Sendai International School
of Japanese**
1-3-1 Kakyouin, Aoba-ku
Sendai 980-0811
sjls.ac.jp/eng

Sendai Language School
1-14-32-8F, Ichibancho, Aoba-ku
Sendai 980-0811
sendai-lang.com/english

**Toyo International
Culture Academy**
1-4-18 Miyamachi, Aoba-ku
Sendai 980-0004
toyo-kokusai.com

TOKYO
Tokyo Foreign Language College
7-3-8 Nishi Shinjuku, Shinjuku-ku
Tokyo 160-0023
tflc.ac.jp

**Tokyo International
Japanese School**
2-13-6 Shinjuku, Shinjuku-ku
Tokyo 160-0022
tijs.jp

Tokyo Japanese Language Center
3-5-4 Shiba Park, Minato-ku
Tokyo 105-0011
tjlc.jp

Tokyo Nihongo Volunteer Network
tnvn.jp/guide/tokyo-23-wards

STARTUP EVENTS ▼

FUKUOKA
Startup Go!Go!
startupgogo-thepitch.biz

Myojowaraku
myojowaraku.net

KYOTO
**Kyoto Startup Summer
School (KS3)**
kyotostartupschool.org

Monozukuri Hardware Cup
monozukuri-startup.jp/
hardwarecup

Startup Weekend Kyoto
communities.techstars.com/japan/
kyoto/startup-weekend

OSAKA
Get In The Ring Osaka
innovation-osaka.jp/gitr/en

Hack Osaka
innovation-osaka.jp/hackosaka/en

Startup Bootcamp Scale Osaka
startupbootcamp.org/accelerator/
scale-osaka

SENDAI
Ignite Sendai
ignitesendai.com

**Techstars Startup
Weekend Sendai**
communities.techstars.com/
japan/sendai/startup-weekend

TOKYO
FuckUp Nights Tokyo
fuckupnightstokyo.doorkeeper.jp

Pechakucha night
pechakucha.com/cities/tokyo

**SDGs meetup (by Social
Innovation Japan)**
meetup.com/Social-Innovation-
Japan/events/265462559

Some of the websites in the Directory require the 'www' prefix.

Shinto Gates in the Sea

Rinno-ji Temple, Sendai

glossary

A

accelerator — an organization or program that offers advice and resources to help small businesses grow

acqui-hire — the process of buying out a company based on the skills of its staff rather than its service or product

AI (artificial intelligence) — the simulation of human intelligence by computer systems; machines that are able to perform tasks normally carried out by humans

angel investment — outside funding with shared ownership equity typically made possible by an affluent individual who provides a startup with starting capital

[see also: **business angel**]

API (application programming interface) — an interface or communication protocol between a client and a server that simplifies the building of client-side software

ARR (accounting or average rate of return) — the calculation generated from net income of the proposed capital investment

B

B2B (business-to-business) — the exchange of services, information and/or products from a business to a business

B2C (business-to-consumer) — the exchange of services, information and/or products from a business to a consumer

B corporation — a certification issued to for-profit companies by the nonprofit B Lab, which certifies that businesses meet standards of social and environmental performance, accountability and transparency

blockchain — a digital public collection of financial accounts in which transactions made in bitcoin or another cryptocurrency are recorded chronologically

BOM (bill of materials) — a list of the parts or components required to build a product

bootstrapping — to self-fund, without outside investment

bridge loan — a loan taken out for a short-term period, typically between two weeks and three years, until long-term financing can be organized

burn rate — the amount of money a startup spends

business angel — an experienced entrepreneur or professional who provides starting capital for promising startups

[see also: **angel investment**]

Business Model Canvas — a template that offers a coherent overview of the key drivers of a business in order to bring innovation into current or new business models

C

C-level — a corporate title given to high-ranking executives responsible for making company-wide decisions

CAC (Customer Acquisition Cost) — the amount needed to pay in marketing and sales in order to acquire one user

cap table — an analysis of ownership stakes in a company

carbon dioxide equivalent (CO2eq) — a unit of greenhouse gas that has the equivalent global warming potential (GWP) as one ton of CO2. Essentially a measurement of environmental impact.

CEO (chief executive officer) — the highest-ranking person in a company, responsible for taking on managerial decisions

circular economy — an economic system aimed at eliminating waste by sharing, leasing, reusing, repairing, refurbishing and recycling existing materials and products for as long as possible

CMO (chief marketing officer) — a corporate executive responsible for marketing activities in an organization or company

cold calling — the solicitation of potential customers who had no prior interaction with the product or business

convertible note/bond — a type of short-term debt often used by seed investors to delay establishing a valuation for the startup until a later round of funding or milestone

COO (chief operating officer) — a high-level executive running the operations of a company

coworking — a shared working environment

CPA (cost per action or acquisition) — the average cost for a conversion from one's advertising campaign

CPC (cost per click) — an internet advertising model used to drive traffic to websites in which an advertiser pays a publisher when the ad is clicked

cybersecurity — computer security; technologies, processes and practices designed to protect against criminal or unauthorized use of electronic data

cytokine — category of small proteins that are important to how cells communicate and function, for example, by aiding in immunity and inflammation.

D

dealflow — a term for investors that refers to the rate at which they receive potential business deals

deeptech — companies founded on the discoveries or innovations of technologists and scientists

diluting — a reduction in the ownership percentage of a share of stock due to new equity shares being issued

E

early-stage — the stage in which financing is provided by a venture capital firm to a company after the seed round; a company stage in which a product or service is still in development but not on the market yet

elevator pitch — a short description of an idea, product or company that explains the concept

Ethereum — a blockchain-based software platform and programming language that helps developers build and publish distributed applications

exit — a way to transition the ownership of a company to another company

F

fintech — financial technology; a technology or innovation that aims to compete with traditional financial methods in the delivery of financial services

flex desk — a shared desk available for temporary use in a coworking space

H

hyperspectral imaging camera — collects detailed data on light intensity in each pixel in an image

I

immune aetiology — an immune-related pathology

incubator — a facility established to nurture young startup firms during their first few months or years of development

installed base — the number of units of a product that have been sold and are actually being used

IP (intellectual property) — property which is not tangible; the result of creativity, such as ideas that can be patented and protected by copyright

IPO (initial public offering) — the first time a company's stock is offered for sale to the public

K

KPI (key performance indicator) — value that is measurable and demonstrates how effectively a company is achieving its key business objectives

L

later-stage — the stage in which companies have typically demonstrated viability as a going concern and have a product with a strong market presence

lean — lean startup methodology; the method proposed by Eric Ries in his book on developing businesses and startups through product-development cycles

Lean LaunchPad — a methodology for entrepreneurs to test and develop business models based on inquiring with and learning from customers

M

machine learning — a form of artificial intelligence that enables computer systems to learn, perform specific tasks and improve without the need to be specifically programmed to do so

M&A (mergers and acquisitions) — a merger is a process by which two companies join to form a new company, while an acquisition is the purchase of one company by another where no new company is formed

MAU (monthly active users) — a performance metric for the success of an internet product

MVP (minimum viable product) — a product with just enough features to satisfy early customers who can provide feedback for future product development

N

natural language processing (NLP) — a subfield of AI concerned with how computers understand and process human language and speech

O

opportunity fund — an investment vehicle in companies or sectors in areas where growth opportunities are anticipated

P

P2P (peer-to-peer) — a network created when two or more PCs are connected and share resources without going through a separate server

pitch deck — a shorter version of a business plan that presents key figures generally to investors

pivot — the process when a company quickly changes direction after previously targeting a different market segment

polyurethane — a man-made fabric that is often used in clothing production as an alternative to leather due to its durability

PR kit (press release kit or press kit) — a package of promotional materials, such as pictures, logos and descriptions of a company

product–market fit — a product that has created significant customer value and its best target industries have been identified

pro-market — a market or capitalist economy

R

retinal — related to the retina of the eye

regenerative medicine — a branch of medicine that focuses on treatments that regenerate, restore or replace damaged or defective cells, tissues and organs

S

SaaS (software as a service) — a software distribution model in which a third-party provider hosts applications and makes them available to customers

scaleup — a company that has already validated its product in a market and is economically sustainable

SDGs (Sustainable Development Goals) — a United Nations agenda that covers seventeen global goals that can be achieved by reaching 169 defined targets

small data — data in a format and quantity that can be comprehended and acted upon by humans

SDG Indicators — an indication used to measure the progress in reaching the Sustainable Development Goals

[see also: **UN Goals for Sustainable Development** and **sustainable development**]

seed funding — the first round of venture capital funding (typically called the seed round); a small, early-stage investment from family members, friends, banks or an investor, also known as a seed investor

series A/B/C/D/E — the subsequent funding rounds that come after the seed stage and aim to raise further capital (up to $1 million) when the company demonstrates various increase factors

shares — a unit of ownership of a company that belong to a shareholder

social entrepreneur — a person who establishes an enterprise with the aim of solving social problems and/or effecting social change

social impact investing — investment that brings together capital and expertise from the public, private and not-for-profit sectors to achieve a social objective

solopreneurs — a person who sets up and runs a business on their own and typically does not hire employees

stabilized lignin extraction method — a technology that prevents undesired reactions when removing the biopolymer lingin during the cellulose extraction process allows, for the first time, the full valorization of lignin

startup — companies under three years old that are in the growth stage and starting to become profitable (if not already)

sustainable development — defined by the UN World Commission on Environment and Development as an organizing principle that "meets the needs of the present without compromising the ability of future generations to meet their own needs."

SVP (senior vice president) — an officer of an organization who reports to the president or CEO and functions as the second in command in rank within the company

T

term sheet/letter of intent — a document between an investor and a startup including the conditions for financing (commonly nonbinding)

therapeutic — an agent used for therapy of disease

U

unicorn — a company, often in the tech or software sector, worth over US$1 billion

UN Goals for Sustainable Development (SDG) — seventeen intergovernmental development goals established by all 193 members of the United Nations in 2015 for the year 2030. The SDGs' non-binding targets provide a framework for organizations and businesses to think about and begin addressing the world's most important challenges

[see also: **SDGs**, **SDG Indicators**, and **sustainable development**]

USP (unique selling point) — a factor that differentiates a product from its competitors

UX (user experience design) — the process of designing and improving user satisfaction with products so that they are useful, easy to use and pleasurable to interact with

V

valuation — the amount of money a company is worth; typically happens at every stage of funding

VC (venture capital) — a form of financing that comes from a pool of investors in a venture capital firm in return for equity

vesting — a process that involves giving or earning a right to a present or future payment, benefit or asset

Z

zebra — a company that aims for sustainable prosperity and is powered by people who work together to create change beyond a positive financial return

sources

P. 16-17 Tech in Asia, "Japan is open for startups, but assimilation may prove difficult," techinasia.com/japan-open-startups-assimilation-prove-difficult

P. 16-17 Jetro, "JETRO Invest Japan Report 2019," jetro.go.jp/en/invest/reports/report2019/ch1.html

P. 16-17 Impact Investment, "The Social Impact Investment Landscape in Japan," impactinvestment.jp/

P. 16-17 The Government of Japan, "ABENOMICS," japan.go.jp/abenomics/_userdata/abenomics/pdf/2003_abenomics.pdf

P. 16-17 Journal of Biotechnology & Biomaterials, "Potential and Challenges for Start-Ups in Japans Biotech Industry," omicsonline.org/open-access/potential-and-challenges-for-startups-in-japans-biotech-industry-2155-952X-1000204.php?aid=64557

P. 16-17 The Government of Japan, "Digital Farming makes agriculture sustainable," japan.go.jp/technology/innovation/digitalfarming.html

P. 16-17 Fukuoka Facts, "Fukuoka Basic Information," facts.city.fukuoka.lg.jp/data/land-area

P. 16-17 Fukuoka City, "Fukuoka statistics (monthly report)," city.fukuoka.lg.jp/soki/tokeichosa/shisei/toukei/geppou/index.html#r1

P. 16-17 Real Estate Japan, "Living in Tokyo - What is the average salary in Tokyo?," resources.realestate.co.jp/living/what-is-the-average-salary-in-tokyo

P. 16-17 Ministry of Internal Affairs and Communications Statistics, "Retail Price Statistics Survey 2018," stat.go.jp/data/kouri/kouzou/pdf/g_2018.pdf

P. 16-17 Fukuoka Asian Urban Research Center, "Fukuoka Growth 2018 NEXTera," urc.or.jp/fukuoka-growth-2018

P. 16-17 Jetro, "Regional Information, Sendai City," jetro.go.jp/en/invest/region/sendai-city

P. 16-17 Tohoku University, "Cost of Living in Sendai," sup.bureau.tohoku.ac.jp/tips/cost_en

P. 16-17 Osaka Convention & Tourism Bureau, "Osaka for beginners," osaka-info.jp/en/page/osaka-beginners

P. 16-17 World Population Review, "Osaka Population 2020," worldpopulationreview.com/world-cities/osaka-population

P. 16-17 Invest Osaka, "Overview of Osaka City," investosaka.jp/eng/chance/about_osaka

P. 16-17 GSG, "Current State of Social Impact Investment in Japan 2016," impactinvestment.jp/doc/Current_State_of_Social_Impact_Investment_in_Japan_2016_eng.pdf

P. 16-17 Statistics Japan, "Annual Rate of Unemployment," stats-japan.com/t/kiji/11187

P. 16-17 Real Estate Japan, "Living in Tokyo - What is the average salary in Tokyo?," resources.realestate.co.jp/living/what-is-the-average-salary-in-tokyo/

P. 16-17 Numbeo, "Cost of Living in Osaka," numbeo.com/cost-of-living/in/Osaka

P. 16-17 World Population Review, "Tokyo Population 2020," worldpopulationreview.com/world-cities/tokyo-population

P. 16-17 World Economic Forum, "These will be the most important cities by 2035," weforum.org/agenda/2019/10/cities-in-2035

P. 16-17 Just Fun Facts, "Interesting facts about Tokyo," justfunfacts.com/interesting-facts-about-tokyo

P. 16-17 Encyclopedia Britannica, "Kyōto," britannica.com/place/Kyoto-Japan

P. 16-17 Jetro, "Regional Information, Kyoto," jetro.go.jp/en/invest/region/kyoto

P. 16-17 Kyoto University of Foreign Studies, "Living in Kyoto," kufs.ac.jp/en/faculties/livinginkyoto.html

P. 16-17 Facts and Details, "Kyoto," factsanddetails.com/japan/cat25/sub167/item1000.html

P. 16-17 e-Stat, "Housing and Land Survey, 2018," e-stat.go.jp/en/stat-search/files?page=1&toukei=00200522&tstat=000001127155

P. 16-17 Statistics Bureau of Japan, "Labour Force Survey, 2019," stat.go.jp/english/data/roudou/index.html

P. 16-17 OECD, "Regional GDP per Capita," stats.oecd.org/ (Regions and Cities > Regional Statistics > Regional Economy > Regional GDP per Capita, OECD.Stats)

P. 16-17 Harvard Business Review, "How the Japanese Government's New "Sandbox" Program Is Testing Innovations in Mobility and Technology," hbr.org/sponsored/2020/02/how-the-japanese-governments-new-sandbox-program-is-testing-innovations-in-mobility-and-technology

P. 32-33 Fukuoka Asian Urban Research Center, "Fukuoka Growth 2020 - The Evolution of Fukuoka City in the 2000's," urc.or.jp/fukuoka-growth-2020

P. 32-33 Startup Fukuoka, "Why Fukuoka," startup.fukuoka.jp/why-fukuoka

P. 32-33 FUKUOKA Smart East, "Creating the World's Most Liveable Smart City," en.smartcity.fukuoka.jp

P. 32-33 BBC Future, "Why Fukuoka Is Japan's Most Innovative City," bbc.com/future/article/20190508-why-fukuoka-is-japans-most-innovative-city

P. 32-33 Line, "What Is LINE Fukuoka?," linefukuoka.co.jp/en/facts/index

P. 32-33 Bloomberg, "Japan's Startup Founders Are Flocking to this Seaside City in Japan," bloomberg.com/news/features/2017-03-28/forget-tokyo-japanese-startup-founders-are-flocking-to-fukuoka

P. 68-69 Kyoto City Official Website, "Basic Information," city.kyoto.lg.jp/sankan/page/0000088894.html?SLANG=ja&TLANG=en&XMODE=0&XCHARSET=utf-8&XJSID=0

P. 68-69 Forbes, "Why Companies Like French Chemicals Maker Arkema Are Choosing Kyoto," forbes.com/sites/japan/2020/02/06/why-companies-like-french-chemicals-maker-arkema-are-choosing-kyoto/#7fa516ce5094

P. 68-69 Federation of Kyoto Prefecture Chambers of Commerce and Industry, "Wisdom for Future," kyo.or.jp/kyoto/e/wisdom/wisdom_for_future.pdf

P. 68-69 Global Destination Sustainability Index, "Performance Overview 2018 - Kyoto, Japan," gds-index.com/destinations/explore/view/kyoto/japan/2018/22

P. 68-69 Federation of Kyoto Prefecture Chambers of Commerce and Industry, "Wisdom for Future," kyo.or.jp/kyoto/e/wisdom/wisdom_for_future.pdf

P. 104-105 Osaka Innovation Hub, "Why Osaka Is the Best Place to Start Your Business in Japan," innovation-osaka.jp/startup-ecosystem

P. 104-105 Osaka Innovation Hub, "Osaka Start-Easy Guide," innovation-osaka.jp/startup-ecosystem/guide

P. 104-105 Japan Association for the 2025 World Exposition, "Expo 2025," expo2025.or.jp/en

P. 104-105 Kansai Airports, "Kansai International Airport Statistics," kansai-airports.co.jp/en/company-profile/about-airports/kix.html

P. 104-105 Forbes, "Why Osaka Is Becoming the Hottest Spot for Startups in Asia," forbes.com/sites/japan/2018/08/02/why-osaka-is-becoming-the-hottest-pot-for-startups-in-asia/#21d133452d33

P. 104-105 Osaka Innovation Hub, "Why Osaka Is the Best Place to Start Your Business in Japan," innovation-osaka.jp/startup-ecosystem

P. 104-105 Osaka Innovation Hub, "From Osaka to the World," innovation-osaka.jp/companies

P. 104-105 CNBC, "Japan's Second-Largest Metro Area Aims for a Slice of the Start-Up Pie," cnbc.com/2018/03/23/japans-second-largest-metro-area-aims-for-a-slice-of-the-start-up-pie.html

P. 138-139 Sendai City Business expansion guide, "Basic Resident Register," city.sendai.jp/invest/miryoku/jinzai.html

P. 138-139 Sendai City Economic Growth Strategy 2023, "Economic Census Survey," city.sendai.jp/kezai-chose/kurashi/machi/kezaikoyo/koyo/jore/documents/02_senryaku2023shiryou.pdf

P. 138-139 Sendai City National Strategic Special Zone Official Website, sendai-tokku.jp

P. 138-139 Jetro, "Sendai City," *jetro.go.jp/en/invest/region/sendai-city*

P. 138-139 Nikkei XTECH, "10 December 2018," *xtech.nikkei.com/atcl/ nxt/column/18/00001/01410*

P. 138-139 issue+design, "Creative City INDEX 2015," *issueplusdesign.jp*

P. 174-175 Startup Genome, "How Tokyo Is Building a Smart, Diverse, and Data-Driven City," *startupgenome.com/blog/how-tokyo-is- building-a-smart-diverse-and-data-driven-city*

P. 174-175 BRIDGE, "Japanese life science startup accelerator to launch shared wet lab in central Tokyo," *thebridge.jp/en/2018/11/bnv-to-launch-beyond-biolab-tokyo*

P. 174-175 KURTOSYS, "The Fintech World Series: Japan," *kurtosys.com/blog/2018/04/18/the-fintech-world-series-japan*

P. 174-175 Slash Gear, "Society 5.0: Japan's Plan to Take Civilization to the Next Level," *slashgear.com/society-5-0-japans-plan-to-take- civilization-to-the-next-level-14595383*

P. 174-175 Medium, "Summary of Listed Ventures from Universities," *medium.com/@BeyondNextVentures*

P. 174-175 Nikkei Asian Review, "Japan's Top 20 Startups Surpass 1tn Yen in Total Value," *asia.nikkei.com/Business/Startups/Japan-s-top- 20-startups-surpass-1tn-yen-in-total-value*

P. 174-175 Informa Connect, "Venture Capital in Japan: The Current Startup Ecosystem," *informaconnect.com/venture-capital-in-japan- the-current-startup-ecosystem*

Cycler in Osaka

STARTUP GUIDE NORDICS   The Entrepreneur's Handbook

STARTUP GUIDE JOHANNESBURG   The Entrepreneur's Handbook

STARTUP GUIDE TRONDHEIM   The Entrepreneur's Handbook

STARTUP GUIDE HAMBURG   The Entrepreneur's Handbook

STARTUP GUIDE AMSTERDAM   The Entrepreneur's Handbook

STARTUP GUIDE CAPE TOWN   The Entrepreneur's Handbook

STARTUP GUIDE LUXEMBOURG   The Entrepreneur's Handbook

STARTUP GUIDE VIENNA   The Entrepreneur's Handbook

STARTUP GUIDE TEL AVIV   The Entrepreneur's Handbook

STARTUP GUIDE MADRID   The Entrepreneur's Handbook

STARTUP GUIDE VALENCIA   The Entrepreneur's Handbook

STARTUP GUIDE COPENHAGEN   The Entrepreneur's Handbook

STARTUP GUIDE PARIS   The Entrepreneur's Handbook

STARTUP GUIDE REYKJAVIK   The Entrepreneur's Handbook

STARTUP GUIDE LOS ANGELES   The Entrepreneur's Handbook

STARTUP GUIDE STOCKHOLM   The Entrepreneur's Handbook

STARTUP GUIDE MUNICH   The Entrepreneur's Handbook

STARTUP GUIDE FRANKFURT   The Entrepreneur's Handbook

STARTUP GUIDE ZURICH   The Entrepreneur's Handbook

STARTUP GUIDE LONDON   The Entrepreneur's Handbook

STARTUP GUIDE TOKYO   The Entrepreneur's Handbook

STARTUP GUIDE LISBON   The Entrepreneur's Handbook

IMPACT GUIDE SERIES STARTUP GUIDE SWITZERLAND   The Entrepreneur's Handbook

STARTUP GUIDE SINGAPORE   The Entrepreneur's Handbook

STARTUP GUIDE NEW YORK   The Entrepreneur's Handbook

STARTUP GUIDE BANGKOK   The Entrepreneur's Handbook

STARTUP GUIDE BERLIN   The Entrepreneur's Handbook

STARTUP GUIDE OSLO   The Entrepreneur's Handbook

STARTUP GUIDE CAIRO   The Entrepreneur's Handbook

startupguide.com

Join us and #startupeverywhere

About the Guide

Based on traditional guidebooks stocked with information you might need to know about starting your next business adventure, **Startup Guide** books help you navigate and connect with different startup scenes across the globe. Each book is packed with exciting entrepreneur stories, insightful interviews with local experts and other useful tips and tricks. Today, Startup Guide has featured over thirty-five cities and regions in Europe, Asia, the US, Africa and the Middle East. Our second regional impact book, *Startup Guide Japan* aims to highlight the most purpose-driven and innovative startup scenes and entrepreneurs in Japan's most socially impactful cities.

The Startup Guide Website

Since the first Startup Guide book was published, our network has grown and the possibilities to reach new audiences have expanded. One of the reasons we decided to start producing content through a digital platform was to be able to take a deeper look at the cities, regions and ecosystems where our books take place. We want to make it more accessible for new entrepreneurs to understand the process of getting a startup off the ground through the stories of those who were once in their shoes. Through educational content and an inspirational community, our website looks into every stage of a startup's journey, all while maintaining the core purpose of why we do what we do: to guide, empower and inspire people beginning their entrepreneurial path.

For more details, visit our website at startupguide.com

Where to find us:
The easiest way to get your hands on a Startup Guide book is to order it from our online shop: startupguide.com/shop or by visiting our team at our Lisbon & Copenhagen office:

Want to become a stockist or suggest a store?
Get in touch here:
sales@gestalten.com

Rua do Grilo 135
1950-144 Lisbon, Portugal
lisbon@startupguide.com

Borgbjergsvej 1,
2450 Copenhagen, Denmark
copenhagen@startupguide.com

Want to learn more, become a partner or just say hello? ♥
Send us an email at info@startupguide.com

Follow us: @StartupGuideHQ

Startup Guide Japan

EDITORIAL
Publisher: **Sissel Hansen**
Editor: **Marissa van Uden**
Proofreaders: **Ted Hermann, Michelle Mills Smith, Hazel Boydell**

DESIGN & PHOTOGRAPHY
Designer: **Joana Carvalho**
Illustrations by **Joana Carvalho**

PRODUCTION
Global Production Lead: **Eglė Duleckytė**
Local Production Manager: **Lee Wang Jong**
External Community Managers: **Jiske van Straaten, Daphne Frühmann**
Researchers: **Phineas Rueckert, Daniel Neves**

PARTNERSHIPS
COO: **Anna Weissensteiner**
anna@startupguide.com

Printed in Berlin, Germany by
Medialis-Offsetdruck GmbH
Heidelbergerstraße 65, 12435 Berlin

Paper: **MultiOffset**

Published by **Startup Guide World ApS**
Borgbjergsvej 1, 2450 Copenhagen
info@startupguide.com

Worldwide distribution by **Die Gestalten**
Visit: gestalten.com

Visit: startupguide.com

ISBN: 978-3-947624-30-0

LOCAL RESEARCH AND DATA
Fukuoka chapter: **Nobuto Muroi**
Kyoto chapter: **Sabrina Sasaki, Kawaguchi Takashi**
Osaka chapter: **Megumi Ishitobi, Nae Nakamura**
Sendai chapter: **Yuuya Shirakawa**
Tokyo chapter: **Kody Ueno, Shino Tsuchiya, Yuko Mishio**

WRITERS
Anthony Griffin Tom Brooke P. 46,
Kumiko Sasaki and Eihiro Saishu P. 50,
Isshu Rakusai P. 84, Kenshin Fujiwara P. 88,
Genki Kanaya P. 120, Mitsuki Bun P. 124

Carter Witt
Keihanna Global Acceleration Program (KGAP+) P. 92

Connor Kirk The Company P. 56,
Engineer Cafe - Hacker Space Fukuoka P. 56,
Fukuoka University P. 59,
engawa KYOTO P. 94, Impact Hub Kyoto P. 94,
SPACE KANTE Co & Co KYOTO P. 95,
Kyoto Makers Garage P. 95, AIDOR P. 128,
Kindai University P. 133, Tohoku Social Innovation
Accelerator P. 163, cocolin, enspace P. 164, THE6 P. 165,
Tohoku Gakuin University P. 167, Etic P. 200, FoundX P. 201

Dylan Parish Le Wagon Coding Bootcamp P. 26,
Open Network Lab P. 27, Jump Start Program P. 55,
Fukuoka Growth Next P. 57, Kyoto Design Lab ME310/
SUGAR P. 92, Kyoto Startup Summer School P. 97,
Startupbootcamp Scale Osaka P. 129, RISING! P. 129,
THE DECK P. 130, Global Venture Habitat Osaka P. 131,
GVH#5 P. 131, SENDAI X-TECH Innovation Project P. 162,
Tohoku Growth Accelerator P. 163, INTILAQ P. 165,
Miyagi Gakuin Women's University P. 166,
Tohoku University P. 167, ischool P. 207

Kathryn Wortley Doreming P. 38, Kyulux P. 42,
On grit P. 44, Dogan beta P. 60, mui Lab P. 78,
Stroly P. 82, Next Innovation P. 112, Wefabrik P. 118,
HHP Co-creation Fund P. 135, Adansons P. 144,
Brain Innovation P. 148, Iot. Run P. 152, Kenji Suzuki P. 154,
Miho Koike P. 158, Heralbony P. 182, Wota P. 190,
Emi Takemura, Naofumi Iwai & Yuji Fujita P. 192,
Toshiki Abe P. 196, J-Startup P. 202,
D4V (Design for Ventures) P. 208, DEEPCORE P. 209

Copyright © 2020 Startup Guide World ApS All rights reserved.

Although the authors and publisher have made every effort to ensure that the information in this book is correct, they do not assume and hereby disclaim any liability to any party for any loss, damage, or disruption caused by errors or omissions, whether such errors or omissions result from negligence, accident, or any other cause. No part of this publication may be reproduced, distributed, or transmitted in any form or by any means, including photocopying, recording, or other electronic or mechanical methods, without the prior written permission of the publisher, except in the case of brief quotations embodied in critical reviews and certain other non-commercial uses permitted by copyright law.

onetreeplanted.org

L. Isaac Simon EDGEof P. 26, Fukuoka City article P. 34, Kyoto City article P. 70, Kyoto University Graduate School of Management P. 97, Osaka City article P. 106, Sendai City article P. 140, Eirene University P. 206, Graduate School of Management GLOBIS University P. 207, Experts P. 213-233

Phineas Rueckert Japan Region P. 16, Fukuoka Overview P. 29 P. 32-33, Kyoto Overview P. 65 P. 68-69, Osaka Overview P. 101 P. 104-105, Sendai Overview P. 137 P. 138-139, Tokyo Overview P. 171 P. 174-175, Tokyo City article P. 176

Phoebe Amoroso Essentials P. 18-21, Kids Code Club P. 40, FGN ABBALab P. 61, Gx Partners P. 62, aceRNA Technologies P. 74, Atomis Inc. P. 76, Space Power Technologies P. 80, Kyoto iCAP P. 98, Gochiso P. 110, Review P. 116, Remohab P. 114, Hack Ventures P. 134, AI Silk P. 146, Co-LABO MAKER P. 150, MAKOTO capital P. 168, TOHOKU University Venture Partners P. 169, Crono P. 180, Infostellar P. 186, Holoeyes P. 184, JobRainbow P. 188, SEA Fund P. 210

Rachel B Velebny Venture Café P. 27, Co-necto P. 54, Hirameki Sprint P. 54, UPDRAFT P. 55, fabbit P. 57, Kyushu University P. 59, Phoenixi P. 93, Doshisha University P. 96, Monozukuri Ventures P. 99, OIH Seed Acceleration Program P. 128, Kansai University P. 132, Osaka City University P. 133, Sendai: DA–TE APPS! P. 162, Team360 P. 201, Anchorstar P. 204, Impact Hub Tokyo P. 205, Ryozan Park P. 205

PHOTOGRAPHERS
Christina Sawka P. 141-145, P. 148-161

Geraldine Barizo P. 177-179, P. 186-187, P. 190-191

Jesse Whiles P. 222-225

Reylia Slaby P. 110-111, 114-115

Said Karlsson P. 27 (top right), P. 184-185, P. 192-199, P. 202-203, P. 209, P. 214-217, P. 226-229

William Fritsch P. 30, P. 35-53

Yoshiaki Suito P. 66, P. 74-87, P. 99, P. 230-233

Yuji Hirai P. 102, P. 107-109, P. 112-113, P. 116-127, P. 135, P. 218-221

ADDITIONAL PHOTOGRAPHY
Tomokazu Matsukawa P. 10,
World Innovation Lab (WiL) P. 21
Takanobu Ikeda (Jump Start program P. 55),
Updraft (Updraft program P. 55),
Engineer Cafe – Hacker Space Fukuoka (Engineer Cafe – Hacker Space Fukuoka P. 56), fabbit Global Gateway"ACROS Fukuoka" (Fabbit space P. 57),
Ikunori Yamamoto (Fukuoka Growth Next space P. 57),
Kyushu University (Kyushu University school P. 59),
Fukuoka University (Fukuoka University school P. 59),
Dogan Beta (Dogan Beta investor P. 60),
Gx Partners (Gx Partners investor P. 62),
Kyoto City (City Article P. 71, P. 73),
Hacarus (Kenshin Fujiwara founder P. 88-91),
©2019 ATR All Rights Reserved (Keihanna Global Acceleration Program P. 92),
Sugar Network (Kyoto Design Lab ME310/SUGAR P. 92),
Yoshitaka Orita (Phoenixi program P. 93),
Space Kante Co & Co (SPACE KANTE Co & Co KYOTO P. 95),
Shinichi Yasuda (engawa KYOTO space P. 94),
Impact Hub Kyoto (Impact Hub Kyoto space P. 94),
Doshisha University (Doshisha University School P. 96),
Sushi Suzuki, KYOTO Design Lab (Kyoto Startup Summer School P. 97), AIDOR (AIDOR program P. 128),
Rising! (Rising! program P. 129),
The Deck (The Deck space P. 130),
GVH#5 (GVH#5 space P. 131),
Kansai University (Kansai University school P. 132),
Kindai University (Kindai University school P. 133),
Osaka City University (Osaka City University school P. 133),
Kanae Nakayama (Hack Ventures investor P. 134),
AI Silk (startup P. 146), DA–TE APPS! (program P. 162),
Tohoku Growth Accelerator (program P. 163), enspace (space P. 164), Miyagi Gakuin Women's University (school P. 166), Tohoku University (school P. 167), Makoto Capital (investor P. 168), 日本仕事百貨, Tokyo Metropolitan Government All Rights Reserved (Etic program P. 200), FoundX (program P. 201), Impact HUB Tokyo (Team360 program P. 201), anchorstar (space P. 204), Impact Hub Tokyo (space P. 205), (Eirene University school P. 206, GLOBIS University school P. 207) courtesy of D4V (Design for Ventures), Sea Fund (investor P. 210) and unsplash: Matthew Buchanan P. 14, P. 18, JJ Ying P. 22, Romeo A. P. 34, Jason Chen P. 58, DEAR P. 63, Kristin-Wilson P. 70, Yasuhiro Yokota P. 93, Alejandro-Barba P. 106, Alex Williams P. 108, Misuto Kazo P. 132, Jonas Jacobsson P. 204, Alan Ko P. 206, Vincent Camacho P. 211, Ryoji Iwata P. 234, P. 243, Rogerio Toledo P. 244 and Laura Thonne P. 249.

Japan Advisory Board

Daisaku Kadokawa
Kyoto City Mayor
Kyoto City Office

Hiro Okahashi
Founder,
Managing Partner
MIYAKO Capital

Ikuo C.Hiraishi
Founder and CEO
DreamVision Inc.

Jacques Deguest
Cofounder and CEO
Angels, Inc

Junichi Anazawa
Manager
Startup Cafe

Kazuya Minami
Managing Partner
Mitsubishi Estate Co., Ltd.

Kazuya Umeda
Executive Officer
KYOTO RESEARCH
PARK CORP.

Kenji Tanaka
Director
Economy, Tourism &
Culture Bureau,
Fukuoka City Government

Kiyoshi Nakazawa
Founder
Innovation Collective
Japan (ICJ)
Director
Ministry of Economy,
Trade and Industry,
Japan (METI)

Kumiko Hidaka
Vice President,
Public Affairs
WeWork Japan

Mariko McTier
Cofounder and Director
Social Innovation Japan

Meghan Bridges
Marketing Director
Rainmaking Innovation
Japan / Startupbootcamp
Scale Osaka

Narimasa Makino
CEO and Cofounder
Monozukuri Ventures

Nobuto Muroi
In-house Venture
Capital Associate
Fukuoka Growth Next

Philip Sugai
Professor of Marketing
Doshisha University,
Graduate School
of Business

Sabrina Ayumi Sasaki
Corporate Business
Development Manager
Monozukuri Ventures

Sushi Suzuki
Associate Professor
Kyoto Institute
of Technology

Taisuke Alex Odajima
co-CEO
EDGEof, Inc.

Toshihiro Kishihara
CEO and
Managing Partner
GxPartners LLP
/ Startup GoGo Inc.

Yuichiro Uchida
Chief of Secretariat
Fukuoka Growth Next

Zachary Cruz
Startup Operations
BARK

With thanks to our **Partners**

Ecosystem Collaborators

Ambassadors

cïc tokyo

Startupbootcamp
SCALE Osaka

Connectors

SOCIAL
IMPACT
LABJAPAN

Booster

wework